Merry Christmas
1980
from The Strings

The Making of Golden Gate Park

Raymond H. Clary

The Making of
Golden Gate Park
The Early Years: 1865-1906

Raymond H. Clary

with an Introduction by Alan D. Cline

A California Living Book

All photographs from the Raymond H. Clary collection.

To Carol

My inspiration, crutch, friend, and wife for more than thirty-eight years.
I met Carol while I was a soldier at the Presidio of San Francisco in 1941
when she was introduced to me by another soldier on a blind date.
We spent that first date and many more in Golden Gate Park.

Acknowledgments

No book of this type could be written without the help and cooperation of countless people. I am indebted to Joan Dillon of the San Francisco Public Library, who was working in the General Reference Section in 1965. When I asked her for a good history of Golden Gate Park, she replied, "We get at least a dozen such requests each day, and no such book exists. Why don't you write one?" Rising to the bait, I replied in an offhand manner, "I might just do that." And so the original idea came from her.

The library visit was also the beginning of my long friendship with Gladys Hansen, the city archivist and head of the San Francisco History Room. She introduced me to the complexities of research and read my first poor attempts at writing, gently suggesting that I had not researched deeply enough. Gladys Hansen has my deepest appreciation and gratitude for her help and warm friendship.

Another person I can never hope to repay is Julia Smith Martin, assistant public information officer of the Virginia Military Institute. She has been of invaluable help over many years.

The people at the Mechanic's Institute Library, Bancroft Library, the California Room of the Oakland Public Library, the Society of California Pioneers Library, the California Historical Society Library, and the Henry E. Huntington Library have all been a tremendous help. Special thanks go to Ray Brian, the librarian at the California

Academy of Sciences, and to Elizabeth McClintock of the Academy, who gave me access to material that I would not otherwise have found. Richard Dillon, head of the Sutro Library, has been a tremendous help. I have been helped many times by the staff of the History Department, Government and Documents Section, and the Newspaper Section of the San Francisco Public Library.

I owe special thanks to Mary Connolly, former secretary of the Recreation and Park Commission. She opened her office to me in the early years of my research and graciously helped in every way. Her successor, Kitty Colzani, also has my gratitude.

I am indebted to many former and current park employees: Frank Foehr, Roy Hudson, Jack Spring, Carl Poch, Ed Schuster, Clarence Shaw, Frank Morgan, Aldo Cima, John Nihill, Bernard Barron, and Joseph Bestresky among them. I wish to thank all of these individuals for their tolerance, patience, and friendship.

And I would be remiss if I failed to mention Miss Ero Cartwright (now Mrs. Jacob McCoy of Columbus, Ohio), the schoolteacher who taught me from the second through the eighth grades. She was not just a teacher, she was my idol. She taught me that you can do anything if you try hard enough.

The life of a researcher is a lonely one for both a husband and his wife, and I am grateful for the understanding my wife, Carol, has shown during the fourteen years I have spent accumulating material for this book. If this work gains a measure of acceptance, much of the credit belongs to her.

To all who have had any influence on this book, my heartfelt thanks. I only hope that the existence of this work will express my thanks better than I have been able to in this brief acknowledgment.

I have set forth the history of Golden Gate Park in this book in roughly chronological sequence. Where a partic- ular episode or the involvement of a given person extends over a number of years, and where the story itself requires them, certain exceptions have been made to that order. William Hammond Hall, for instance, appears in many contexts, both as park consultant and as public critic, long after his retirement from the park as its first superinten- dent. This overlapping nature of the text is necessary in order to preserve its anecdotal essence.

Maps

Contents

Introduction

Golden Gate Park ranks among the finest of the many wonders of San Francisco. In a city saturated with beauty, the park is a jewel carved mainly from sand dunes.

In 1868, when the real work of creating a park had begun, its site was described in a Santa Rosa newspaper as a "dreary waste of shifting sandhills where a blade of grass cannot be raised without four posts to keep it from blowing away." In 1980, although the shifting sandhills have been transformed into parkland, there's a danger of their returning.

Unlike many great urban parks, Golden Gate Park is not at the hub of the city it serves. But as is true of the parks that are — Central Park in New York City, the Tuileries Garden in Paris, Hyde Park in London — San Francisco's park is an attraction that transcends local and even regional description. Although it does not hold the official title, Golden Gate Park is in essence a National Historic Landmark.

Today's hordes of park users arrive by auto, public transportation, and sightseeing bus, by bicycle and on foot, and on roller skates. The park's main drive, closed to cars for more than a mile on Sundays, comes close to bedlam when the newest park arrivals — the skaters — jam the roadway, carrying their own music boxes and dancing to disco in a scene more closely atune to Coney Island than to a park setting.

One September Sunday in 1979, with a free opera concert in the band concourse and the treasures of King Tut a few hundred yards away in the M. H. de Young Memorial Museum, park attendance surpassed 200,000.

Despite the swirl of activity and the ever-increasing use, little is known of the history of the park, which is as unique in its origins as in its present layout.

With this book, published in Golden Gate Park's 110th year, Raymond H. Clary fills the historical void in a work capturing in exciting detail the beginnings of the three-mile long playground.

Clary, a retired watchmaker and state government worker, has had a forty-year love affair with the park. At sixty-five, he continues to fight for the park, arguing for adequate maintenance — such efforts have been reduced to practically nothing — and against more buildings and more activities that bring swarms of visitors but detract from the park as a retreat. As the self-appointed historian of Golden Gate Park, he has demonstrated the tenacity of a pit bull.

Clary spent fourteen years on his history, poring over microfilm copies of the newspapers of San Francisco and neighboring areas, reading reports, minutes, and every other word available from the early-day meetings of the Park Commissions, Boards of Supervisors, and State Legislatures. His research has turned up a lot more than just park history. It adds to the lore of San Francisco and gives us a graphic picture of what the city and its people were like in its early days.

But Clary's story is essentially of Golden Gate Park. From his exhaustive studies comes a tale of occasional genius, intrigue, political power plays, "good guys" and "bad guys," and some one-of-a-kind characters.

Clary tells us that when Leland Stanford, railroad baron, manipulated City Hall to run a new rail line through the park lands, Con Mooney, a sand-lot orator of local renown, figured that if a tycoon could be a land grabber, so could he. He promptly established a squatters' village — Mooneysville — at the ocean's edge.

And when the wealthy wanted a speed track for their horses, they got it. Its establishment was one of the earliest "invasions" of Golden Gate Park.

Open space seems to offer a great temptation to the politically powerful, and Golden Gate Park has always been a prime target. The park invaders added Kezar Stadium (now abandoned and decaying), museums that might have been situated in more centrally located sections of the city, a municipal sewage-treatment plant, and a water-treatment plant behind a barbed-wire fence. The casual stroller comes upon the seven-foot barricade which bears this sign:

DANGER KEEP OUT

DANGER HIGH VOLTAGE

CHLORINE GAS

KEEP OUT

William Hammond Hall, the visionary who laid out Golden Gate Park, did not have such displays in mind. By Raymond Clary's calculations, nearly 30 acres of the parkland that Hall fought so long to plan and preserve are covered with buildings, while nearly 250 acres have been paved over.

Although Golden Gate Park still sparkles on the outside, today it is an abused and neglected chunk of San Francisco real estate. Park management officials admit that efforts are concentrated on maintaining an appearance of clipped lawns and shrubs in the areas most heavily visited. But let's check a little further.

William Hammond Hall created a forest woodland at the west, or ocean, end of the park as a buffer against the stiff and constant winds blowing off the Pacific. Many of the Monterey cypress holding back the pounding ocean gales are sick or dead.

Should those trees drop, the winds will come roaring into the park unchecked, endangering inland trees and shrubs. Gardeners describe the situation as a form of "domino effect," with the threat of disaster growing as neglect continues.

A State Forestry Department study, concluded in 1979, found that nearly one-fifth of the 33,342 trees in the park were in poor or dying condition, or were dead. The study noted:

> In the original forestation of the sand dunes, the park was designed as an even-aged stand. No reforestation has occurred in this forest. Subsequently, natural and man-made obstacles have compounded this problem.
>
> Many individual attempts to reforest parts of the park have had minor successes due to the lack of time, equipment and expertise.

Contrary to the report, reforestation has been a constant process, but not on an adequate scale. As we enter the 1980s, a serious tree replacement problem exists — compounded by a doubly severe need for irrigation and a continuing crisis in equipment and maintenance.

One recommendation made by the state foresters was that a wind barrier — a 10-foot-high, 35-foot-wide wooden structure — be built along the ocean frontage. The city has obtained $370,000 in federal funds to build the fence.

The foresters also suggested that park management create a program for recycling the fallen trees and leavings that could serve as valuable soil nutrients. Currently, this debris is buried in giant dumps built inside the park — dumps used not only for park refuse but for the waste from many of the other 170 units in the San Francisco Recreation and Parks system. Park as dump! — an incredible waste of irreplaceable land. The major reason for transforming parkland into dump site is the absence of wood chippers. Golden Gate Park has four. None work.

The 1979 park budget included no funds for equipment. The maintenance budget for all of the Rec-Park system was $300,000, enough to pay the salaries of one foreman and three-plus mechanics and to buy a smattering of spare parts.

One park official, asked to estimate the cost of a Golden Gate Park rehabilitation "wish" list, put a price tag of between $15 and $25 million on upgrading the three out-of-date and inefficient irrigation systems. Between $6 million and $10 million over a 25-year period would be required for the reforestation program. An adequate maintenance budget was set in the neighborhood of $2.5 million a year.

At present, the park maintenance yard resembles a graveyard of lawn mowers, of all sizes and shapes. The story of the worker mowing a huge meadow with a tiny, backyard-size machine is a standing joke among park employees. The worker is asked when he expects to finish his assignment. His answer? "Never."

In an election year, the city picked up from Uncle Sam's urban park kitty $439,000 for rehabilitation of the once-prized Chain of Lakes, $162,000 for ten reforestation projects on small plots, and $315,000 for the historic restoration of two wings of the Conservatory of Flowers, along with the $370,000 for the wind fence.

With $1,286,000 in federal aid and several hundred thousand dollars more in state money now available, it can be said that something is being done to save Golden Gate Park.

It might also be argued that the present programs are illusionary, that the task goes far beyond a few projects financed through the largesse of outside bureaucracies.

City Hall officials appear unwilling to make a commitment to Golden Gate Park, perhaps because the park is not yet in a state of actual crisis. And, although thousands of people use it, the organized constituency speaking on the park's behalf is miniscule.

If parks are to be saved, it appears, the public will have to draw upon private resources.

In the newsletter of the gardeners' William Hammond Hall Society, a Golden Gate Park gardener suggested that a Save Golden Gate Park League, along the lines of the Save the Redwoods League, be formed. The organization could serve as a single-purpose, private, nonprofit agency, able to accept gifts from corporations and individuals — gifts that could be used to buy lawnmowers and repair machinery and hire gardeners, not to add buildings and monuments. Meshing the interests of the public and private sectors would not be easy, but the problems of doing so are not insurmountable.

And so the battle against decay, noise, personal memorials, vandalism, and trash continues. Returning Golden Gate Park to the work of art envisioned by its original planners is certainly worth the effort.

Alan D. Cline

Author's Prologue

Over the past thirty years, I have read about the sad fate of New York City's Central Park and watched with dismay the changes in San Francisco's Golden Gate Park. I am convinced of one inescapable fact: *You cannot add to a park without subtracting far more than you have added.*

Each new generation and each new social trend places added pressure on the woodland park originally designed to balance the effects of urban living. Each change serves to defeat the very purpose of the park — to serve as a quiet retreat, a natural environment. Although the setting aside of park areas for buildings or specific uses may be important to certain groups of people, in total, these changes destroy the woodland park.

Many people firmly believe that a museum or a library adds to a park, but they fail to realize that such a feature brings with it elements of destruction — automobiles and huge concentrations of people — which completely ruin the fragile beauty of a park. Others cast covetous eyes on parks as free land — places to pursue their own hobbies and use their playthings. And some people even believe that open space is wasted space, that the setting aside of land which does not return a profit on investment (at least in dollars) is foolish in the extreme. But many of these same critics enjoy mountain or seaside homes, trips abroad, or annual vacations to natural areas — without which they too would be clamoring for a breathing spot, or a large city woodland park.

The average citizen is often just as active in demanding "improvements" that will destroy the very place that serves as one of the few means of retaining sanity in a city environment. Motorists want to drive fast throughout the park; pedestrians are ignored. Pedestrians in turn walk wherever and whenever they please, with no regard for greenery or other people. Bicyclists and equestrians often stray from areas set aside for their use.

Others demand that the city provide buildings, lawns, or lakes for their exclusive use — at the taxpayers' expense. Model yachting, flycasting, professional football, lawn bowling, kite flying, skateboarding, roller skating, and the flying of model airplanes — any outdoor activity popular at a given time — make demands for more of the open space that was originally reserved for the use of all.

Such special interests could easily be provided for elsewhere, in smaller areas all over the city. This shift away from the park would preserve the trees, shrubs, and lawns within the park as a refuge for those who have no means or time to travel away from the noise and tensions of the urban environment.

Some city officials remain unconvinced that urban parks are a necessary expense of city government. They mistakenly advocate charges for many areas that have traditionally been free. Golden Gate Park officials are considering charging admission to the Conservatory, the Japanese Tea Garden, and the Arboretum. Attempts have been made to install parking meters in the park. Concessions are given out as political patronage, and then the profit motive prices many facilities beyond the reach of average citizens. To ride the park merry-go-round, for instance, schoolchildren, who are given preferential treatment on public transportation, must pay the same fee as adults.

We need to change our thinking about urban parks. A renaissance has recently revived New York's Central Park, where concerned citizens' groups and park employees have begun to restore that once-fine park to its former beauty and charm. Rustic bridges and shelters have been built. Car traffic has been greatly reduced, and buildings and plantings have been restored. Once again, a weekend day spent in Central Park is safe, enjoyable, and, most of all, relaxing and refreshing.

A park is robbed of open space and needed greenery in a variety of ways: by neglect of the park; by the filling up of the park with trash, noisy events, or unattractive equipment; and as a result of allowing special-interest groups to have their way. At the root of this neglect and misuse lies apathy on the part of the public, the city administration, the park administration, and even the average park worker.

William Hammond Hall, the first superintendent of Golden Gate Park, once said, "Destroy a public building and it can be rebuilt in a year; destroy a city woodland and all the people living at the time will have passed away before its restoration can be effected."

Hall's words have served as warning throughout the history of the park, and they have often gone unheeded. But never before has the need to respond to them been so great.

RHC

The Making of Golden Gate Park

The Birth of American Parks

Until about the 1830s, little demand arose in America for large city parks. With so many natural areas all across the country, easily accessible to all, little thought was given to the preservation of natural areas. But as cities expanded into suburbs and pavement replaced greenery, it became apparent that steps must be taken to find a balance for the disturbing aspects of city life.

Many notable country parks remained along the Hudson River, but these areas were private and belonged to the extremely wealthy. The average city park consisted mostly of one or more undeveloped city blocks, with a few benches and perhaps a lawn. It could scarcely be called a park.

For every cause, however, there usually comes a champion, and in the 1840s Andrew Jackson Downing came to the attention of the public. Downing's writings reminded people that America already had beautiful natural parks which needed only to be developed and preserved. He had already created a beautiful park at Newburgh, New York, on the Hudson River. His father had been a nurseryman, and Downing became the first American landscape gardener. He was really more than a gardener though, and became the foremost authority on landscape gardening in this country. *Rural Essays* and *Downing's Landscape Gardener* are among his written works.

Henry Winthrop Sergeant, born in 1810, was next to champion the cause. He became the leader in the de-velopment of large estates. Inspired by his neighbor Downing, Sergeant made his estate, Wodene, into the most famous private home park of its time. Like Downing, Sergeant also wrote books and contributed to periodicals.

Henry Winthrop Sergeant was succeeded by a younger cousin, Charles Sprague Sergeant, born in 1841, who adapted the writings on rural private parks to the concept of the city woodland park. Charles Sergeant taught agriculture at Harvard for years and wrote many books on forestry.

Frederick Law Olmsted, who was born in 1822 in Hartford, Connecticut, became widely known for his interest in parks and landscapes. Olmsted took a special course in farming at Yale and then farmed for a few years. He then took a walking tour of Europe to study the parks of Great Britain, France, Germany, and Italy. In many subsequent trips to Europe, he took notes on the art of park making and the management of parks.

In 1856 he formed a partnership with Calvert Vaux, an architect of reputation, and, in competition with thirty-two others, they submitted a design for the creation of Central Park in New York. Their plan, called Greensward, was awarded first prize, and Olmsted was made superintendent of Central Park. Within a few years, he and his partner were also engaged to design Prospect Park in Brooklyn. They were in charge of both parks for many years. Olmsted later laid out the plan for the University of

California at Berkeley and did preliminary work for the grounds of Stanford University.

After the Civil War, while Olmsted was in California as part of a commission on Yosemite, he was engaged by Mayor H. P. Coon to report on the subject of a possible park for San Francisco. His report was widely quoted in nearly all the local newspapers. He was of the opinion that parks with trees and shrubs were out of the question for San Francisco, and he stated his opinion forcefully.

The Municipal Reports of 1865–66 quoted Olmsted as saying:

> It must, I believe, be acknowledged, that, neither in beauty of greensward, nor in great umbrageous trees, do these special conditions of the topography, soil, and climate of San Francisco allow us to hope that any pleasure ground it can acquire will ever compare in the most distant degree with those of New York or London.
>
> There is not a full-grown tree of beautiful proportions near San Francisco, nor have I seen any young trees that promised fairly, except perhaps, of certain compact, clumpy forms of evergreens, wholly wanting in grace and cheerfulness. It would not be wise nor safe to undertake to form a park upon any plan which assumed as a certainty that trees which would delight the eye can be made to grow near San Francisco.

Anyone who has visited Golden Gate Park can readily see how wrong Olmsted was in this opinion. And eleven years after making this statement Olmsted cheerfully admitted his mistake.

Olmsted's expert opinion was no doubt sought as a direct result of a petition signed by many citizens and taxpayers in 1865 and presented to the Board of Supervisors. This petition — or memorial, as it was then called — asked that thought be given to the matter of public parks:

> The great cities of our own country, as well as of Europe, have found it necessary at some period of their growth, to provide large parks, or pleasure grounds, for the amusement and entertainment of the people. When they have set about their work early in their history, the grounds have been secured near the centers, and so made easily accessible, and the expense has been comparatively light.
>
> No city in the world needs such recreation grounds more than San Francisco. . . . Until some provision is made to meet this need, however successful and impressive the business growth of San Francisco may be, it will not be an attractive and impressive place for families and homes.
>
> With this fact patent to everybody, and the certainty that every year's delay adds to the difficulties to be overcome, it would seem to be wisdom, before the suburbs of the city are more thickly populated, to have some general plan adopted for the pleasure grounds and connecting avenues, and to secure the required land as early as possible. However slowly or rapidly the work in the grounds may be prosecuted, all the other developments of the city, in buildings, railroads, sewers, gas and water pipe, etc., will then be adapted to the plan of the park, and thus the great expense of subsequent changes will be avoided.

The citizens of San Francisco had reason to be concerned. The city had not been born or planned, it had grown up overnight. From a sleepy pueblo of a few hundred people, San Francisco grew by leaps and bounds during the gold rush days. The early rude board shelters and tents were later replaced by more permanent buildings. Expediency was the watchword. When lumber became scarce, abandoned ships in the harbor were turned into shelters, places of business, and even a jail.

Such urban niceties as streets, fire protection, sewers, lights, and other public utilities were unknown at first. Major parts of early San Francisco burned down six times. Water was delivered to the city European style, on the backs of donkeys, and later by flume around Fort Point to the Plaza, which came to be known as Portsmouth Square. Garbage has been unceremoniously dumped into the Bay for decades, and to this day San Francisco still has no permanent solution to this problem.

Parks were not even considered in the early years of San Francisco. As late as 1868, the *San Francisco Daily Evening Bulletin* ran an editorial on the need for open space:

> Within a mile circle drawn from Portsmouth Square, there are but two large open spaces, Washington and Union Squares — and these are nearly a mile apart. As the few vacant lots fill up and wood buildings are replaced with lofty bricks, the streets will appear to become narrower and the want of clear sky spaces will become more than ever felt.

Yerba Buena Park, the area in the sand dunes bounded by McAllister, Polk, and Market streets and Van Ness Avenue, had been set aside as a "future park." But already a corner of it at Polk and McAllister had been preempted for a city cemetery. Later, in 1870, the Market Street frontage was sold by the city fathers as business lots to raise money for the new City Hall. Today, the entire greenery at the site of what was once meant to be parkland consists of a small green lawn surrounding the City Planning Department at 100 Larkin Street.

In the 1850s and 1860s, the built-up part of San Francisco ended near this park. Beyond Divisadero Street lay the area referred to as the "Outside Lands," consisting of 13,765 acres of land, mostly sand dunes. The federal government claimed this land on the grounds that it had been acquired by treaty with Mexico. The city of San Francisco claimed that the acreage was part of the Pueblo of the City of Saint Francis. To add to the confusion was the indisputable fact that several people had already homesteaded the land, and they too claimed ownership. District and federal courts, the state legislature, the California Supreme Court, and the United States Supreme Court ruled on the question of ownership of the Outside Lands. In addition, according to a close observer, "The United States Congress took a couple of whacks at it."

Possession counted heavily in the days when homesteading was still practiced, and no one in his right mind would try to evict a homesteader by force. Other more subtle means were sometimes employed, however.

As were mining claims, homesteads were generally marked off by piles of stone. But stones had a way of being moved during the night. No one could be certain that he would not wake up within the boundaries of his neighbor's claim. One determined homesteader near Mountain Lake went so far as to build breastworks and install a ship's howitzer for protection. When his dogs barked at night, he would rush out and fire the gun to scare off claim jumpers.

The fight over the Outside Lands was a grand one, lasting more than twenty years — from the 1850s until the Congress finally gave up its last claim to Seal Rocks in the 1880s. The gradual withdrawal of the United States government narrowed the field to two opposing factions, the city and the squatters, both of whom claimed the land as their own. Marches on City Hall, torchlight parades, and sandlot orations were led by both sides. But somehow the issue did not disappear. Finally the Board of Supervisors appointed an Outside Lands Committee, composed of C. H. Stanyan, chairman; A. J. Schrader; R. Beverly Cole, a society doctor; Monroe Ashbury; and Charles Clayton.

Another battle also had an effect on the Outside Lands. Following the Civil War, the widespread belief prevailed that England intended to capture California and that the United States government was so war weary that the capture might, in fact, be easy. To dispel these rumors, the War Department sent Gen. Barton S. Alexander to San Francisco to erect fortifications. General Alexander was a hero of the Civil War, having been in charge of the fortifications that prevented Gen. Robert E. Lee from capturing the nation's capital.

General Alexander soon discovered that he would have to devise some method to control the drifting sands; as fast as he built gun emplacements the wind filled them up with sand. In a methodical manner, he sent to Europe for studies on sand reclamation. The general knew that thousands of acres had been reclaimed by Spain, France, Belgium, Holland, and England. England had also had a problem with drifting sand when building the Suez Canal, and her experience was also put to use. The art of reclaiming sand dunes had been practiced for over four hundred years. The task facing the general was to determine the cheapest and best method. In spite of the fact that nearly every Board of Park Commissioners since 1870 has taken credit for reclaiming the sand dunes to build Golden Gate Park, it was in reality the Army Engineers under Gen. Barton S. Alexander who assembled the information on sand reclamation that made the work possible.

Working with the general was a civilian surveyor named William Hammond Hall, who was to become the first designer and superintendent of Golden Gate Park. He had gone over the entire Outside Lands many times and had mapped them for the army. Working in the general's office during inclement weather, he became intimately acquainted with sand-dune reclamation.

The Outside Lands Committee, after months of negotiations, reached a compromise whereby all the settlers agreed to give up one-tenth of their holdings in return for clear title to the remaining land. Each landholder was to pay a one-time tax of 10 percent of the appraised value. This tax would be collected by the city and then used to reimburse those who had lost all or part of their land because of the proposed park or another municipal project.

On December 7, 1868, the Outside Lands Committee made their report to the Board of Supervisors. They described all the land secured for the city as in the table appearing at right.

The report was adopted by the Board of Supervisors on May 3, 1869, by Resolution No. 9,721. And thus, by authority of Order Number Eight Hundred, adopted by the Board of Supervisors in 1868, the question was finally

	Acres	Assessed Value
1 Main Park	1,013.00	$ 801,593.00
2 Buena Vista Park	36.22	88,250.00
3 Public Squares	15.53	12,025.00
1 Cemetery (Lincoln Park)	200.00	127,465.00
1 Mountain Lake Park	19.93	19,930.00
1 County Hospital Lot	9.54	68,607.00
1 County Jail	1.37	2,750.00
1 City Hall and Library	2.92	35,425.00
1 Asylum for Foundlings	3.30	6,600.00
1 Home for Veteran Soldiers	0.82	1,462.00
1 Home for Inebriates	0.82	2,100.00
1 Women's Hospital	0.81	5,500.00
1 Ladies Relief	0.82	1,283.00
1 Academy of Sciences	0.86	3,200.00
91 School Lots	68.21	115,077.00
32 Engine Lots	2.31	5,700.00
139	1,376.55	$1,297,027.00

settled. Some of the settlers who signed the compromise later refused to pay their portion of the tax. Not until 1870 did the money actually change hands, under threat of condemnation by the tax assessor.

In his search for parkland in San Francisco, Frederick Law Olmsted had completely ignored the Outside Lands and had proposed a park in Hayes Valley, near what is now the Fillmore District of San Francisco. He observed that the Hayes Valley area was sheltered on the north, west, and southwest by hills and that plants retained their greenery during the dry season. Since he was an acknowledged authority on the subject, Olmsted's report had been used by all the local papers and periodicals to thwart plans to locate a large park in the sand dunes near the ocean.

Few citizens had been in favor of locating a great park in the sand dunes. Transportation was a problem. The people in the Mission District felt that they had the best land and the most people, along with the warmest climate. Citizens in Cow Hollow, between Telegraph Hill and the Presidio, felt that the Mission was far too distant for a park, and that the government should turn over the Presidio for a large park. Attempts are still being made in this direction, and nearly all coastal portions of the Presidio are now part of the Golden Gate National Recreation Area.

Some men realized, however, that San Francisco would grow into a great city and pushed for a park as large as five thousand acres in the Outside Lands. This group included Frank McCoppin, who was later mistakenly called "The Father of Golden Gate Park." McCoppin, who was first a supervisor, then mayor, and later a state senator, was one of the staunchest supporters of a park in the sand drift.

Interestingly, McCoppin was also the principal stockholder in a firm known as the San Francisco Grading Company, which was busily engaged in hauling dirt from the hills around Lone Mountain to the tidelands of the Mission District. He reasoned that if the park were located in the hilly section of the Outside Lands, he could get the contract to level it. He could then be paid for scooping the dirt from the park and paid again for dumping that same dirt in the Mission District, thus doubling his profits.

William Hammond Hall learned of this scheme while working as a surveyor for the army. He told General Alexander, who appeared before the Park Commission to state that the hills should be preserved as they were to help control prevailing westerly winds. It was General Alexander's opinion that if the land were made level, the task of reclamation would be infinitely harder. McCoppin's nefarious scheme was thus scotched before it ever got off the ground, and Hall made an enemy — one with a long memory indeed.

Then the five illustrious gentlemen who had comprised the Outside Lands Committee — Stanyan, Schrader, Cole, Ashbury, and Clayton — presented the Board of Supervisors a bill totaling $50,000 for their services. The auditor refused to honor the bill, and the case was taken to court. Judge Elisha W. McKinstry, who heard the case, severely discounted the bill and awarded each claimant $2,100, instead of the $10,000 each had sought.

As a sop to the injured pride and pocketbooks of these dedicated public servants, the Board of Supervisors later named a street at the eastern end of the main body of Golden Gate Park after each of them. If you begin to walk westward on Oak Street from Masonic Street, you will find these men immortalized on street signs as you walk toward McLaren Lodge in the park.

William Hammond Hall, surveyor and designer of Golden Gate Park and superintendent from 1871 to 1876.

William Hammond Hall

The role of William Hammond Hall in the making of Golden Gate Park was many-faceted. He helped win the battle for its location, surveyed it and made a topographical map of it, drew up a farsighted plan for its development, became its first superintendent, and later acted as a consultant from 1886 to 1890.

Hall was born in Hagerstown, Maryland, on February 12, 1846, the son of John Buchanan Hall and Anna Marie Hammond Hall. The Hall family moved to Stockton, California, in 1853, where the young boy was enrolled in a private academy from 1858 to 1865 under the tutelage of an Episcopal clergyman.

The family had planned that he would go to West Point, but with the outbreak of the Civil War his mother declared that he could never be an officer in an army arrayed against her own people, so Hall never attended college. Since all his education had been directed toward West Point, he was well versed in mathematics.

He began his practical education as an engineer by taking work with a surveyor, A. J. Bender, in the summer of 1863. He worked first as a rodman and then as a leveler.

The winter was spent in further schooling under a private tutor, and during the summer of 1864 he did barometrical work under a Colonel Williamson on Mt. Hood and Mt. Adams in Oregon.

The next winter was spent in further schooling. In 1865, he became permanently employed by the Board of Military Engineers in San Francisco. Hall remarked ruefully that his former experience as a leveler carried no weight with the Board of Military Engineers and that he had to go to work as a rodman. Within two months, he was promoted to leveler. Before the season was over he was in charge of a party of levelers and transit men.

He worked for the army for three years, spending each summer in the field and each winter in the office with army engineers. He was an apt pupil and spent much time studying everything he could find on engineering.

He then worked on the Outside Lands Survey under City Surveyor William P. Humphreys to prepare new block books of the Outside Lands for the city assessor. His knowledge of the area was complete when he later took the contract to survey and mark the boundaries of Golden Gate and Buena Vista parks.

In 1869 Hall went to White Pine District, Nevada, to do mining engineering in the vicinity of Ely.

In August 1870, Hall, as the low bidder, was awarded the contract to survey and make a topographical map of Golden Gate Park. Following that report, he prepared a plan for the development of the park and a year later, in August 1871, he was appointed engineer and superintendent of the park. He remained in this capacity until the spring of 1876, when he resigned.

During this five-year period, he also did inspection work and made weekly reports on the construction of the

Palace Hotel. He became very friendly with William C. Ralston, who was impressed by the work of the young engineer.

In 1870, when Hall was twenty-four, he and Emma Kate Fitzhugh, member of a very distinguished Southern family, were married. They had three daughters — Anna Hammond, Margaret Fitzhugh, and Katherine Buchanan Hall.

After his resignation from the park, Hall was employed as chief engineer of the West Side Irrigation District, which is still in existence. Money for this project was furnished by the Bank of California, of which William C. Ralston was second in command.

On January 23, 1878, Hall assumed command as chief engineer of the Central Irrigation District, including the canals that have made Fresno famous.

In May 1879, Gov. William Irwin appointed Hall as the first state engineer of California. Hall helped to prepare the first environmental law in California — that controlling the placer mining debris and the protection of the rivers of the Central Valley. He was reappointed to that position by four successive governors.

In 1886, still as state engineer, Hall was asked by Governor Stoneman to act as consulting engineer for Golden Gate Park. He served as consulting engineer until 1889, when he again resigned.

In March of that year, he was appointed supervising engineer of the United States Irrigation Investigation (the forerunner of the United States Reclamation Service), for all of the region west of the Rocky Mountains. He served in this capacity until June 1890, when he went into private practice as a civil engineer on irrigating projects in central and southern California.

The next two years Hall spent in England and South Africa, acting as consulting engineer on irrigation and waterworks. He was in charge of constructing a large plant for supplying water to the mines around Johannesburg in the Transvaal for the Cecil Rhodes-Warner Breit Syndicate.

In 1899 Hall went to Russia, where he made examinations and reports in the Russian Transcaucasus and in Central Asia to the Minister of Agriculture, M. Yermoloff, and on works in the Merve Oasis, where he made reports on the Imperial Estate.

When Hall returned to the United States, he entered into business as a civil engineer and land developer.

In 1905 he went to Panama and made a report of engineering studies on the Panama Canal to Senator George C. Perkins of the United States Senate.

In 1918 Hall went to Turkey, where with a Mr. H. A. Hatch, he made a report on conditions in Turkey for the American Committee of Armenian and Syrian Relief. The report, in book form, was written by Mr. Hall.

When Mr. Hall returned to the United States in 1900, he soon acquired control of the land in the Cherry Creek region of Yosemite Park for about $165,000. The City of San Francisco was seeking the same land for a water supply — known later as Hetch-Hetchy. Hall demanded a million dollars from the city for his holdings, and the city promptly instituted condemnation proceedings. During the controversy, a cousin of Hall's made some disparaging remarks about Hall's demand and was sued for $150,000 for his pains. The cousin, John Hays Hammond, later apologized to Hall, saying that he had been misinformed about the case. The lawsuit was dropped. Hall eventually realized about $600,000 on his investment of $165,000, which he paid to one Elmer C. Smith for about a section of land in the area.

Hall was a member of the American Society of Civil Engineers, in which he was the holder of the coveted Norman Medal.

He joined the Pacific Club in San Francisco on June 15, 1874, and retained his membership when that club and the Union Club became the Pacific-Union Club in 1889. He resigned from the Pacific-Union Club in 1901.

Hall passed away on October 16, 1934, at the age of 88 years and 8 months. He was buried in Colma.

VIEW FROM CLIFF HOUSE
1865.

The "Outside Lands" as they looked from the Cliff House in 1865.

Sand dunes of the "Outside Lands" about 1865.

The Beginning of Golden Gate Park

An Act to Provide for the Improvement of Public Parks in the City of San Francisco

The People of the State of California, Represented in Senate and Assembly, Do Enact as Follows:

SECTION 1.   The lands designated upon a map of the Outside Lands of the City and County of San Francisco, made in pursuance of Order Number Eight Hundred, by the word "Park," to wit, extending from Stanyan Street on the east to the Pacific Ocean, is hereby designated and shall be known as the "Golden Gate Park"; and the other parcel of land fronting on Haight Street, and also marked "Park" is hereby designated and shall be known as "Buena Vista Park"; and also the land marked on said map "Avenue," extending from Baker Street westward until it crosses Stanyan Street, shall be and remain public parks of said city and county, and shall be improved as such by the commissioners hereinafter mentioned and their successors.

SECTION 2.   The said Parks and Avenue shall be under the exclusive control and management of a board of three commissioners, who are hereby designated as "Park Commissioners."

SECTION 3.   The Governor of the State of California is hereby authorized and directed, within thirty days after the passage of this Act, to appoint three commissioners, who shall hold their offices for four years, and who shall receive no compensation for their services. In case of a vacancy, the same shall be filled by the remaining members of the board for the residue of the term then vacant; and all vacancies occasioned by expiration of terms of office, or neglect or incapacity of qualification, shall be filled by the governor aforesaid.

The above act, approved April 4, 1870, was the final step in the long fight to secure a park for San Francisco. It is also the first official mention of the name Golden Gate Park. California Governor Henry H. Haight then appointed Samuel Fowler Butterworth, David W. Connelly, and Charles F. MacDermott as the first commissioners. Butterworth was president of the Quicksilver Mining Company of New York. Connelly was a former state assemblyman from San Mateo County. MacDermott was president of the People's Insurance Company of San Francisco. These three gentlemen organized as a commission on May 3, 1870, with the election of Butterworth as president. They then appointed Andrew J. Moulder as secretary.

On May 6, 1870, the commission advertised the sale of $100,000 in bonds, bearing interest at the rate of 6 percent. Those opposed to the park had managed to tack onto the measure enacted by the legislature an amendment prohibiting the sale of any bonds under par. All other city bonds could be sold at ninety-two, and many people hoped that no one would bid on the park bonds.

There were wealthy landowners in the Outside Lands, however, who felt that improvement work on the park would greatly enhance their holdings. On July 1, 1870, only one bid had been received. That one bid was by Abraham Seligman, who bid for fifteen bonds of $1,000 each and the bid was awarded to him. With this paltry sum, the commissioners began work on a park that was destined to become world famous. On May 1, 1871, Seligman made a bid for sixty more bonds at par. With a total of $75,000, the work was advanced. Seligman then made an offer to become treasurer of the Park Board for 1 percent per annum on the monthly balance in the park fund. His offer was accepted.

Specifications for a detailed topographical survey of the Avenue (now called the Panhandle) and Golden Gate Park were prepared, and a number of competent engineers were invited to put in sealed bids. On August 8, 1870, the bids were opened, and the contract was awarded to William Hammond Hall for the sum of $4,860. This award marked the beginning of Hall's twenty-year involvement in the making of Golden Gate Park.

Today, it is difficult to visualize the immensity of the area set aside for the park and the problems in building it up from raw ground. The area was almost inaccessible by horse and carriage. It was served by only the Point Lobos Toll Road, beginning at Central Avenue, and the Ocean House Road, a poorly maintained thoroughfare that began in the vicinity of Eddy and Divisadero streets and ran its tortuous way among sand dunes to the south of Lone Mountain, across the southeast corner of what is now the park. From there it continued winding past the Giant Powder Factory and ended at the Ocean House, a popular out-of-the-way roadhouse.

The entire area was windswept nearly all the time. When a stiff breeze sprang up, it was difficult to get a horse to face west because of the blowing sand. Aside from the few homesteaders, visitors to the area were few — except for young boys who liked to explore their "Sahara Desert." Other boys and men visited the natural lakes in the sand dunes to shoot wild ducks and gather wild rice and frog legs to be sold to the French restaurants in the city.

Fourteen year-round lakes fell within the area of the newly located park. About a third of a mile from the beach, a ridge ran from north to south; just east of this ridge was a series of natural lakes. Several hundred willow trees and many wild lupine bushes grew along the lake, as well as grasses, tules, watercresses, cattails, and other minor plants. About the turn of the century, this series of smaller lakes was changed by then-Superintendent John McLaren into what is now the Chain of Lakes. Elk Glen Lake, near South Drive, was also one of the original lakes.

A series of high ridges was located east of the lakes, comprising Strawberry Hill, Prayerbook Cross Hill, and another hill to the north past what is now Fulton Street. This last hill has since been completely quarried away for material to build roads and walks in the park. Strawberry Hill was thickly covered with a low growth of scrub oak and California cherry, as well as the wild strawberry plants for which the hill was named.

The North Ridge, near Fulton and Stanyan streets, was covered with scrub oak of a second growth. All the larger trees in this area had been cut for firewood during the gold rush, as had almost all the trees on the entire peninsula south of San Francisco. The southern exposures on these ridges were covered in California cherry, the red-berried elder, native lupine (silver leaf), yellow lupine, gooseberry, and other plants and grasses.

The lower areas of the park were covered with constantly drifting sand. The eastern end of the park and the ridges were of good, arable soil consisting mostly of decomposed rock and leaf mold. Near the juncture of the Panhandle (a block-wide strip of land extending beyond the park proper to the east, then called the Avenue) and the main park was a large deposit of clay that was later used as a base for the earliest roads built in the park and the Avenue.

For more than a decade after the work on the park was started, public transportation to the new park was nonexistent. The Geary Street Cable Road went as far as Central Avenue, and then it was a long dreary trudge through the sand dunes to the corner of D (now Fulton) and Stanyan streets.

The remaining transportation available was a horse-car line that went out Eddy Street as far as Pierce Street. From there, it was a ten-block walk to Oak and Baker streets. The streets were unpaved, and the walk was either dusty or muddy, depending on conditions. Either way, it was unpleasant. That district was inhabited by many undesirable characters who had been evicted from San Francisco by the Vigilante Committee. A walk through the area was sure to subject any lady to cheers, jeers, and insults, so it is understandable why the sand dunes were an unpopular choice for a park. Indeed, the area was so disreputable that the sheriff authorized early park workers to carry guns on their way to and from the new park.

One can imagine the Herculean job facing the park commissioners, and especially the person who would actually plan and direct the work, the first superintendent of Golden Gate Park. Had someone had the temerity to suggest at that time that within fifteen years Golden Gate Park would become famous, he or she would have been rushed off to an insane asylum. It was generally agreed that the making of the park was just another job for the politicians to cash in on. Even if trees and grass could be grown, which many people doubted, no one would ever visit the place. The habit of looking askance at any proposal labeled as a benefit to the city was becoming ingrained even in 1870.

William Hammond Hall, however, went to work as soon as he had won his bid. With a corps of assistants, he laid out the park and Avenue in connection with the existing city surveys.

The maps and plans for the early work on the park that Hall prepared were adopted by the Park Commission on February 15, 1871.

In November 1870, three months after Hall won his bid, Patrick Owens, the first park worker, was employed as keeper of the grounds at a salary of $75 per month. His appointment was considered necessary to protect the few trees and shrubs that did exist in the park and to prevent trespassing. He was further charged with the care of the greenhouse, which had been erected for $300, as well as the nursery and the young trees that were to be grown from seeds purchased for a total of $40.

On May 2, 1871, the commissioners asked that bids be offered for grading the Avenue from Baker to Stanyan streets. The low bid was awarded to B. Kenny, who agreed to do cutting for 4½¢ per cubic yard and filling for 6¢ per cubic yard. The Board of Supervisors was asked by the park commissioners to approve changes in the grades along Oak and Fell streets so that the Avenue might be made level, as it is today. Because of the unevenness of the ground, a total of 101,500 cubic yards of cut had to be made and about the same of fill. The total cost of leveling the Panhandle was $10,657.50.

In August 1871, William Hammond Hall was appointed engineer and superintendent of Golden Gate Park. He remained in this capacity until the spring of 1876, when he resigned.

The next big project was preparation of a roadbed, macadamizing the road in the Avenue, and construction of a redwood sewer to connect with the city sewer in the Western Addition. The contract for the sewer was awarded to James Gaffney at a cost of $2.97 per running foot.

The work of the park went on in the face of opposition from every source. The nurserymen of the city became violent opponents of the park as soon as they learned that Hall intended to raise his own trees and shrubs instead of buying them. Hall's reasons were twofold: he would have the plants on hand when he needed them, and his own men could raise them cheaper than they could be bought. Another group criticized Hall for working in the eastern end of the park without trying to control the encroachment of new sand from the ocean. Still another group found fault with his method of grading the land in conformation to his plan for the park.

But by the end of 1871, in slightly over a year, the following had been accomplished: 11,700 feet of roadbed, 40 feet wide, had been prepared; 20,000 cubic yards of fill had been added to the main valley; 5,000 cubic yards of cut had been done in the main valley; a quarry had been opened in the park; 16,000 square feet of macadamizing had been done; and a nursery had been established (on the future site of McLaren Lodge). All this work was in addition to the work in the Avenue.

In his work, William Hammond Hall encountered an old recluse who lived with his chickens, ducks, and geese on the little hill formerly referred to as Chicken Point, at the junction of what is now John F. Kennedy and Middle drives. The old man lived in a shack he called home and had built some rude structures for his flock. The poultry ran loose in the daytime, but at night the old man had to catch the flock and lock it up to protect it from coyotes. This evening roundup was quite a chore, because the ducks and geese roamed toward the lakes. One night as he tried to round up the strays, the old gentleman fell and broke his leg and was hauled away to the hospital. He was so frantic about the safety of his charges that Hall assigned one of his men to stay in the old man's cabin until he returned from the hospital.

During this period, the commission and the city were saddened by the death of Commissioner David W. Connelly. The two remaining commissioners filled this void by appointing Gen. Barton S. Alexander, who declined. On May 10, 1872, Charles J. Brenham, who had been San Francisco's second mayor in 1851, was appointed to the position. He was in the banking and exchange business, with a partner, under the name of Sanders and Brenham.

While the surveying crew was camped in the sand dunes during the survey of the park, a saddle horse spilled its nosebag onto the sand dunes. The bag contained soaked barley, which was scooped up and put back in the nosebag. But the horse refused to eat it because of the sand, and barley was scattered on the ground. A week later Hall happened by the spot and found it covered with fresh green sprouts of barley.

Experiments had already been made with soaked lupine seed, but the lupine grew so slowly that it would become covered with drifting sand before it took hold. But the barley patch presented a possible solution. Soaked barley mixed with soaked lupine seed was broadcast on a small area, and then the seed was covered over by dragging brush as a harrow behind a saddle horse. The barley sprouted within a week and lasted for several months, giving the lupine time to grow tall enough to control the movement of the sand. Lupine could live at least two years without additional plant food. That would be ample time to get small trees started.

The following season, over an acre of land just east of one of the lakes was successfully planted with this technique. Since plenty of wild lupine grew over certain parts of the Outside Lands, Hall put his men to work gathering lupine seed when it became ripe for picking.

Over time, most of the sand area was reclaimed in this manner. Near the ocean, however, beach grasses were used, because the barley and lupine would not sprout on sand freshly washed up from the sea. The first beach grass seed was purchased in Paris by William Alvord, a former San Francisco mayor, who brought it to the park in 1873.

When Hall first went to survey Buena Vista Park, he found a cabin on top of a hill inhabited by two "roughs," as they were then termed, who had been "invited" out of San Francisco by the vigilantes and had settled on the spot outside the city limits. The two men drove Hall's survey party off the hill with gunfire. The sheriff was summoned, a posse was gathered, and the area was taken by force.

Then Hall detailed two armed men to live in the cabin and hold it for the city. (At that time park workers actually lived in the park.)

The next night, the two roughs came back and fired several shots into the cabin, hoping either to kill or scare off the park men. The following night, Hall hid in the brush with his men and waited. Soon the displaced settlers appeared with a log that they intended to use as a battering ram. A few shots were fired over their heads, and they ran off. Hall reported that his armed guards lived in that cabin for almost a year before it was considered safe to remove them.

To understand the many problems Golden Gate Park has had in irrigating the land, watering the trees, and filling the lakes is often difficult. Early in the park's history, William Hammond Hall reported in minute detail on all of the area's resources, including the water and drainage:

> The natural drainage of the Park and Avenue Reservation is excellent. The eastern boundary of the main reserve being on the crest of the watershed, its drainage slope is to the west, into the ocean, while that of the Avenue is toward the east, through the city sewers, into the bay. The general fall in each direction is such that an effectual system of drainways may be readily constructed at an expense much less than that generally accompanying this feature of park improvement. As has been described, the character of the soil is such that there are no marsh lands or stagnant pools to be drained before the grounds can be made pleasurable to the public. There is, however, an abundance of water to be had throughout the eastern portion of the Reservation, at a depth of twenty-five to thirty-five feet below the surface of the ground in the valleys. Under the clay formation, at the western end of the Avenue, it is even nearer the surface.

His comments were recorded in the First Biennial Report of the San Francisco Park Commission, 1870–71.

At first, water was taken from lakes in the eastern portion of the park area to irrigate the Panhandle. Then an experimental well was drilled near Stanyan Street, and a redwood tank was placed on the elevated area at the northeast corner of the reservation so water could flow by gravity to the Avenue, or Panhandle. A steam pump apparatus was purchased to get the water into the tank. When it proved defective, Hall recommended that the bill for it not be paid. Because the well did not produce enough water, this approach was discontinued.

Water was then purchased from the Spring Valley Water Company until early in the 1880s, when new attempts were made to provide an independent water supply for the park. The city had many problems with the Spring Valley Water Company. Before long, water bills for the park were amounting to $1,100 per month, and the Park Commission was advised by the city auditor not to pay them. This nonpayment resulted in the company refusing to pay taxes to the city, and the dispute went on for years. Meanwhile Golden Gate Park suffered from lack of water.

Although park commissioners have known since 1871 that an "abundance of water [exists] throughout the eastern portion of the Reservation," on numerous occasions the park has suffered from lack of water. Yet the park is situated over an immense underground water storage, a source that has never been known to fail, even during periods of extended drought.

Early in 1872, Samuel Fowler Butterworth resigned from the Park Commission, and the two remaining members appointed Eugene L. Sullivan. Butterworth later returned to the commission in December 1872, when he was reappointed after the resignation of Charles J. Brenham.

Sullivan was prominent in the city, having been a state senator and author of the bill creating Golden Gate Park. He had also authored a bill that was unfavorable to the railroad interests during his years in the state senate,

Ocean Beach from the Cliff House prior to 1873.

and the word in political circles was "Get Sullivan." He had long fought the battles of San Francisco, but by the time he became a park commissioner, he was tired of fighting and was growing old. In order to "Get Sullivan," Golden Gate Park's needs were sacrificed.

At the time, one of the most pressing problems of the park, aside from a general lack of money, was the sand that blew into the park from privately owned property to the north or the south. Many efforts were made to get people owning land adjacent to the park to reclaim their land, but these efforts were unsuccessful. Hall even furnished lupine seed and equipment to landowners — and was severely criticized in the process. But little progress was made.

In addition to his work in the park, Hall did engineering work with the knowledge and written consent of the park commissioners. One of his jobs was to make weekly inspections of the extensive brick work of the new Palace Hotel. This grand edifice was being built by William C. Ralston, a man who has often been called "The Builder of San Francisco." Ralston and Hall became good friends, and Ralston often detoured through the park to talk to Hall on his trips to his home in Belmont.

Ralston was ever alert to any project that might benefit San Francisco. When he learned of the problem of drifting sand, he immediately devised a plan to reclaim the entire area. The Bank of California would advance the money to the landowners, and a contractor would be hired to reclaim the entire area at one time. Landowners who would not cooperate could be bought out. Apparently nothing stood in the way of William C. Ralston once he made up his mind. Just as the preparations were getting under way for this grand scheme, the Bank of California failed, and its failure was closely followed by Ralston's death. The plan was abandoned, and the sands were not reclaimed in some areas for over fifty years. One can speculate that had Ralston lived, the enemies of Hall, and of Eugene L. Sullivan, who shared many of Hall's views, would not have dared to show the animosities they did in later park politics.

In August 1873, Charles F. MacDermott's position on the Park Commission was declared "vacant by operation of law."

In March 1873, a woman of questionable virtue known as Lizzie Gannon, or "Little Genoa," had walked up behind MacDermott on Market Street and fired point-blank at his head. Fortunately, or otherwise, she missed. At the hearing on the assault charge, MacDermott hired one Judge Mee to represent his assailant and to plead insanity in hopes of getting the young woman committed, thus avoiding scandal.

The defendant objected that she had not hired the man and that she was not insane. She had known what she was doing: she was only sorry that she had missed. She was bound over for trial and released on bail. When the trial came up in July, it was postponed because the complaining witness was absent. In August 1873, the trial came up again, but MacDermott was touring in Europe with his wife. One newspaper suggested that the charges would be dismissed for lack of prosecution.

The Park Commission minutes made no mention of the scandal. "Vacant by operation of law" was apparently intended to mean that he did not attend meetings.

William Alvord, former San Francisco mayor, was appointed as a park commissioner to replace MacDermott. He became a favorite of William Hammond Hall.

Another park problem at this time was the widespread habit of hauling heavy loads on wagons with narrow tires, which ruined the roads. The City Street Department was one of the biggest offenders in this regard. Hall held several demonstrations to prove that a heavy load could be moved more easily on wider tires. But the Street Department would not change, because if it did, it would not have to repair the streets so often, and jobs would be lost. In 1873 the Park Commission passed an ordinance prohibiting heavy wagons on park roads unless they had tires at least five inches wide. Street Department wagons were then turned away at the gates. In retaliation, the Street Department refused to let the park commissioners have any of the street sweepings, including horse manure, to fertilize the park. Not until the mid-1890s was this high-level dispute settled; after that, street railways were used to haul horse droppings and other sweepings to the park. Before that, the sweepings had been dumped into the Bay, rather than used to improve the city park.

In 1873 Hall began the task of trying to stop the encroachment of sand from the ocean. He was again criticized for his methods, his detractors maintaining that he should work westward from the arable portion of the park. But no roads went to the beach, with the exception of the Point Lobos Toll Road, where one had to pay to take a team and a wagon. Besides the money, it took a great deal of time to drive a team down First Avenue to Point Lobos Road, then to the beach, and south to the park. Time was money to Hall, so he determined to build a road through the park. It was called the North Ridge Road, and it began

In 1870 the Hayes Valley Horsecar Line ended at Pierce and Eddy streets.

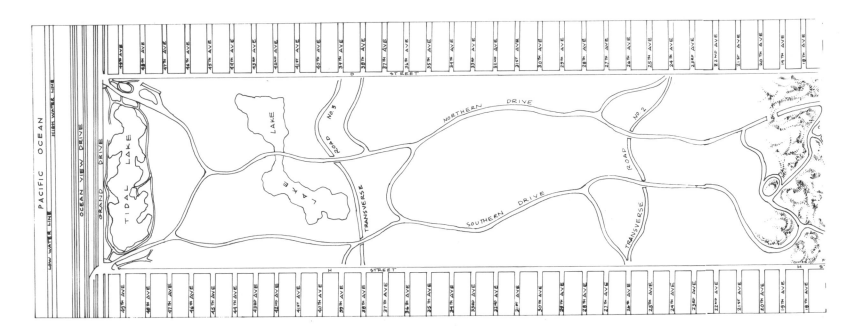

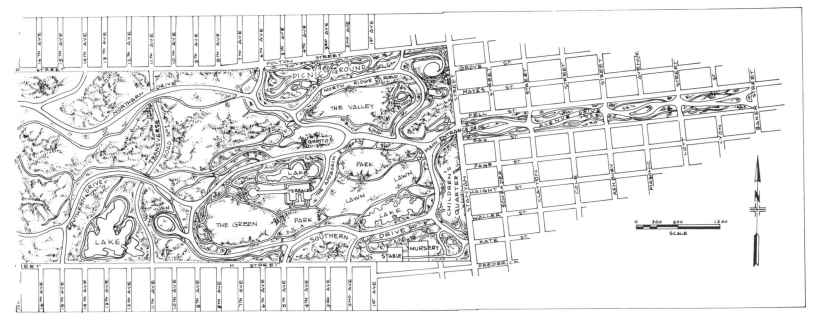

Golden Gate Park in 1872.

just west of the present Lodge and followed North Ridge to the ocean. At that time, you could not drive a team and wagon into Conservatory Valley from the east. Strawberry Ridge, which ran beyond what is now Fulton Street, was too steep to drive over with a team and wagon.

The road was built to the beach in record time at a total cost for grading, draining, and paving of 6¢ per square foot. One newspaper mentioned this cost, remarking that not a single street in the city had cost less than 12¢ per square foot and wondering why it cost the city twice as much to build a road as it did the Park Commission. (This penny-pinching habit of Hall's did not endear him to the local political machine. In addition to the Street Department, which already had an unsavory reputation, the City Hall Commission was rapidly catching on to the game of fleecing the taxpayer. The old City Hall, which took thirty years to build, collapsed in thirty seconds in 1906, leaving the steel framework standing amid the rubble of poorly constructed brick walls.)

During the building of the North Ridge Road through the park, a young boy named Patrick Henry McCarthy was working with his older brother, a teamster employed by Hall. The younger McCarthy, later known as "White Hat" McCarthy, was standing astride his brother's team as they hauled rock down the road, singing "Pop Goes the Weasel" in a thick Irish brogue. Coming down the road in the opposite direction, in a hired horse and buggy, were two distinguished gentlemen, Irving M. Scott and William T. Coleman. Coleman had been the leader of the Vigilante Committee, and Scott was head of the Union Iron Works in Cow Hollow. Young McCarthy's singing disturbed their horse, which responded by running away. The runaway upset the buggy, broke one of the wheels, and dumped the two solid citizens unceremoniously into a muddy ditch. Hall, who was working nearby, took the men into a tent he had erected in case of rain and consoled them with some Christmas cheer that he always carried in his buggy. One of the park workers was sent to the nearest livery stable to rent another rig to take the shaken gentlemen home. The young boy who caused all the commotion became the mayor of San Francisco in 1910. Sometimes called "Pinhead" McCarthy for his initials, P. H., he often bragged that he got his start in Golden Gate Park.

Another story was told about "White Hat" McCarthy in his youth. It concerned the time he and a friend were making the rounds of the saloons in the city. In time they came to a bar owned by a man named Clancy. The hitching rack was full, and there was no place to tie the horses. "I'll fix that," said McCarthy, and he went into the bar and came out with one of Clancy's free doughnuts. He tied the reins to the delicacy and said, "That'll hold 'em," and the two men went inside to have a drink. In just a few moments, a heavy hand came down on McCarthy's shoulder and an Irish voice announced, " 'White Hat,' ye're under arrest for leaving a team unattended on the street." "I'll fight it," vowed McCarthy, and he demanded a trial.

In court "White Hat" told the judge, "Yer Honor, those horses could not get away. They were tied to one of Clancy's doughnuts!" And the judge said, "I hev niver seen wan uv those doughnuts that did not weigh at least 150 pounds. Case is dismissed!"

When the North Ridge Road was finished, and the park workers could get to the beach easily, Hall had them drive posts into the sand at close intervals. They placed boards between the posts; then they leaned lupine and other brush against the boards. The wind then drifted the sand up to the brush and raised the level of the sand barrier. As the brush became covered, the boards were raised and more brush was placed against them to pile up more sand. This method is still used to stop snow from drifting and blocking highways in the snow country. It was estimated that it would cost about $15,000 per year to arrest the sand until a barrier was built high enough to protect the park. But many unforeseen events interrupted the completion of this plan.

Rustic wooden bridge over North Lake, built in the 1870s.

The Visionary Plan
of William Hammond Hall

Much has been said and written in recent years about the need for a plan for Golden Gate Park. But the park has had such a plan since December 30, 1871, when the plan of William Hammond Hall was adopted by the Board of Park Commissioners.

From the first the plan emphasized that Golden Gate Park was to be natural in appearance — a woodland park. Nothing in the park was to be suggestive of the city. Bridges were to be made of wood and were to be rustic in appearance. Even the use of windmills for pumping water was discouraged. Hall said that a steam plant for pumping water could be built underground and then completely hidden.

Hall's plan for the park and Avenue included underpasses at alternate streets of the Avenue to remove city traffic from the area. Between Stanyan Street and the ocean three roads were to cross the park from north to south, but these roads were to be separated from park drives by underpasses. Lack of funds prevented adoption of this part of Hall's plan, and the park suffers today because of it. Fully 95 percent of the daily traffic in the park is actually nonpark traffic. Crowd-attracting features such as museums, aquariums, and libraries have damaged the natural look that was originally designed into the park.

In the 1872–73 Biennial Report to the Legislature, Hall elaborated on his plan in detail:

FIRST: The improvement of the Avenue of approach and about three hundred acres of the main reservation as a finished modern pleasure ground. . . .

SECOND: The reclamation of the sand dunes, the cultivation of forest trees thereon, and the construction of two drives — one near the northern boundary and one near the southern boundary — westward through the forest to the Ocean Beach. . . .

THIRD: The improvement of this beach by the erection of an artificial sand dune upon its outer half; the building of a broad, sheltered drive upon its inner half; the outer sand dune in time to be surmounted by a drive and the construction of a large tidal lake of salt water inside of this drive and within the boundaries of the park.

The plan noted that, unlike eastern parks, Golden Gate Park could be used twelve months of the year. Thus, particular care would have to be given to providing shelter from prevailing winds for those who wished to walk or drive in the park or otherwise enjoy it. Roads were deliberately made crooked, both to discourage fast driving and to prevent the creation of a wind-tunnel effect, which would hinder the healthy growth of trees and shrubs.

Walks were designed for the lower portions of the park and to provide maximum shelter from the wind. These carefully planted low spots, or dells, attracted birds and small wildlife. The walks were kept away from drives as much as possible to avoid large paved areas and too great a width of land devoid of greenery and sheltering foliage.

Hall anticipated that four distinct groups of people would use the park: first, eminently respectable and well-behaved groups of people of the adult community, who would demand a first-class reception; second, ladies with their families, children in the charge of nurses, and boys and girls who wished to enjoy themselves in a homelike manner; third, large picnic parties and people who would approach the park on foot or by public conveyance, and who would enjoy having more freedom; and, fourth, gentlemen who wished to speed their horses and required a place where such privilege was allowed.

For the first group, a "Manor House" was contemplated at the west end of the Main Lawn Valley. It was to be a one-story building that would serve food and refreshments and include a reading room. The area would also have horse sheds, hidden from view by trees.

The children, of all the groups in San Francisco, most needed a place designed to their own needs. Ten acres were planned in the southeast corner of the main reservation. The building for this area was to be called "The Dairy," after that in Central Park. Special places were to be available for croquet, rolling hoop, blindman's buff and such games for quiet children; ball grounds were to be laid out for older boys. The building would serve refreshments suitable for mothers and children. Use of the grounds by adults without children was to be discouraged. Due to lack of funds, Hall stated that the public could not expect a tank of seals or a pair of camels or other such luxuries for some time to come. For the present, he wanted a warm, sunny, protected nook with a decidedly rural air, equipped with appliances for children's games and entertainment.

For the picnic crowds, rustic shelters were contemplated on the North Ridge where a good stand of native oak provided the most privacy for this type of pleasure seeker. That area would also be located closest to the main reservation for those who came on foot or by public conveyance when such transportation became available.

For the fast-driving group, Hall proposed using the Lower Great Highway when it was completed. He envisioned a house for refreshments and sheds for horses at the southwest corner of the park. This plan would provide a drive, two and a half miles in length, that would not interfere with the proper use of the park by other groups of people.

Beyond a music concourse and a conservatory of flowers, no other plans were made for this great woodland park that was designed to meet the needs of city residents for generations to come. Hall felt that the writings of Charles Sprague Sergeant, who had applied the rural park experience to urban needs, had no equal in the English language. It is obvious from Hall's writing that he had avidly studied the writings of Sergeant.

Hall's long-range plan was followed closely until the early 1890s, when W. W. Stow became a commissioner and park policy changed radically.

When buildings such as picnic shelters and meeting places became needed, an expert was employed to do the work. He was Anton Gerster, who was the leading architect for rustic buildings in the country, having been employed for several years in Central Park.

Four large, rustic shelters were built in the park in 1874. They were behind the present Conservatory site and behind the present Lodge on the hills. One was for the exclusive use of women and children, one was for moonlight dancing, and others were for general use in case of inclement weather. The last of the rustic shelters was torn down in the 1960s.

Even the earth toilets used at the time were made of wood and then hidden discreetly from public view by shrubs and trees. In addition to rustic shelters, other buildings had to be erected in the park. Stables must be built. Small homes were planned to house the foreman teamster and other workers because of the distance from town. A small lodge was built for the gatekeeper at Stanyan Street. In 1874 a large two-story Victorian was built on the Oak Street side of the Main Drive for the superintendent. One of the original small three-room cottages can still be seen at the West Side Stables, where it is being used as a gardeners' headquarters. As the park grew, the need for a larger nursery became evident. The first nursery site, where McLaren Lodge now stands, was abandoned in favor of a larger nursery built in 1873–74 on the southeast corner of the park, where Kezar Stadium is today.

In 1874 the Bell Tower, located on the ridge south of Conservatory Valley, was built. It was a substantial rustic tower of heavy timbers built on a brick foundation. This tower was a landmark in the park for years. The bell tolled morning and evening, announcing the start and end of the workday. The tower was destroyed by a fire of unknown origin in 1939. The following morning the bell was a mass of molten metal.

A huge wooden water tank was also built in 1874 along the Main Drive near what is now the south end of North Lake. A windmill pumped water to this tower, which in turn filled the water wagons that were used to sprinkle the drives daily. This water tower is still remembered by old-timers who once worked in the park.

A young Civil War veteran from the South named William Bond Prichard was in charge of most of this construction. He was assistant superintendent under Hall and took complete charge of building the two-story Victorian Lodge in 1874.

The first gardener and forester hired by Hall was Arthur Lowe, who had been employed in the 1830s and 1840s on English estates. He had come to California during the gold rush and earned a small fortune in the mines. Then he had worked for Gen. H. M. Maglee on his estate near San Jose; he was also in charge of the grounds of the James Lick estate. These two estates were considered to be the most important private estates of that day in the Bay Area. Lowe was hired in 1872 to oversee the planting of Golden Gate Park, but he was more than sixty-five years old and could not endure San Francisco's climate. He returned to San Jose the following year. At the time he was

hired, Lowe probably had greater gardening experience than any other man in the history of Golden Gate Park.

Another gardener of note was F. W. Poppey, who was hired in 1874 from Central Park in New York. Poppey's father had been in charge of the estate of Emperor William of Germany for many years. Young Poppey was graduated from the Royal Horticultural College in Berlin and then worked under his father. He was later sent to England and France to study the art of park building. The Franco-Prussian War broke out while he was in Paris, and he could not return home. He came to America and went to work on Central Park and Prospect Park under Frederick Law Olmsted. With his broad experience and education, he was highly regarded by Hall. Poppey left Golden Gate Park in 1876, and returned to New York, where he resumed his employment under Olmsted.

All park workers were required to work a nine-hour day, six days a week. They had one working day per month off, with proper advance notice given to the superintendent. They were forbidden to engage in idle conversation or to use profane or disrespectful language to their co-workers or superiors. Any infractions of these rules were to be reported to the superintendent.

On December 1, 1873, Hall addressed a letter to one of his foremen. This letter, seemingly insignificant at the time, proved noteworthy within a few years:

To Louis Enricht, Keeper
Golden Gate Park

Sir: I observe that you have sent to my house from the park, blocks or post ends for my use as kindling wood. You will have this material taken back to the park. If you have permitted any of like nature to be taken to the residence of any of the other Park Commissioners, have it brought back.

In the future, as in the past, I desire that all property, however valueless, belonging to the park, and all labor paid for with park funds will be retained and expended exclusively on the reservation, or upon other matters connected directly therewith.

Very respectfully yours,
Wm. Hammond Hall

The Third Biennial Report of the Park Commission for the years 1874–75 reported the death, in May 1875, of Commissioner Samuel Fowler Butterworth and his replacement by Louis McLane. The board was now composed of President Eugene L. Sullivan and Commissioners William Alvord and Louis McLane. McLane was a prominent man who had been one-time head of the entire Pacific Coast Section of Wells Fargo & Co. He was the owner and incorporator of the California Telegraph Company and one of the original shareholders in the Bank of California. He had interests in Pacific Insurance Company, California Dry Dock Company, Sacramento Gas Company, Pacific Rolling Mills, Overland Stage Company, and Pioneer Stage Company. In the early years, Golden Gate Park did not lack leadership on the Park Commission. Louis McLane had few detractors.

Central Park in New York was begun when that city was well into its third century. San Francisco's Golden Gate Park was begun while the city was still in its third decade. The *San Francisco Chronicle,* which had bitterly opposed the park from the beginning, became positively lyrical in praise of the new park. The Sunday *Chronicle* of October 24, 1875, gives a long description of the progress in the park.

> The park is approached by a serpentine drive, winding among the groves of shrubbery. . . . The average number of vehicles entering the park each weekday is six hundred; on Sundays, one thousand to twelve hundred. . . . The drives are many and have been laid out judiciously. Picnic grounds with lovely rustic buildings and dancing pavilions are being laid out by skilled workmen. The picnic area

embraces twenty-five acres. . . . The chief improvement is the reclamation of the sand and establishing thereon a young growth of forest trees. . . . The management of the park is in excellent hands. Everything is done according to routine and the discipline of the force is admirable. . . . The expense of constructing and maintaining the park since the beginning is $385,927.71.

In contrast, on the other side of the Golden Gate, the *Marin County Journal* had this to say about the "Manor House" advocated by Hall on December 16, 1875:

> What do you think of that Golden Gate Park Hotel project? The Palace is considered by some old fogies quite a hotel, but wait till you see this. The building is to be two miles wide by three miles long. In place of elevators, balloons. Shaving and hair brushing will be done by electricity. The waiters are all to be on horseback. Meals will be announced by cannon.

The park was becoming immensely popular, however, both as a place of resort and as an example of how to spend the people's money to the best advantage. The entire park had been planted with lupine, and small trees covered the eastern section. One newspaper remarked, "The desert had been made to blossom as the rose."

In the June 1875 report, issued just before the civic storm broke, Hall remarked: "In presenting this report, I cannot refrain from expressing the hope that the near future has in store a bright prospect for Golden Gate Park."

Hall recommended that the street connecting Van Ness Avenue with the Panhandle or Avenue be improved by park money, since the city did not seem inclined to do so. He also recommended that First Avenue from Point Lobos Road to Golden Gate Park be improved with park moneys to make it easier for "the masses" to enjoy the park. He deplored the lack of public transportation to the park and exhorted the city and the street railroad companies to remedy the situation.

Rustic shelter built by Anton Gerster in 1874.

At that time, there were 35,882 running feet of road-ways and more than 17,000 feet of water pipe laid. The buildings included the Lodge, the Bell Tower, four rustic houses, a carpenters' shop, a plumbers' shop, storerooms, and two open sheds for storage. The stables had been enlarged to accommodate twenty horses. Trees and shrubs had been planted: in 1871–72, 1,800; in 1872–73, 16,745; in 1873–74, 15,700; and in 1874–75, 25,435 — for a total of 59,680. Of this figure, 17,854 trees and shrubs had been planted in the sand district and the balance in the eastern portion and the Avenue. Nearly a mile of the Great High-way barrier had been started, and the sand bulwark averaged a height of nine feet for the entire distance. Hall recommended strongly that sufficient money be appropriated to continue this work to extend it all the way to Sloat Boulevard.

Hall's plan divided the park as follows:

	Area in Acres
Drives for pleasure	50.53
Crossroads for business travel	5.80
Saddle roads for riding	7.65
Walks for foot traffic only	25.00
Freshwater lakes	12.30
Saltwater lake near beach	15.00
Highly finished park	120.00
Picnic grounds, rambles, and the like	90.00
Nursery, yard, shops, office	20.00
Forest land	672.72
Total	1019.00

One hundred years later, the park has nearly 30 acres of permanent buildings, exclusive of nurseries and rest rooms; nearly 250 acres of pavement for roads, parking lots, and the like; and plans exist for expansion of all the major buildings presently in the park. Park management still talks of a plan for the park while acting steadily to increase the number of buildings and parking lots. No Golden Gate Park will remain a hundred years hence unless citizens demand that the land be returned to its original purpose: to be "a green oasis in the arid desert of business and dissipation."

Frederick Law Olmsted, the builder of Central Park and a renowned expert on parks, had advised in 1865 against the possibility of growing trees in San Francisco. In January 1876, he wrote the following letter to Hall:

Dear Mr. Hall: Since I wrote you this morning, I have received your Third Biennial Report, and have read it with

Another example of Gerster's work, about 1874.

great interest. I cannot too strongly express my admiration of the spirit and method which characterize your undertaking, and I do not doubt that it will be rewarded with results such as I have not hitherto thought reasonable to expect under the circumstances. There is no like enterprise anywhere else which, so far as I can judge, has been conducted with equal foresight, ingenuity and economy.

Very truly yours,

Fred. Law Olmsted

While all this was happening at the park, the scandal of the City Hall Commission was reaching great proportions in late 1875. Clamors for reform in city government were hard to ignore. And so, in Hall's words, "a shovel full of blinding dust was thrown into the air." Hall's detractors were determined to get him, and by spring 1876, they succeeded.

Hall had once fired a blacksmith named D. C. Sullivan because he had "padded his bill more than 100 per cent." Sullivan eventually settled for half the amount. This peculiar quality of character seemed to fit Sullivan well for politics, and he was duly elected to the state legislature. He had sworn to get even with Hall, and he was used by his fellow legislators in the debate as the "shovel full of blinding dust" which persuaded the legislature not to approve new bonds to build the park. Instead they approved bonds that allowed the skullduggery at City Hall to continue.

Sullivan brought all kinds of charges against Hall on the assembly floor. He accused Hall of using wood from the park (an interesting accusation in light of Hall's letter on the matter). He accused Hall of stealing monuments from the park. And Hall was accused of drawing a city salary while at the same time, working outside the park. The charges were fiction based on a bit of fact, but they made headlines in the papers that sided with City Hall. Frank McCoppin, Hall's old enemy, through his influence in the state senate, blocked the report that might have cleared Hall's name.

Sullivan was named chairman of the Assembly Investigating Committee, but when it was brought out that he had been fired from the park for dishonesty, he retired in disgrace. The committee nevertheless came to San Francisco and took an entire volume of testimony. They held hearings on two different occasions, questioned forty-one witnesses, and examined the park records. Then their report was postponed and not made public until after the legislature had adjourned. The damage to the future of the park was done.

The wood, as implied in Hall's letter, had been returned to the park as soon as Hall learned of it. The "monuments" were granite markers that Mr. Hall had brought on the site under contract to lay out the boundaries of the park. He had supplied more than required, and some that had not been needed were removed from the park and used in San Rafael on a private surveying job.

Hall's work outside the park was done with the knowledge and written consent of the park commissioners. His outside jobs were completed a long time before he began receiving a full salary.

City Hall got the bonds they sought, but the park did not get any bonds. The tax rate for park purposes was reduced by half to 1½¢ on each $100 of taxable property. The superintendent's salary was reduced from $400 to $200. No provisions were made to rent an office for the commissioners or to pay a secretary to the commission.

The entire Park Commission resigned in disgust along with Hall. Hall was forced to turn the park over to his successor, William Bond Prichard, who was appointed superintendent at $200 per month in 1876.

For the next ten years, because of the infamous City Hall Gang, Golden Gate Park was deprived of the funds necessary even to maintain what had already been accomplished. Plantations were not watered, and trees were not thinned; roads were not maintained, and horses and equipment were sold because the budget did not allow the hiring of men to drive or operate them. The majority of the western district returned to a sand waste, and even the work of preventing the inroad of sand at the Great Highway had to be discontinued. It was a shameful ten years in San Francisco's history, and a period that has been neglected, in a large measure, by historians to date.

William Bond Prichard, park superintendent from 1876 to 1881.

William Bond Prichard

The second superintendent of Golden Gate Park, William Bond Prichard, followed in William Hammond Hall's footsteps. Like Hall, Prichard was both a Southerner by birth and an engineer.

He was born February 17, 1842, in Petersburg, Virginia, and received his education in private schools. He was graduated from Virginia Military Institute (VMI) in 1861 and served in the Confederate Army from April 1861 to April 1865.

At the age of twenty, Prichard was a captain of Company B, 38th Virginia Infantry, C.S.A., and led his company of forty-one men in Pickett's Charge at Gettysburg. He and six men survived that charge. Four of them were wounded; Captain Prichard was wounded twice. Prichard surrendered with Gen. Robert E. Lee on April 10, 1865, at Appomattox Court House, and was given parole.

Captain Prichard was assistant professor at VMI from 1867 to 1871, when he was advised to seek a better climate because of his wounds. He went to California in that year and was hired as assistant engineer to William Hammond Hall, working in Golden Gate Park until 1881, when he resigned and went to Southern California.

One of his first major works in the park was to oversee the construction of the first Park Lodge in 1874. It was a two-story Victorian frame house located on the Oak Street side of the Main Drive, near the Stanyan Street entrance to the park.

His major contribution to the park was the beautiful job of grading and landscaping Conservatory Valley. A great deal of earth was moved to provide the magnificent setting for the Conservatory, and millions of visitors to Conservatory Valley owe their enjoyment of that portion of the park to his engineering skill.

When Hall resigned in 1876, Prichard was appointed superintendent. In spite of crippling legislation that deprived the park of adequate funds to pursue the final reclamation of the park, he persevered until 1881, when he finally resigned in disgust.

During his final year at the park, Prichard drew the plans for a huge irrigation reservoir on the east side of Strawberry Hill. Not only would the reservoir be used for irrigation, but it would also serve as a lake for boating and other forms of healthful exercise. Since no funds were available for construction, the plans were deferred. In the 1890s, after W. W. Stow had been appointed to the Park Board, the plans were revived with adequate funding, and Prichard's reservoir was named Stow Lake.

In 1876 Prichard and Margaret Johnston were married. She was the daughter of Gen. Albert Sidney Johnston, commander of Benicia Arsenal until the outbreak of the Civil War, when General Johnston resigned his commission and made his way to Los Angeles by horseback. There he joined other Southern sympathizers in a flight to Texas, where they joined the Confederate forces.

Stow Lake, built in 1895, was named for W.W. Stow, a park commissioner.

Prichard lived in Los Angeles, where he was a civil servant, until 1886, when he moved to San Luis Obispo and became interested in fruit farming.

From 1896 until 1899, Prichard followed his profession as a civil engineer in private practice. He returned to San Francisco in 1899 and became deputy assessor in this city.

He was prominent in the Democratic Party and was a member of the convention that nominated James D. Phelan for mayor of San Francisco.

Prichard died in 1915 and is buried in Cypress Lawn Cemetery in Colma, California.

Great Highway, Life Saving Station, and Dutch Windmill, about 1902.

Politics in the Park

The first five years of Golden Gate Park's history had been a time of growth and expansion. With the reduction of funds due to the action of state legislation, work on the park nearly stopped. The money and the greenery both dried up. At the board meeting in April 1876, the secretary reported that cash on hand for the operation of the park amounted to $10,532. The board president reported that he had revised the work force and pared it down to a maintenance crew paid at the very low rates the board had adopted.

At the next meeting, on June 30, 1876, William Hammond Hall was appointed secretary pro tem; no money was available to pay a regular secretary. The minutes note that Governor Irwin had asked the board members to accept reappointment to the board, even though they had all resigned. After discussion the board agreed.

On July 12, 1876, the board met again. Eugene L. Sullivan, William Alvord, and Louis McLane presented their new commissions. On the motion of McLane, Sullivan was elected president of the board.

In spite of the action of the legislature, which severely crippled the board, the community in general supported continuing the work on the park. In the twentieth Annual Report of the Mechanic's Institute, delivered on June 10, 1876, Andrew S. Hallidie, president, said:

> I must . . . refer to the excellent work done by the park commissioners in laying out and reclaiming the sandy and forbidding soil, which, by their careful management and patient experiments, has become a spot of beauty and an ornament to the city. The Golden Gate Park bids fair to outrival any park in the United States, as to extent and natural beauties. The volunteer service of the commissioners, and excellent results of their engineer, Wm. Hammond Hall's skill, deserves more than passing mention, and I join in the general feeling in expressing my regret that the work is in danger of serious interruption by the resignation of the commissioners and their engineer, than whom no citizens in the community command more respect.

Though park policy was initially determined by people of importance in the city, this practice changed somewhat. As the park became an established part of life in San Francisco, members of the wider community began to make their needs felt. A special meeting of the commissioners was held on August 31, 1876, in response to a request by the mayor of San Francisco, and many citizens argued that the gates of the park be kept open at night. After due deliberation, the board decided that the gates would be kept open until 11:00 P.M. At 10:30 P.M. the great bell in the Bell Tower would toll, notifying all that the gates would close in thirty minutes. The order was then amended to read that the park would be open until 11:00 P.M. only on moonlit nights.

On March 21, 1877, James Scott Henderson was employed as the head gardener at a sum of $5 per working day. Henderson was a Scot and a gardener of wide experience. After he left Golden Gate Park, he was in charge of the James Flood grounds in Menlo Park and was highly regarded in horticultural circles. In later years Hall stated that if he had been able to find Henderson when he was searching for a superintendent in 1887, in his capacity as consulting engineer, he would not have hired John McLaren.

The pay of Sgt. Thomas Sloan of the park police was ordered increased that year to $3.25 per day and that of the day watch increased to $3.00 per day.

Charles Webb Howard, president of the Spring Valley Water Company, wrote the board that unless the water bills were paid at once, the company would be forced to shut off the park's water supply. Eugene L. Sullivan, president, was authorized to reply to Howard that the board was not authorized to pay the bills as long as the matter was in litigation. He was to send a copy of both communications to the mayor.

Superintendent Prichard was then authorized to make inquiries concerning the cost of sinking an artesian well. He later reported the estimated cost as follows: two artesian wells, 12 inches in diameter, with 130 feet of pipe each at $7.00 per foot = $2,100; two tanks, 30,000 gallons each (covered) = $1,800; two pumps, engines, boilers, capacity 800 per hour = $2,400; pipe, 630 feet = $2,205; fittings = $300; and labor and materials = $1,000. The total was $9,805.

At another special meeting in April 1877, the following letter was signed by the president and ordered sent to Howard at the Spring Valley Water Company:

Office of the Park Commissioners
San Francisco, April 19, 1877

Dear Sir: As at present advised, the park commissioners cannot now take action and audit the bills of your company for water furnished in the park or make any contract upon that subject. But to meet the present necessities, we request that your company shall turn the water on at Golden Gate Park and agree that until further notice we will take as much as we shall need for the use of said park at meter measurement, by thousand gallons, and pay for the same at our negotiated rates, auditing the bills therefore monthly.

Yours respectfully,

E. L. Sullivan
President of Board of Park Commissioners

Howard wrote back accepting the offer.

On this same date bids were opened for the drilling of an artesian well in the park. Two months later, Superintendent Prichard was authorized to dig two more wells in Golden Gate Park at a cost not to exceed $200.

Because of the lack of funds, all work was suspended on the Great Highway. With the exception of a mile-long bridle path, no improvements were made in Golden Gate Park, the Avenue, or Buena Vista Park. All work was limited to watering, maintenance, and the establishment of compost piles. During the years 1876 and 1877, the park crew used 17,822,600 gallons of water.

Visitors to the park for the year ending November 30, 1877, numbered 703,658. Of these, 17,259 were pedestrians; 218,266 came in vehicles. This census showed conclusively the need for public transportation to the area, so people without vehicles could still get to the park.

In 1877 the Department of the Treasury sought permission of the board to erect a life-saving station in the western end of the park. This station was to provide protection to persons at the beach and aid in the rescue of sailors on board ships entering the Golden Gate. Approval was finally granted, and construction began in 1878. The building, which was expanded several times, remained in the park until the 1940s. In those days before radio, television, or movies, anything new was of great public interest. The lifeboat drills held on Sundays were attended by thousands of people who watched the launching of the lifeboat, the shooting of life lines, and the staged rescues by the station crews. Crew members received $40 per month plus room and board as pay at that time.

Charles F. MacDermott, one of the original park commissioners, addressed a letter to the editor of the *San Francisco Bulletin* on January 26, 1878. He noted that unemployment was high in the city and that much work remained unfinished in Golden Gate Park. He offered to donate $1,000 to a fund for the employment of men in the park if ninety-nine other citizens would do the same, thus raising $100,000. Since no further mention was made of this offer, it is presumed that he was unsuccessful.

Then David Bush, a private citizen of San Francisco, proposed raising money for the park by donating $100 to a fund to hire unemployed men at a dollar a day. He soon raised over $5,000, and men were put to work immediately. Much of the South Drive was built by the Dollar-a-Day Fund, and considerable work was later done in Conservatory Valley. This fund, known as the David Bush Fund, was continued under one sponsor or another for fifteen years until 1893, when the work of building the Midwinter Fair was begun in the park.

In December 1877, the board received an important letter:

San Francisco, December 29, 1877

Eugene L. Sullivan, Wm. Alvord and Louis McLane.

Gentlemen: The Late James Lick, in his lifetime, at heavy cost, imported and prepared the materials now stored at his homestead in San Jose, where they were designed to be erected, two large and beautiful conservatories, modeled after those in the Kew Gardens, London.

These, after his death, were offered for sale by his trustees and have been purchased by the following named gentlemen, viz: [There followed the names of twenty-eight

prominent citizens of the city, including William Alvord, Leland Stanford, and Charles Crocker] . . ., who, desirous of giving what they believe will be a very desirable addition to Golden Gate Park, and which will contribute to the future pleasure of the inhabitants of this city, have each contributed in equal amounts toward the purchase and for that purpose. Acting as a committee for and in behalf of the purchasers, we respectfully ask you, as the representatives of that great public trust, to accept for the park this gift, exacting only the condition that the conservatories shall be erected in the park within eighteen months from this date, put in good condition and so maintained thereafter for the use and benefit of the public.

Very respectfully,
James Irvine
W. H. Whittier

The board gratefully accepted and stated that "if sufficient appropriations are made, the building will certainly be erected within the time you prescribe." Board president Sullivan was authorized to seek sufficient funds in the legislature to comply with the terms of the gift. The matter of location in the park was deferred, pending developments. The legislature in due time appropriated the sum of $40,000 for "The Improvement of Golden Gate and Bellevue Parks," specifying that no more than $5,000 per month could be spent, adding the condition that the Board of Supervisors approve the expenditure. William Hammond Hall, the consulting engineer, later reported that the task of erecting the Conservatory was done, and that the park commissioners had $13,000 remaining for other uses.

Superintendent Prichard directed the grading of Conservatory Valley and the preparation of the site of the new Conservatory.

The firm of Lord and Burnham was hired to erect the conservatories at a cost not to exceed $2,050. Work was to commence as early as possible and to be completed without unnecessary delay.

The Conservatory as it looked in 1879.

While the original letter offered two conservatories, only one was subsequently built in the park. Some clues to this unsolved mystery remain. In 1881 the *Sacramento Union* mentioned that Mrs. Edwin Bryant Crocker, wife of a Sacramento judge, had erected the Bell Conservatory on the family's estate. Charles Crocker, one of the original donors of the conservatories, was a Sacramento native.

Although the Bell Conservatory was torn down in 1954, Bert Geisreiter, the last owner, wrote to the Park Commission in an attempt to learn more about the replica of the park's conservatory which he and his father had used as a commercial nursery. Photographs from his collection show that, in all respects — those of shape, scroll work, and the design of the entrance — the two conservatories were identical except for size. The one on the Crocker estate was one-half the size of its larger mate in Golden Gate Park. The photographs show the Bell Conservatory and the Golden Gate Park Conservatory before its roof was burned and replaced with one of a different

shape. No known records remain, however, to explain how one of the conservatories wound up on the Sacramento Crocker estate. That is anyone's guess.

At a regular meeting of the commission on October 3, 1878, President Eugene L. Sullivan resigned, giving as his reason other pressing business. On November 7, 1878, the board met to consider the appointment of a new commissioner. Commissioner Alvord submitted the name of Capt. Oliver Eldridge of San Francisco. Captain Eldridge had had a long career as a sailor in the Merchant Marine and the United States Navy. During the Civil War he had joined the transport service and had worked with Gen. William Tecumseh Sherman in the famous expedition through Georgia. Afterward Eldridge had commanded the U.S.S. *Constitution,* and then he had gone to California. No other nominations were forwarded, and Captain Eldridge was appointed to fill the board vacancy. The new appointee was not of the same political persuasion as the governor of California. On November 28, 1878, a communication from the governor was read to the board. It protested the appointment of the new commissioner and called attention to several laws regulating the appointment of park commissioners. The board instructed the secretary to point out in his reply to the governor the precedent of commissioners electing a replacement when one of their number resigned or died before completion of a term. Captain Eldridge was given the oath of office, and the board was reorganized, with Louis McLane as its elected president.

Bicycling had become a popular sport. The San Francisco Bicycle Club appeared before the board to ask for the privilege of riding on the excellent park roads. Superintendent Prichard recommended that the cyclists be allowed to use the South Drive between the hours of 5:00 and 7:00 A.M. and from 5:00 to 8:00 P.M. on weekdays, and on Sundays from 5:00 to 10:00 A.M. and from 4:00 to 8:00 P.M. The report was ordered filed, and the privilege was granted only to members of the San Francisco Bicycle Club for a period of thirty days on a trial basis. Speed was to be held at not more than ten miles per hour. Any violations of the rules would subject culprits to arrest and forfeiture of their permits to ride in the park.

The mounted police had a field day. When one of them caught a cyclist in violation of the rules, he galloped after the bicycle and lassoed the rider. Then he would halt his horse and let the bicycle continue on its merry way, minus its rider. After a few such episodes, violations were few and far between.

The park area remained wild. One day early in 1879, Dr. J. A. Bauer of the city was driving through the park

Music Stand built in 1881 in front of the Conservatory.

when his dogs startled a wildcat from its cover. The wildcat was trailed by the dogs and treed in a willow near the Chain of Lakes. Dr. Bauer and one of the park policemen shot it from its perch.

In May 1879, the Board of Supervisors appropriated $2,000 for a road to be built from the Cliff House to the Park entrance on the Great Highway. The funds were allotted in spite of the fact that the sand barrier was neither complete nor stable. Hall estimated that several years would be needed to complete the work, but influential people in the city did not want to wait. They put pressure on the city government to build the road right away, with no thought of the future. The sand was never completely controlled in that area, because the road was put in too soon. Thousands of dollars have been spent each year since then to clear the road of sand. Several times over the years sand has closed the road to traffic. Maintenance and digging out costs, paid for with city tax money, stem from the impatience of people who influenced civic affairs one hundred years ago.

Getting to Golden Gate Park during its early decades was very trying to those who had horses and carriages. The *Alta Californian* remarked on September 17, 1878:

At length the supervisors have discovered the fact that the principal roadway to the park is in such condition that a resident cannot invite a visitor to drive out to our only pleasure ground lest the visitor might be tempted to ask: "Why don't your city lay out a road to the park?" A portion of McAllister Street is in worse condition than the poorest country road in the state. A resolution of intention to pave the roadway with granite blocks was introduced to the Board of Supervisors last night.

But if you were too poor to own a horse and carriage, the task of getting to the park was almost insurmountable.

On May 10, 1878, the *San Francisco Examiner* had reported on the development of the Victoria Regia, a water lily, in the Conservatory. The seeds for the plant had been donated by Her Brittanic Majesty's Consul, William Lane Booker of San Francisco. Many San Franciscans made the grueling trip to see the new plant, and the *San Francisco Chronicle* of August 30, 1879, told a sad story:

A party of San Franciscans residing in the vicinity of Rincon Hill who yesterday assayed a visit to Golden Gate Park via horse cars to see the Victoria Regia now in bloom are much prostrated by the journey. . . .

Among the lines daily advertised to carry passengers to Central Avenue, the starting point of the Geary Street Dummy, is the Sutter Street Railroad, and it was deemed most convenient to take those cars at Sansome Street. It is not exactly a pleasant thing to have a car pass within six feet of one, an absent-minded conductor failing to perceive your signals, and then be compelled to walk four or five rods over a too-much sprinkled pavement to overtake the car; but this was a minor grievance. Arriving at Buchanan Street, two blocks from Central Avenue, the conductor, who had been giving guilty back glances for a block or two, opened the door and announced a change of cars. "But we want to go to Central Avenue," said a passenger. "Don't you keep right on out there as you advertise?" "Well, no," was the response. "We shall, though, in a few days. You take the next car and it will carry you on farther," he added deprecatingly. . . .

The party took up the line of march through dusty streets to the City Central Road, three blocks away. "Do you run to Central Avenue?" "Yes, Marm," said the urbane conductor. "How far from where the Geary Street Dummy runs?" Answer, "Just one block." "You are sure you don't stop before you get there?" "We run all the way there."

Halfway up the hill the car stopped, and the driver, changing the horse about, prepared to return. "What is the matter?" "Oh, it's all right, Mum, I'll put you on the next car coming up." Passing down the hill several blocks, the contents of the car was transferred to the up-coming car, which proceeded, miraculously, without stopping, to Central Av-

The Geary Street, Park and Ocean Railway began operations in February, 1880.

enue. Then it became necessary to hastily plow a block through the sand to take a dummy train, where a conductor stood upon the platform ringing the bell as if there was no time to be lost.

When some time had elapsed and those who had hurried to secure seats had grown somewhat impatient, another dummy with car attached came steaming down the road.

"This is the car to take," came another announcement, and several more minutes of waiting ensued. . . .

The ride to the park occupied but seven minutes and the troubles were at last over. "I can go from here to England with less trouble," an Englishman was heard to grumble as he left the car.

One newspaper writer pointed out that the park had distinct phases, as far as visitors were concerned. From 6:00 to 10:00 A.M. equestrians of all ages prevailed. One could see a father and his daughters, who rode decorously on sidesaddles. Groups of young boys rode tough ponies on their Mexican saddles, and the visiting Englishman on his English saddle looked disdainfully at "those fellahs,

who ride all over their mounts, you know." The period between 10:00 A.M. and 2:00 P.M. was the dullest of the day. Pony phaetons and family carriages with nurses and children were the most common sight. Some phaetons, drawn by two fast horses, carried blonde "painted" women who stared with interest at the men. About 2:00 P.M. the park filled again, when the carriages were going to the beach or the Cliff House. By 4:00 P.M. the tide turned. The road was filled with carriages returning from "the Cliff."

One hundred iron settees were purchased and distributed throughout the park for the convenience of its patrons. Young lovers soon took advantage of the seats on moonlit nights — to escape the chaperoned front rooms of the young ladies' homes. Charges were made that the park was undermining the morals of the youth of the city by providing such comforts. The *WASP* carried the following editorial on "Hugging in the Park":

The law-abiding people of this community were startled a few days since, and the greatest indignation prevailed at an editorial article in a contemporary, denouncing

South Drive in the 1890s, looking east toward Strawberry Hill.

the practice of hugging in the public parks. The article went on to show that the placing of seats in the park leads to hugging, and the editor denounced hugging in the most insane manner possible.

Parties who object to hugging are old, usually, and are like the lemon that has done duty in the circus lemonade. If they had a job of hugging, they would want to hire a man to do it for them.

Let us call attention to that powerful paper, the Declaration of Independence, where it asserts that "All men are created free and equal, endowed with certain inalienable rights, among which are life, liberty and the pursuit of happiness."

When the framers of that great Declaration of Independence were at work on that clause, they must have had in view the pastime of hugging in the parks. Hugging is certainly a pursuit of happiness. People do not hug for wages, that is, except on the stage. It is sort of spontaneous combustion, as it were, of the feelings, and has to have proper conditions of the atmosphere to make it a success. . . .

A man who complains of a little natural, inspired hugging on a seat in a park, of an evening, with a fountain throwing water all over little cast-iron cupids, has probably got a soul, but he hasn't got it with him. . . .

The couple, one a male and the other a female, will sit far apart on the cast-iron seat for a moment, when the young lady will try to fix her cloak over her shoulders, and she can't fix it, and then the young man will help her, and when he has got it fixed, he will go off and leave one arm around the small of her back. He will miss his arm and wonder where he left it, and go back after it, and in the dark he will feel around with the other hand to find the hand he left.

Certainly the two hands will meet; they will express astonishment, and clasp each other, and be so glad that they will begin to squeeze, and the chances are that they will cut the girl in two, but they never do. Under the circumstances, a girl can exist on less atmosphere than she can while doing a washing.

It is claimed by some that young people who stay out nights and hug are not good for anything the next day. There is something to this, but if they didn't get any hugging, they wouldn't be worth a cent anytime. They would be all the time looking for it.

After Conservatory Valley was filled and leveled, the commissioners decided to cover the floor of the valley with gravel to make a huge music concourse, 100 feet wide by 500 feet long. A wooden band shell was planned as soon as some means could be found to hire a band.

Behind and to the east of the Conservatory was what was known as "the Ramble." This area was devoted to lawn tennis and croquet, as well as picnics.

The commissioners announced plans for a Casino and also for a Speed Track, where the owners of fast horses could ride or drive them without restriction. For the first time, demand was made that an area be set aside for the exclusive use of a certain group of people, to the exclusion of others. But many more such demands were to be made on the park as time went on.

At a regular meeting of the board in August 1880, a letter from the directors of the Park and Ocean Railroad Company was read. This company, owned by "Leland Stanford and Others," asked for a franchise lasting fifty years to build a steam railroad from Haight and Stanyan streets, across the southeast corner of Golden Gate Park, out H Street (now Lincoln Way) to the Great Highway, and then across the park to the base of the Cliff. The secretary was instructed to answer, pointing out that under Order Number Eight Hundred establishing the park, the Park Commission was allowed to lease land for no more than three years. The commission signified its willingness to lease the land at the southeast corner of the park, but under no circumstances would they allow a railroad to be built across the park at the western end, thereby cutting off access to the beach. Further, they said, the railroad company would have to fill in the southeast corner of the park with a minimum of twenty-seven thousand cubic yards of earth. This response, which served to block the plans of "Leland Stanford and Others," was not considered acceptable behavior on the part of public officials in those days. On August 27, the board received a letter from the Park and Ocean Railroad Company stating that they could not accept plans to utilize the southeast corner of the park unless they could also cross the park at the Great Highway.

In September the bicycle riders presented a request that they be allowed to use all roads in the park from 6:00 to 10:00 A.M. and from 6:00 P.M. until closing. Permission was granted for a period of thirty days on a trial basis.

The mayor then sent a letter to the Park Commission stating that if the commission had no objections, he would grant James McMichael permission to care for horses in the park. The secretary was instructed to write the mayor to inform him that the commission most assuredly did object. A pamphlet covering the laws for the government of the park was enclosed with the letter. This incident was the first recorded attempt to use jobs in the park for political

The original Park Lodge after a twelve-inch snowfall on February 5, 1887.

patronage, but it was not the last. The practice soon became common. At the board's next meeting, Commissioner Eldridge moved that no person be employed in the park or fired therefrom without the express approval of the board. The motion carried.

On January 11, 1881, the resignation of T. B. Mortee, secretary of the board, was accepted. Commissioner Alvord then recommended F. P. Hennessey to fill the vacancy, and his appointment was ordered. Hennessey had been employed in Central Park for about seventeen years and was apparently highly recommended by Frederick Law Olmsted. Little is known of him, as the personnel records of Central Park for that period are not available, and little mention was made of him in the San Francisco newspapers. At the same meeting, the order granting use of all park roads to bicycle riders was rescinded, so that riders were restricted as they had been in the past.

That same year, Isaac P. Allen and about a hundred other members of the Archery Club requested archery privileges in the park. They were granted. Foreman Patrick Quigley was also ordered to set up two tents from the storeroom for the club's use. The club agreed to keep the tents in repair.

On February 3, 1881, Superintendent William Bond Prichard submitted his resignation, effective March 1, 1881. It was accepted and the order filed.

Deer Glen (now de Laveaga Dell) on Middle Drive, about 1895.

The Dark Years

At a special meeting of the board held on May 9, 1881, F. P. Hennessey was elected superintendent of the park. He was also to serve as secretary of the board at no extra salary.

J. J. Daemon submitted to the board plans for a house of refreshment in the park. The superintendent was ordered to stake out the lines for this project and to assist Daemon in the final determination of the matter.

On June 7, 1881, the immediate resignation of James Scott Henderson, the head gardener, was accepted. The resignations of the secretary, the superintendent of parks, and the head gardener, all within a few weeks, were not explained in the minutes. Perhaps the cause was lack of money; the superintendent was ordered to take charge of all work that had been the responsibility of the head gardener, in addition to his own duties as superintendent and as secretary of the board. However, on June 30, 1881, Edward Sheldon was named to be secretary to the board. The superintendent was ordered to move his family into the Park Lodge, so he would be on hand when needed.

In August 1881, the *Pacific Rural Express* carried a long description of improvements in Golden Gate Park. The writer described the Conservatory as being "Oriental in style, graceful in outline and highly ornamental." He went on to say that the park had recently received some sixty-five varieties of "Sikkam and Bootan" rhododendrons.

But it was plain to the knowing eye of consultant William Hammond Hall that the park was deteriorating rapidly. Trees that had been planted in the western end of the park had received no water. Roads were neglected, except to water and roll them. And the growing trees needed to be thinned out to give them room. This period was one of the barest minimum of maintenance and care, with little thought for the future. It was also a period of rapid turnover in park personnel. The clerk in the office of the Park Lodge was notified that his services would no longer be needed, and James Taylor was hired as head gardener at $3 per day.

Telephone communication between the park and the city was established in September 1881, at a cost of $25 for the connection and $2.50 per month for rental of the instrument and maintenance of the batteries.

In November 1881, the secretary reported that the money in the bank was insufficient to cover the monthly vouchers. Commissioner William Alvord stated that the vouchers could be cashed at the Bank of California for that one month, pending receipt of more funds from the Board of Supervisors.

The mounted police were notified that, as of December 1, 1881, they would have to furnish and feed their own horses. But they would be paid $3.33 instead of $3.00 per day.

At a special meeting of the board on December 16, 1881, a contract was ordered drawn up between the Park

Commission and Rhinehart Daemon to operate the Casino for a period of three years.

For the building of the Casino in the park, a contract of $1,950 was awarded to McCannot and Jeffers for "mechanical and other work." The minutes of the board do not make clear whether the Casino was being built by the commissioners themselves or by J. J. Daemon.

On December 30, 1881, the *San Francisco Examiner* described the Casino and told how it would benefit the park.

The Casino stood on the hill west of the Conservatory, facing east. It was a one-story building with a long veranda. It held a dining hall, but one could also dine discreetly, without disclosing the identity of one's companion, in one of the private dining rooms, after the manner of the city's Poodle Dog Restaurant. Since no sewers had yet been built in the vicinity, no modern toilet facilities were available in the Casino. Casino guests had to use the earthen "closets" outside the building, but the guests in the private rooms had adult "potty chairs" for their convenience. These handsome chairs were made of three kinds of hardwood. The backs of the chairs were made of maple and intricately carved. The rungs and legs of the chairs were made of hickory, and the seat and arms made of oak. One or two of the "potty chairs" still exist; one is on display at the San Francisco History Room of the San Francisco Public Library.*

To raise money for the park, an auction sale was held, and seven of the park horses, two park mules, and miscellaneous gear were sold. There was no point in keeping horses and mules if the park had no money to hire men to drive them or to buy feed. After all expenses were deducted, the total amount put into the Park Improvement and Maintenance Fund was $770.64.

---

*The potty chair in the library is owned by the author and was purchased from a descendant of the Daemons.

President Louis McLane announced to the board that he must make a trip to the East in March and would be absent for six weeks. Commissioner Alvord was appointed president pro tem of the board.

On May 4, 1882, Frank M. Pixley presented his commission along with the new commission for William Alvord. Pixley was editor of the *Argonaut*, and it was common knowledge that he was under the influence of the "Big Four" railroad kings — Mark Hopkins, Leland Stanford, Collis P. Huntington, and Charles Crocker. He replaced Oliver Eldridge, who had become one of the pilot commissioners of San Francisco Harbor. The commission of Louis McLane was ordered filed, pending his return from the East, and Alvord was ordered to continue as president pro tem of the board.

Frank Pixley's presence was immediately felt. A long list of charges against Sgt. Thomas Sloan of the mounted police was read, as well as charges against an Officer Leeper. The superintendent was ordered to investigate the particulars and report to the board. Sergeant Sloan was the first mounted "Range Rider" in the park and had always been praised by William Hammond Hall. But the creed of Frank Pixley was "to the victor belong the spoils," and he soon put his beliefs into practice.

At the board's next meeting, testimony was heard regarding the behavior of the entire force. The secretary was instructed to notify all the park police that their positions had been declared vacant as of May 1, 1882. The secretary also reported that he had received a communication from McLane, declining his new commission. Apparently McLane was not willing to work with Pixley.

When Superintendent Hennessey reported that Bernard Collins, who had charge of the first watering trough in the park, was seldom sober, Collins's position was declared vacant. Hennessey also reported that he could obtain men from the Bush Fund labor force to act as policemen until the necessary appointments could be made.

Commissioner Pixley pompously announced, on June

The Casino, built in 1874 on a ridge west of the Conservatory.

8, 1882, that he had made the following appointments to the police force — all new men: Ralph Smith, Walter Tilton, John J. McEwen, and James Dailey, with Ralph Smith as sergeant of the guard. He also announced that Simon Kelleher, a member of the old force, had been reinstated, since it had been shown that he had no part in the "late unpleasantness."

Superintendent Hennessey then reported that he could see no reason for the "keep off the grass signs" in Golden Gate Park. No such signs were posted in Central Park in New York, and in San Francisco, where the grass was green year-round, the signs were unnecessary. Com-

missioners Pixley and Alvord ordered that children be allowed to play on the grass on Thursdays and Saturdays on a trial basis. A few months later, still in 1882, the order was made permanent. It remains in effect.

The secretary reported that $4,500 remained in the Park Fund — barely enough to meet the month's expenses. Further, the tax levy for the following year had been reduced from 2½¢ to 1½¢, which would give the park only $31,000 for the next fiscal year. Commissioner Pixley was appointed to plead with the Board of Supervisors for more money.

John Rosenfeld reported on June 26, 1882, that he had

received a commission from the governor and was allowed to take his seat on the board. His appointment made William Alvord a minority of one on the board.

The office of superintendent of the Parks and Avenue was declared vacant as of July 1, 1882, purportedly because of lack of funds; Hennessey was let go. Commissioner Pixley was again appointed to see if further layoffs could be made in addition to the police and the seventeen other men who had been dismissed since Pixley's arrival on the board. At the July meeting, Commissioner Alvord resigned as president pro tem of the board and nominated Pixley as president.

Several years before, Alvord had donated the money to improve the lake that now bears his name. He had insisted that it be called "The Lakelet," and it had been so named. But Alvord had made a trip out of the city after the governor had appointed Pixley to the board. During his absence, John Rosenfeld and Pixley held a ceremony in his honor and named the lake "Alvord Lake." Alvord was furious at this betrayal of his wishes, and when the board would not rescind its action, he resigned, exactly as Pixley had planned. Leland Stanford was then appointed to the board by Rosenfeld and Pixley, and the way was at last clear for the Park and Ocean Railroad Company to build its railroad through and across the park. It was not long in coming.

Little is known about John J. McEwen, the next superintendent, who kept the job for four years, as long as Pixley remained on the board. He was a teamster, and he resided on Pixley property in Cow Hollow. On July 7, 1882, the *San Francisco Chronicle* charged that McEwen was Pixley's brother-in-law. Pixley, through the *Argonaut*, hotly denied that he had any male relatives, save his brother's sons, who were not yet fifteen years old. About this time, however, Mrs. Pixley adopted a little girl whom she identified as her niece. This relationship may have led the *Chronicle* to assume that McEwen was Pixley's brother-in-law.

Hennessey was not mollified, however. He wrote a scorching letter to the board, denouncing his dismissal as superintendent. The letter was published in a *Chronicle* article, but it was not entered in the minutes of the board.

Golden Gate Park
San Francisco, July 6, 1882

To the Honorable, the Board of Park Commissioners:

Gentlemen: For some reason not clear to my mind, I received on the 27th of June a notice from the Secretary of your Board stating that on account of lack of funds my position as Superintendent of the Park was declared vacant on the 1st of the present month. I thought at the time that it was rather short notice and I think so now. I also thought at the end of the fiscal year it would not be for the best interest of the Park when there was so much data in my hands to be put in order for future use and reference. I thought that the Commissioners, as businessmen, would recognize this.

I thought the time and circumstances would prevail to some extent and allow me sufficient time to place before the Commissioners a correct statement of the Park affairs.

More especially did I think so because a majority of the Commissioners were new and for that reason had no practical knowledge whatever of the Park and its workings. I know also that I have spent thirty-five of the best years of my life in the study of engineering, rural architecture and landscape gardening, and in justice to myself, I will say I think I have got a fair knowledge of my profession, and I think so without egotism.

In support of this assertion, I ask the Commissioners to consider my work on the Park since my connection with it. Should the Commissioners decline to do me this justice, I will be compelled to call on the people of San Francisco for their verdict, whom I know I have served faithfully while in their employ.

Now, Gentlemen, I ask you in all honesty and ernestness if you conscientiously believe that you have improved the Park management by the change; placed yourselves in a position in keeping with the dignity of Park Commissioners and done me justice! If you think you have, be kind enough to permit me to submit the following for your consideration:

Is the Gentleman whom you have replaced me with cheaper at $125 a month than I would be at $200, when he admits that he doesn't know anything about the place he is trying to fill? Why not have asked me to agree to a reduction, if necessary, as many people think I could serve the Park better at a reduced salary than the present incumbent, who admits his inability. If I had been spoken to by the Commissioners, I would and could afford to give them three or four months gratuitous.

Is the present Superintendent a gardener? Because the Act of the Legislature creating his position, approved April 3, 1876, Section 2, and not repealed, says he must be. The same Act of the Legislature says he shall receive $200 per month and no more. While I am not a lawyer, I think he can recover $200 per month, because the law says so.

I have done the engineering and architectural work for the Park during my administration without charge. Can the present incumbent do the same?

Gentlemen, I ask you as business men, are cheap workmen always the most profitable? Are the Commissioners making the following savings by the appointment of the new Superintendent, as claimed by one member of your Honorable Board?

Superintendent-Salary per month	$200.00
Secretary	100.00
One Park Policeman's duty	105.00
One messenger	45.00
Savings on rent by having offices in Park	25.00
	$475.00

I may be mistaken, but I don't think or believe he can fill all these places, because while he was doing police duty under my instructions, I found that he could not do two hour's duty as it should be done out of his whole watch.

One more observation and I am done. I have been charged by one of the Commissioners with a crime, and I will acknowledge it as a shame as well if the gentleman can prove it. This Commissioner says the only thing he ever heard against me was, that when discharges took place on the Park, the Irish Roman Catholics were favored to the disadvantage of the Protestants. To this I will say that up to the 1st of last May, Louis McLane was Chairman of the Park Commissioners, and as such made out all the discharge rolls, and he never once to my knowledge asked what any man's religion was, but he would not discharge a man who was competent. The interests of the Park was his first consideration, and I think he will say the same of me.

The same Gentleman told me that he was told there were only two Protestants on the Park works. I then made it my business to inquire the religion of the Park employees, and I found fifteen Protestants, the greater part of which were employed by me, or I recommended their employment. There was a portion of the late Park Guard I recommended to be taken back, which were also Protestants, but this Commissioner refused. I am, Gentlemen, your obedient servant.

/s/ F. P. Hennessey.

The *Chronicle*, in the same edition, had this to say in conclusion of the long article:

It should be mentioned in justice to Mr. Hennessey that he has stepped into another position so much better than the one from which he has been removed that he would not again accept the place of Superintendent should it be offered him; and it should be mentioned in justice to Commissioner Pixley that the new Superintendent who was appointed at his (Pixley's) solicitation, is strangely, but characteristically, his (Pixley's) brother-in-law.

Pixley became an instant expert, the first of many. When an appointing authority calls on a political supporter and offers the position of park commissioner — regardless of the appointee's qualifications (or lack of them) for the job — the offer is hard to refuse. Such a person often instantly blossoms into an expert on all matters pertaining to the maintenance and governing of public parks. And so it was. Pixley immediately wrote a long letter to the Board of Supervisors, outlining the plans and needs of the park. The excellent plan of William Hammond Hall was completely ignored. Instead of winding roads to cut down on the effects of a prevailing westerly wind, Pixley proposed a driveway 150 feet wide from the vicinity of the Conservatory to go in a straight line to the Great Highway. On either side would be a walk and a "fast" lane for the owners of fast horses, with a divided road in the center for others.

He proposed sowing the entire park in bent grass, in spite of the fact that bent grass is coarse and long, usually brown, and unattractive. He ignored experiments that had shown that lupine and barley were the most economical means of reclaiming the sand and that the bent grass had been used principally at the beach or western end of the park.

For once, having no money to spend on the park was a boon. Had the money to carry out all of Pixley's plans been available, Golden Gate Park would have been doomed to oblivion.

The *San Francisco Chronicle,* archenemy of Pixley's *Argonaut,* carried several articles derogatory of the new Park Commission. One was entitled "Poverty Park" and another "Park Retrenchment." On August 5, 1882, a barbed story on Golden Gate Park appeared in the *Chronicle.* A portion of it follows:

Until very recently the people of this city were felicitating themselves that Golden Gate Park was rapidly being put into shape of a poor man's pleasure ground. It seems, however, that the plan which held out this promise is to be abandoned, and that hereafter the commissioners will devote themselves to converting the tract of land specially set aside as a breathing space for the people into an immense race track, where our bloated millionaires and owners of blooded horses can speed their animals. One of the commissioners, Mr. Pixley, has informed a *Chronicle*

reporter that "It has been virtually decided to preserve the Conservatory and the Amphitheater, and to utilize the remaining space in the park for tracks or drives where blooded horses can be speeded, and to a frenzy."

Just think of it! It has actually been decided to preserve the Conservatory. There is something to be thankful for — at least for the present. Next year, perhaps, the commissioners will decide to sell out the Conservatory and plants in order to increase the number of drives and racetracks, for what use is a public conservatory to the owners of blooded horses when they nearly all possess handsome greenhouses of their own. It is the beautiful colors and fragrance of the flowers in this public collection that are enjoyed by the clodhoppers who ride out there on the streetcars, but the park is not designed for such people anyway.

Aside from the fact that the park was dry and brown and neglected, another immediate effect of Pixley's presence on the board was a rise in crime in the park. His handing out of policemen's jobs as patronage brought no professionalism to the force. It brought no experienced men to what is always a difficult job. As a result crime flourished, and soon the park was not safe for anyone. A letter to the editor of the *Examiner* suggested that the park was now being frequented by hoodlums and pimps:

Editor: Sir: I should like to call (through your valuable paper) the attention of the chief of police to the conduct of certain hoodlums, who are in the habit of driving through Golden Gate Park almost daily with fast horses, and who are supported by a class of the women styled "fast women." They do not work but live on the proceeds of the ill-gotten gains of those women. I have occasion to drive through the aforesaid park daily with my wife and family, and it seems that a certain hoodlum among the number will insist on annoying my daughter, greatly to the distress of both my wife and myself, and also by my daughter, by throwing insults and likewise writing anonymous letters to her to meet them in the Park. . . .

Conservatory Valley in the mid-1880s.

By inserting this, you will confer a great favor on the parents of many respectable families.

Yours respectfully,
Paterfamilias

Leland Stanford, as a park commissioner, never attended a single meeting. Although the minutes stated that he was "absent" or away "due to ill health," he was careful not to attend. Had he done so, he would have been guilty of conflict of interest, a felony as outlined by Order Number Eight Hundred creating the Park Commission. His membership was strictly to give Pixley a majority and to get rid of Alvord, who opposed the Park and Ocean Railroad. As soon as the Park and Ocean Railroad became a certainty, Stanford resigned from the board, pleading "other interests" — which was certainly true.

On September 16, 1882, Gustave Fuchs led a twelve-piece band through its paces in the new Music Stand in the park. It was the first known band concert in a series that has since become a tradition in San Francisco. The concert was paid for by a group of citizens who hoped to continue the concerts by means of public subscription.

On January 5, 1883, more disaster occurred in the park. A fire broke out in the heating apparatus behind the Conservatory. Before it could be extinguished, the entire dome of the Conservatory was burned and with it many rare and valuable plants. Fire Chief David Scannell and Sergeant Nichols hurried to the fire, along with Hose Company Number Two. The hose company proved to be of little use, since no fire hydrants had yet been installed near the Conservatory. Damage was estimated at $9,000 to $12,000, and restoration of the building was not finished for almost a year. The city's children particularly mourned the loss of a gorgeous Brazilian parrot that had amused them with its chatter.

The *Bulletin* and the *Call* kept the city aroused by their charges that although there were endless streams of water just below the surface the park was dry and brown. They did not bother to suggest where the money would come from to drill the wells, install pump engines, buy pipe to distribute the water, or hire the men to oversee the distribution.

A communication from London was received at a special meeting of the board on June 29, 1883. Through Charles Crocker, Leland Stanford offered his resignation, which was duly accepted. The secretary of the board also resigned, and the vacancy was filled by Valance V. Block. Her appointment took effect on July 1, 1883. Gen. Irwin McDowell was elected to the Board of Park Commissioners at a special meeting held September 1, 1883.

On October 12, 1883, the three new commissioners, Pixley, McDowell, and Rosenfeld, voted to allow Leland Stanford, Collis P. Huntington, Charles Crocker, and their successors or assigns the right to build, maintain, and operate a single- or double-track street railroad across the southeast corner of the park, along H Street (now Lincoln Way), and then across the park at the Great Highway. They also authorized the railroad to construct a depot within the park boundary near the intersection of Haight and Stanyan streets.

However, a month before, the *Chronicle* had reported that a gang of men had already been busy for several weeks building an embankment across the southeast corner of the park for the railroad. A *Chronicle* reporter made his way to the Park Lodge and asked to see the secretary of the board. She was not in. Then he asked to see the minutes of the board so he could determine if the Park Commission had approved the railroad. He was informed that the books were not available, and that he would have to see the secretary. The reporter then made his way to the scene of the activity. When he asked the foreman where the railroad had gotten the right to enter the park, he got this reply: "Why, Mr. Stanford wanted the road. That's all." Both the city of San Francisco and the state of California filed suit in superior court to stop the work, but it was continued without any delay.

During the same period Charles Crocker donated $10,000 for reconstruction of the burned-out Conservatory. Several newspaper writers suggested that this gift was a bribe to get the park commissioners to allow the railroad to enter the park. On September 29, 1883, the *Argonaut*, owned by Pixley, hotly denied this charge.

> It is not true that Governor Stanford, while a member of this Board, ever sought for himself or for his associates any privilege in or about the Park. It is not true, when Mr. Crocker gave ten thousand dollars to restore the conservatory, that he exacted or suggested any conditions to accompany his most generous gift. It is not true that the conservatory is being rebuilt, except according to the plans and drawings and under the direct and personal supervision of Mr. John Gash, an architect employed by the Park Commissioners and paid out of park funds. It is not true that it is being constructed by railroad employees. It is not true that the glass used is inappropriate or improperly laid.

But the facts are plain. The old Park Board, composed of Alvord, Eldridge, and McLane, had denied the use of the park for building the railroad. Now all three men were gone, and their successors had voted unanimously to allow the railroad into the park — *after* most of the work of building it had already been done. In just a few short years, the entire concept and plan of the park as a place for the general public had been changed to that of a park catering to the wealthy. The crime rate in the park was escalating. The lawlessness at the Great Highway was only a reflection of the lawlessness of the park commissioners. They had granted a fifty-year lease to the railroad in direct defiance of Order Number Eight Hundred, which allowed the commission to lease ground for no more than three years — and then only if it were not needed for park purposes at the time.

During 1883, the park commissioners complained about the lack of water for the park. When William Hammond Hall, then the state engineer, was questioned about the problem by a *San Francisco Call* reporter, he remarked:

> The whole park can be put into a presentable condition with very little more water than is now being used. . . . It is my opinion that the expense of supporting blue grass out there is unnecessary. Blue grass is not adapted to this locality, and on a sandy soil, oceans of water is required to keep it going. There are many plants and grasses that will keep the park green all summer with little or no water. . . . I think there is no doubt that a supply of water, abundant for all needs, could be cheaply obtained. . . . It seems to me the problem of irrigating Golden Gate Park is a very simple one.

But a hundred years later, the problem of irrigating Golden Gate Park remains unsolved. And attempts are still being made to change the master plan of William Hammond Hall.

In January 1884, the park commissioners finally decided to build a waterworks that would provide all necessary water and end the controversy with the Spring Valley Water Company. But the bids for the construction of such a system were out of reach of the board. So Commissioner Irwin McDowell had one of his officers, Maj. William A.

Jones, "volunteer" to draw up the plans and oversee the construction of a waterworks.

Preparations were going smoothly, when suddenly Major Jones was transferred by the War Department to The Dalles, Oregon, to do engineering work. United States Sen. William Sharon of Nevada, who made his business headquarters in San Francisco, had an interest in the Spring Valley Water Company and was a close associate of the president of that company, Charles Webb Howard. Many people suspected that the water company, not wishing to lose the park's lucrative business, had acted accordingly. Editorial writers of the day suggested that Sharon may have been asked to pull a few strings.

Petitions were sent to the Congress and to the War Department, but Secretary of War Robert Lincoln replied that he did not deem it advisable to interfere in the assignment of duties in the Department of the Army. So Maj. William A. Jones went to Oregon. To make sure that he stayed in Oregon, someone pointed out that Gen. Irwin McDowell was not a resident of the state of California and therefore was not legally entitled to serve on the board. General McDowell soon resigned.

The Board of Supervisors had appropriated about $28,000 for the waterworks, and in 1885 the park commissioners hired an engineer, Alfred Poett, to proceed with the work. Poett drilled a well in what is now the Arboretum, but since no engine or pump was available, the well was capped and the operations were moved to the beach. Poett reasoned that the land at the beach was lower, so he might not have to drill as far to find water. Unfortunately, he did not also reason that even if he found water, he would have to pump it to an elevation of nearly three hundred feet, near Strawberry Hill, in order to irrigate the park.

Poett ignored the fact that when the Park and Ocean Railroad had built the tunnel under the Main Drive, they had had considerable trouble with underground water. Two wells were dug about fifteen feet deep, and four-foot iron pipe was used to line the wells. The drillers found that at low tide, the water level dropped about two feet, but it returned to normal height at high tide. Thus, they learned at some expense what William Hammond Hall had told them earlier. Ample water was to be had at the beach, as well as all over the park in the low areas. Water was known to exist in this area even before it became a park.

The Spring Valley Water Company, for all its faults, was well run. Its engineers knew every source of water on the San Francisco Peninsula. Many former employees of the company, still living, must laugh to themselves every time a "drought" occurs in Golden Gate Park — or anyplace in San Francisco.

W. B. Bradbury, owner of the Centennial Planing Mills, was engaged to build the waterworks. Bradbury had a well at his home, which "qualified" him to take on the job of providing water for a thousand acres. He promised to supply five hundred thousand gallons of water per day at a cost of $200 per month as compared to the $1,100 per month that Spring Valley was charging for one hundred thousand gallons per day. Further, Bradbury assured the city that he was doing all this not to make money for himself but to provide a service for his city.

A reservoir was built near the crest of Strawberry Hill. It was intended to hold one million gallons of water, but with the faulty construction methods used by Bradbury, the new waterworks could not supply enough water, even before any was drawn off for irrigation, to fill the reservoir. Later the park commissioners also charged that the pumping machinery was built on a faulty foundation, that the machinery was secondhand and not new as required by contract, and that even the pipe laid to the reservoir was secondhand pipe. It was also learned that smaller pipe than that specified in the plans had been used in the entire operation. Six-inch pipe had been substituted for eight-inch pipe, and so forth. When all the valves and fittings were totaled up, this substitution constituted quite an extra profit for the man who wanted only to "provide a service for his city." Bradbury had been paid $10,000 "on

account" at the beginning of his work, and the commissioners refused to pay him any more money.

On July 14, 1885, Charles Goodall was appointed to the board to fill the vacancy left by General McDowell. From that moment, dissension seemed to rend the Board of Park Commissioners. Commissioners Goodall and Rosenfeld voted against paying any more money to Bradbury, and Pixley voted in favor, pompously insisting that Bradbury be paid.

Pixley pleaded his cause in his newspaper, the Argonaut, telling of the great changes that had been made since his appointment to the board. He even took credit for all the railroad lines built to the park. (He was, indeed, responsible for the Park and Ocean Railroad, but he had no part in the Geary Street Park and Ocean Railroad or the California Street Line, which reached the northern edges of the park.) The article recounted how park visitors had been made to feel uncomfortable by the former park policemen, who were "stern, uncompromising and hard-hearted men." Pixley bragged that he had fired them and that the present officers acted as if they owned the park and as if the visitors were their guests.

Soon, he added, the new road opened through the quarry at the west end of Conservatory Valley would be a straight boulevard, one hundred feet wide, from the Conservatory to the ocean. No longer, he went on, would the drivers of fine horseflesh have to slow down for those narrow, winding roads that had been built under the direction of former commissioners. He reasoned that perhaps a few young people might want to wander off into secluded spots and byways, but the vast majority of people wanted to see and be seen. Therefore, the park would be "opened up." And in spite of the fact that the Bay District Racetrack was adjacent to the park between First and Fifth avenues, a track would soon be built in the park for those who wanted to drive without regard to speed regulations.

This long article in the Argonaut gave the impression

that Pixley had found the park a desolate spot when he came to the board. In fact, more than three hundred thousand trees and shrubs had been planted prior to his reign. Previous buildings included a Conservatory, a Park Lodge, barns, maintenance buildings, earthen closets, and homes for some of the foremen who worked in the park, and a huge nursery had been started.

To make sure that the public was kept unaware, a Grand Jury was asked to study the affairs of the park. Their report, published in the *San Francisco Evening Bulletin* on June 12, 1885, read, in part:

> The Golden Gate Park is a feature of our city government in respect to which it is a pleasure to speak in terms of unqualified praise. . . .
>
> Much interest centers in the search for water for park purposes, and Captain Bradbury has been duly interviewed and found full of enthusiasm and confidence in the ultimate outcome of his labors, while he considers very satisfactory results have thus far been obtained. It is but fair to say that from our observations Captain Bradbury at every step is sinking the contractor in the unselfish citizen.

Though the Grand Jury found Bradbury the model "unselfish citizen," it is interesting to note that he was sentenced to San Quentin a few years later for perjury. On September 23, 1885, Bradbury notified the board that he had completed his contract and asked that $28,000 be paid to him. Commissioner Goodall made a motion that no money be paid until the plant and entire system had been approved by Engineer Poett. The motion carried, Pixley dissenting.

On November 6, 1885, the water wells, engines, pumps, and pump frames were accepted, but the reservoir was not. Bradbury was ordered paid all but $10,000, which was reserved until the contract was satisfied. Bradbury was also ordered to turn on the water for irrigation and told that he would be paid $100 per month for water until he had fulfilled his contract.

Spring Valley was ordered to turn off its water and that no more water would be needed from it. The water company turned off the water and acknowledged the board's letter by enclosing a bill for $6,854.83 for water pipe laid in the park, pipe now owned by the Park Commission. The board sent the bill to the Board of Supervisors for payment, because they did not have the funds to pay it.

Alfred Poett, the park engineer, had resigned. The board was forced to hire the firm of Ekart and Scott, Experts, to examine the waterworks. The firm presented a bill for $204.50, which was paid. The secretary was also told to express the thanks of the board for the good work done.

In December the bill from Bradbury was ordered returned to him because it did not have itemized expenditures, as required. Bradbury was also instructed to lay the correct size pipe, which he had not yet done. He was further ordered to install a fireproof floor in the engine house, to cover the boilers with asbestos, and to install meters according to contract. He was told that if he did not do these things at once, the commissioner would do the work, and Bradbury would be billed. Pixley also dissented with this action.

In January 1886, the superintendent was instructed to determine the amount of leakage in the reservoir and to report to the commission. Superintendent John J. McEwen reported that he could not detect leakage in the reservoir, since he had taken water from it every day.

While the debate over the water situation continued, newspaper stories and other criticism induced the park commissioners to pass Ordinance Number Eleven, in which the Park and Ocean Railroad Company was granted a lease for three years instead of for fifty. The new ordinance, passed on April 24, 1886, also provided that the company would have to pay a rental of $100 per month instead of $100 per year.

Band concert in Conservatory Valley, about 1883.

In retaliation, the Haight Street Railroad and the Park and Ocean Railroad notified the commissioners that they would pay that amount. But the $100 per month they had been paying for the upkeep of the band in the park would no longer be paid.

When a new governor was elected in the state, rumors hinted that Frank M. Pixley would not be reappointed to the board. Gov. George Stoneman surprised everybody by refusing to renew the commissions of *any* of the Park Board, an action which created great change. Consultant Hall reported that former commissioner William Alvord was approached to resume his place on the board but had declined unless the governor could find two other men with whom Alvord felt he could work harmoniously. Governor Stoneman apparently was unable to find two other men compatible with Alvord, because he announced the appointment of three new men to the Board of Park Commissioners. They were Maj. Richard P. Hammond, Gen. William H. Dimond, and Joseph Austin.

Austin, of Scotch birth, had arrived in California in 1856. He entered into the dry-goods business under the name of A. Austin & Co. He was appointed port warden of San Francisco by Governors Booth, Haight, and Irwin. He was a veteran fireman and also the adjudicator of claims for the Occidental and Oriental Steamship Company.

Gen. William H. Dimond was born in Honolulu, where his parents were missionaries. He came to the mainland in 1861 and became attached to the Sanitary Commission that did so much good during the Civil War. Later he entered into the shipping and commission business with Henry B. Williams.

Richard P. Hammond was the brother of John Hays Hammond, the famous mining engineer of South Africa, and of William H. Hammond of Visalia. He was also a cousin of William Hammond Hall, who was probably responsible for getting Hammond on the Park Commission. For many years, he was a surveyor general of the state of California. He was a member of the local real estate firm of McAffee, Baldwin and Hammond. With the all-new board came a new regime.

Great Highway about 1904. Smokestack was pumping plant for the Lurline Baths.

Mooneysville, U.S.A.

Fortunately for followers of Golden Gate Park's early history, a little comic relief did emerge during these lean years. The American West is replete with stories of ghost towns that came into being overnight and just as suddenly disappeared. Something like that happened in San Francisco in the 1890s.

At this time of high unemployment, there was lots of public agitation, usually in the form of speeches made to crowds gathered in one of the empty lots in town. The lots were mostly covered with sand; thus the phrase "sand-lot oratory."

The particular eruption of humanity known as Mooneysville, U.S.A., was named after that master of sand-lot oratory, a true son of the "ould sod," Con Mooney. Mooney was an associate of Dennis Kearney, perhaps the most famous of all sand-lot orators. Kearney was a thorn in the side of the so-called Octopus, which included Mark Hopkins, Leland Stanford, Charles Crocker, and Collis P. Huntington. These gentlemen were also referred to as the Big Four.

By 1883, the Park and Ocean Railroad Company, using questionable tactics, had obtained a fifty-year franchise to build a steam railroad across the park along the beach. The route of this new line effectively eliminated all competition on three sides of the park, a fact that did not escape the railroad company's attention. Mayor Bartlett promptly vetoed this illegal franchise. But he was just as promptly overridden by the lackeys of the Big Four, and the railroad was put through.

More as a manner of protest than in the interest of profit, a group of sand-lotters, headed by Con Mooney and Dennis Kearney, came up with a plan of staking out claims on Ocean Beach. The sand-lotters reasoned, with some logic, that if Charles Crocker and Associates could break the law, they had no reason not to cash in on this new "strike" or "bonanza." They put their plan into action overnight. The new railroad was formally opened on December 1, 1883, and by December 10, Mooneysville was a fact. The first claim, running from the base of the Cliff at Sutro Heights, was staked out by Con Mooney. It was 60 feet wide and ran 280 feet to the low-water line.

When a reporter asked Mooney how far west his claim ran, he retorted, "All the way to China!" The property sported a platform covered, more or less, by canvas, and it featured dancing and whiskey — "the finest kind."

The next 60-foot-wide claim was owned by another famous sand-lot orator, Stephen Maybell, alias "the Oregon Poet," who was also a congressional aspirant. His sail-covered platform had a sign that proclaimed "Coffee & Doughnuts — 10¢. Families Supplied — 25¢." If anyone was ever able to stand alone after the second round of coffee at Maybell's stand, the *San Francisco Call* wryly reported, "He has yet to report."

"Dennis [Kearney] and I are partners," said Maybell.

"He has gone into town to buy a ham. We keep no books. We divide the profit every night." On the floor of the establishment were several huge boulders which, Maybell said, were seats for his patrons. They also served as weights to keep the high tide from washing this portion of Mooneysville out to sea. Sad experience later induced owners to build their places of business on stilts in order to protect them from high seas. Nearly all of the shacks were between high- and low-water marks on government land, and the tide claimed many casualties as far as the buildings were concerned.

The curiosities the Oregon Poet displayed for the edification of his customers included a specimen of petrified mud and the petrified hand of "Five-Fingered Jack," a deceased highwayman of the period. The specimens, however, had more the appearance of vegetable matter than petrified animal growth. Following Maybell's claim, to the south, was that of Col. Joe Monaghan, which was also sixty feet in width and ran west "all the way to China."

Early in December who should appear on the scene but Frank M. Pixley, whose position as president of the Board of Park Commissioners was also due to the not-so-subtle influence of the Big Four. On the occasion of this visit, he pompously announced to all within hearing, "I am Frank Pixley, Park Commissioner. You are trespassing, and I give you notice to leave."

At the mention of Pixley's name, dark looks and mutterings came from the crowd, and fingers pointed toward the blue Pacific. "If he comes here again, he gets ducked," someone was heard to say. "Nobody but the Pacific Ocean or the United States Government can drive us away from here," said Colonel Monaghan, "and the United States Government has never been known to do anything in less than three years."

The squatters were careful not to "claim" any land within nine hundred feet of either side of the Life Saving Station. Though they might have sympathizers locally, any interference with the operations of that station would bring down the wrath of Uncle Sam on their heads. That was the last thing they wanted.

Adjacent to Colonel Monaghan's holding was the claim of Capt. P. Curley. This budding businessman had brought two thousand feet of lumber with him. He currently planned a two-story structure after the manner of Noah's Ark, having learned two nights previously that the sea had almost preempted his claim and the lumber with it. He planned to anchor his house securely to the cliff and let the Pacific do its worst.

Alarmed by all this activity, Adolph Sutro, who owned the cliff above called Sutro Heights, had his men construct a high board fence to the northwest, shutting off the rest of Ocean Beach to the sand-lotters. He was, however, too late to erect his fence on the line of his property.

To the south, with the exception of the United States government's Life Saving Station, the sand-lotters had no impediment to progress. Lots were hastily claimed all the way to H Street (now Lincoln Way) on the south side of the park.

Sunday, December 17, 1883, produced the greatest crowd that had ever been seen on the beach — more than ten thousand people. Swarms waited for the cars that left every three minutes; still, many could not get aboard.

Enterprising "Johns" (in those halcyon days, a "John" was a hack driver, not a "trick") parked their hacks on the street and tried to drum up business by saying that the next car would not leave for half an hour. "Here. This way. Take you to the beach without delay. Train won't leave for thirty minutes. Only 25¢. Come right this way." And many did, only to watch the train pull out while they struggled to crowd their huge families into small hacks. It was all grand fun for the crowd.

At the beach, the scene was pandemonium. The crowd found thirty-two shanties and eleven tents, along with sixty-seven wagons, carts, and portable stands. Businessmen — the electrical machine man, the man with the lung tester, the proprietor of a popcorn-ball factory, the

FERRIES, CITY HALL, GOLDEN GATE PARK & CLIFF.

GOLDEN GATE PARK, OCEAN & CLIFF HOUSE   9   VIA MARKET & HAIGHT STREETS

MARKET ST. CABLE RAILWAY CO.

The Market Street cable railway began service to the park in 1883.

telescope man — hawked their wares in coarse variations of English. The telescope man, an enterprising capitalist, had procured an ordinary marine glass and mounted it on a tripod. (Presumably one of his descendants still has the concession at Land's End.)

Along with the shouting rose the incessant crack of rifles in numerous shooting galleries, the roar of the surf, and the screaming of lost children. The resulting cacophony was not exactly what William Hammond Hall had had in mind when he drew up plans for Golden Gate Park. It could best be described as bedlam.

A Recorder's Office was erected on Pacific Street, but a reporter wrote that, judging from the number of barrels stacked in the Recorder's Office, the only thing recorded there was the number of drinks sold.

Since the squatters could not claim the protection of the law, they soon deemed it advisable to hire their own policeman to prevent claim jumping. A young man named W. G. Shaw was engaged to uphold the local law. On December 20, 1883, Shaw was huddled in his office when a huge man burst in and announced, "I am Mack McAuliffe's brother, and I'm going to shoot you." And he did. But his aim was poor, and he succeeded only in shooting off the end of one of Officer Shaw's fingers before he was disarmed. A crowd rapidly assembled, and talked of a lynching, but Officer Shaw made light of the whole affair. While the men went home for their rifles to protect hearth and home, Officer Shaw rode away in the darkness to the receiving hospital to get his wound dressed.

Fearing further violence, the Park Commission held an emergency meeting and passed a resolution denying all privileges for peddling or selling anything on the Great Highway. They also promised to eject Mooney from the premises before Sunday.

PARK AND OCEAN RAILROAD

A NEW STEAM RAILROAD,

EQUIPPED WITH SPACIOUS AND ELEGANT CARS

OBSERVATION CARS ATTACHED TO EVERY TRAIN.

This road runs from STANYAN ST., opposite the terminus of the

HAIGHT STREET LINE OF CABLE CARS,

ALONG THE ENTIRE LENGTH OF

GOLDEN GATE PARK,

And across the GREAT HIGHWAY to the shores of the PACIFIC OCEAN, where many pleasant hours may be spent upon the beach, viewing the SEALS upon the rocks and strolling along THE CLIFF, from which locality a full view of the GOLDEN GATE and northern shores of the Bay may be obtained.

EVERY ONE MUST VISIT THE

PARK, BEACH AND CLIFF

while in the CITY. Always a pleasant route and the only quick and cheap one.

FARE ON THIS ROAD (A DISTANCE OF ABOUT FOUR MILES) 5 CTS. EACH WAY.

FARE ON MARKET STREET CABLE CARS, - - 5 CTS. EACH WAY.

The Park and Ocean line officially opened on December 1, 1883.

In desperation Adolph Sutro had his men drill holes at the edge of Sutro Heights, and he blasted the rock at all and sundry. His bombardment failed because most of the rock merely tumbled down the hill. His enemies promised retribution. Sutro, in turn, threatened all of them with prosecution, but his threats were no more effective than those of Pixley. Mooneysville grew and grew.

Con Mooney, the "Mooneysville Magnate," was arrested on December 22, 1883, for selling liquor. He was promptly bailed out after he pleaded not guilty and demanded a trial by jury. Pixley then demanded that Police Chief Patrick Crowley arrest all the squatters, but the chief declined, saying that his jurisdiction ended at Divisadero Street.

Profit was pouring in far beyond the wildest dreams of the promoters. Maybell claimed to have sold seven thousand cups of coffee in a single day, and Dennis Kearney stated, "If our fragrant mocha is not superior to any on Kearny Street in the city, you don't have to pay for it." The *San Francisco News Letter* bemoaned the fact that they had predicted for years that Kearney would end up as deputy assistant cook at the Almshouse — and he was becoming a capitalist.

Frank Pixley was seething with frustration, and the entire city was laughing in delight at the discomfiture of their enemy, the Octopus. The newspapers, with the exception of the *Argonaut*, had a field day. To further complicate matters, the Board of Supervisors issued a free license to Con Mooney for a refreshment stand "for the reason that it is an actual necessity to travelers seeking refreshment and recreation."

Land to claim became scarce, and a real estate office was set up to handle sales and trades. The fame of Mooneysville had spread far and wide. On January 5, 1884, the *New York Tribune* had this to say:

The crowds which have thronged Ocean Beach, near San Francisco, since the opening of the new railroad to the sea have stimulated the cupidity of the liquor dealers, and hucksters' tents have been erected for the sale of refreshments. Among the venders of coffee and doughnuts is the ex-sandlotter, Dennis Kearney, who has never taken kindly to the hard work of a drayman since his experience in politics. He looks more greasy and unkempt than usual and is an awful example of the demagogue who has sold out for too small a price.

Of all the San Francisco newspapers, only the *Call* had the temerity to suggest that the squatters were not the only ones breaking the law. The *San Francisco News Letter*, tongue in cheek, wrote:

> It is understood that in order to meet the requirements of the inhabitants of Mooneysville by the Sea, a newspaper will shortly be started on the beach. It will be democratic in politics and circulated largely among the sea gulls. Editorials about Con Mooney's and Dennis Kearney's coffee stand will be paid for at the rate of six bits a column, which is an inducement to our local scribes to immediately go out there and interview the new and rising community. Mr. Kearney, assisted by a doughnut, will sing a new duet next Sunday, entitled, "What Are the Wild Waves Saying?" which is alone worth the price of admission to his crab lunch.

Ignoring the Life Saving Station that had operated in the northwest corner of the park since 1879, the new city announced an amateur lifesaving service of its own in January 1884. The residents held a town meeting and formed what they called the "Ocean View Township." A duly authorized sign appeared on the beach as follows:

W. J. MACLEOD
Voluntear
Life Saving,
supported by
collections from
the Publick
on the Beach
Surf Batheing at Low Tyde

At this same meeting a number of residents requested the removal of the night watchman, since he had become a public nuisance. He was alleged to have shot at several peaceful citizens and wounded one. Furthermore he was not a special officer, as he had claimed. No official action was taken on the request.

But the budding *San Francisco Chronicle* took action. An editorial demanded to know why city officials were allowing a new government to be set up in competition with San Francisco. The *Chronicle* demanded that the superintendent of streets "clear the streets." But the superintendent of streets responded that he had petitioned the Board of Supervisors for authority and had been told "The park commissioners have sole jurisdiction in the matter." Clearly, no one wished to face the rifles at Mooneysville, whose citizens included several Civil War veterans.

On the evening of January 6, 1884, a storm blew in from sea. The shooting gallery floated away and had to be lassoed, towed back, and secured by ropes. Maybell's stand also floated out, but the principal damage was to his "other shirt." The following day he entertained his customers with his own version of "What Are the Wild Waves Saying?"

> Oh! wave; Oh, unpitying wave!
> Oh, how could you so vile behave?
> And not let me this clean shirt save,
> Nor give me time, Oh, wave, to shave.

Maybell knew the other seventeen verses by heart, and repeated them in an unrelenting monotone.

The main thoroughfare of Mooneysville was named "Cornella Street," and the town continued to grow. At the barber shop, without which no city can prosper, the problem was the chair — an unstable thing, balanced on a few boards on the sand. To be shaved by an unsteady hand in a wobbly chair was not an inviting prospect. The success or failure of this business endeavor was unrecorded.

Tank house and cottage built on North Ridge Road in 1874.

The Seal Rocks House and the Long Branch Saloon, old landmarks, began to feel the effects of competition. Their proprietors began to make some improvements that had been needed for years.

A. P. Hotaling, the famed liquor merchant, then began erecting a two-story hotel on land between the Sutro property and the park. The building was to be a substantial one with a concrete foundation. According to news reports, a large force of laborers speeded its completion.

The Board of Supervisors was in a quandary. Pressure was growing for them to act, but they professed to have no authority. They had had no problem in granting a franchise to "Leland Stanford and Others" for the railroad, but the rights of the Mooneysville squatters were not something they wished to establish. The supervisors hesitated to declare the squatters in violation of the law, since that action would also render the railroad in violation. Everyone passed the buck, from the Park Commission to the superintendent of streets to the chief of police to the Board of Supervisors.

Pixley averred that the United States government had admitted the jurisdiction of the Park Commission by asking permission to build the Life Saving Station in the park. And the city had admitted the park's jurisdiction by obtaining consent in the matter of the railroad franchise. The immediate problem was Pixley's park police force, which he did not wish to decimate by pitting them against the rifles of Mooneysville. Just two years earlier, Pixley had fired the entire trained police force so carefully assembled by William Hammond Hall and replaced them with men of his own choosing — men who could not be counted on to face anything more dangerous than a frightened horse or a bicycle "scorcher" in bloomers.

At last, taking the bull by the horns, the Park Commission enacted Section Four, a new ordinance, published in the *San Francisco Examiner* on January 17, 1884:

> All persons occupying or squatting upon any portion of the grounds or avenues, or roads or tidelands of said

Golden Gate Park, who, after written notice from the superintendent of said park, to remove therefrom, shall fail or neglect to remove therefrom within twelve hours after receipt of such written notice, shall be punishable according to law, as offending against an order of this board.

The Park Commission stated that the ordinance would go into effect in twenty days. If the street superintendent's orders to move were disobeyed, his forces, the police, a posse comitatus, and the military could be invoked to compel obedience. The threat of using the army could be made because at that time Gen. Irwin McDowell of the Presidio was on the Park Board.

By January 25, a local scribe reported that lots in Mooneysville north of the park were selling at $300 per front foot, while south of the park they were going as high as $175 per front foot. By now the town contained a hardware store, a candy factory, a bakery, a chop house, several wells and pumps, a lumberyard, and fifteen saloons. Beer, which had been selling for 5¢ a glass in the Cliff House the previous week, rose to 10¢ a glass to conform with Mooneysville prices. The crime rate was rising. A businessman's establishment was destroyed by his enemies and erected again by the same men for a friend of theirs.

A new mass meeting was held in Mooneysville, and the following pronunciamiento was unanimously adopted:

> We, the undersigned settlers of Mooneysville-by-the-sea, now assembled and located upon United States property on the great seaboard of the Pacific Ocean between high- and low-water mark, according to the government survey made by Mr. Surrey, do intend to conduct ourselves as law-abiding citizens and earn a living for ourselves, our wives and families. Every man whose name is attached to this resolution pledges himself to see that no man, woman or child who visits Mooneysville will be insulted. We also respectfully petition the chief of police to send a couple of officers to assist us in the carrying out of our object and to

punish offenders. Most of us have some service for the Stars and Stripes and are again ready at any time to build fortifications on the very ground we are now holding. We well know how to defend them should a foreign enemy invade our shores. If we have no right here on this land, we would like to know what right Hotaling has to build on the same land or maintain the Long Branch. It is either because he has become rich or has fought better battles for his country. We know there are a few roughs and toughs who come here flourishing their pretended authority, using bad language and building campfires, but we believe them to be working in the interest of the park commissioners, the Cliff House and the Long Branch, trying to give Mooneysville a bad name. We hope the law will deal with them as they deserve. We protest against building fires outside of the houses or on the beach or obstructing the drive from the park to the beach. We want no deadly weapons in our camp or jumping of each others' claims. A committee shall be appointed to see that this order is enforced and if there are any offensive fences blocking the drives, they must be removed to give the public full access to the beach. It will be better for ourselves and we will gain the respect of the public.

[signed] J. Monaghan, M. Ault, J. Maree, J. Tennis, J. Downey, Phil Coyle, P. Rooney, J. Rooney, C. Cassini, C. P. Rank, J. O'Neill, G. Skippin, F. Brady, J. Brinkhard, P. Brandhouse, J. White, N. P. Limbug, D. Kearney, F. Hetterman, J. Short, J. Masterson, M. Carey, P. Curley, J. Looney, P. Rodgers, J. Brennan, James Nolan, J. F. Schroeder, John Elehrs, Con Mooney [by proxy]

Construction continued at a feverish pace. Fully sixty claims were bought or staked out in the last week of the doomed village. One of the last of the real estate purchasers was one Molly Greenlock, alias "Irish Molly." For $150, this lady of questionable character had purchased from James Nolan a claim fifty feet wide, although the western boundary did not go "all the way to China." Her fictitious deed showed that her ownership ended at the Farallone Islands. She then pawned her clothing and jewelry and raised an additional $300 with which she built a shanty in order to ply her trade, whatever it was. She had barely managed to turn a profit when the roof fell in.

Chief of Police Crowley was authorized to lend all the force necessary to protect park laborers as they played "Hannibal and Troy" — with Pixley playing the role of Hannibal. By January 30, 1884, all the structures in the beleaguered city had been posted with legal notices to vacate. That same afternoon, a deputy sheriff appeared and placed an order of attachment on the business premises of two men named White and Sargent, who had a refreshment parlor. It seemed that since the carpenter who erected the building had not been paid for his labors, he had secured a writ of attachment to secure the money he was owed. White and Sargent were gleeful over this new development. They bragged to everyone that Pixley would never dare to remove their building as long as the "high sheriff" had attached it. But their glee proved to be short-lived.

Mooneysville dominated all the newsprint far and wide, with the exception of Pixley's *Argonaut*. Rumors ran rife. The *Call* announced, "The war cloud that has hung over the park strand is dissipating." Rumors circulated that the coffee sellers had agreed to move but the whiskey sellers were adamant in their resistance. They raised $750 and hired a lawyer, Henry E. Highton, to fight their case in court and to secure an injunction to bar the park commissioners from their own land.

The *Examiner* reported that the troops had been reviewed in front of the Conservatory by General Pixley, and that gallant band had stood at rigid "Present Shovels" all the while. In view of recent rains, it was decided to dispense with the heavy artillery because it would delay the arrival of the troops. Pixley's "Army" left at 10:00 P.M. and, after a forced march to the beaches, bivouacked and posted sentinels until dawn. Instead of the batallion of police requested, only seven men were sent to protect the army of twenty-five laborers. Sergeant Nash and Officers Cummings, Burke, Crosby, Rainsbury, Dwyer, and Keller were chosen to uphold Pixley's honor. Early on the morning of January 31, 1884, these seven gallant men were ordered to the park and placed at the disposal of the Park Commission.

The *Bulletin* referred to the brave attack as "Pixley's March to the Sea," comparing Pixley to General Sherman. Unlike Sherman, Pixley prudently remained in his offices at the *Argonaut* and directed the campaign from the relative safety of his own bailiwick.

When the expeditionary force, under the command of Park Superintendent John J. McEwen, reached Mooneysville in the early dawn, no resistance was offered. As they approached the first shanty, its owner was in the process of dismantling it, so they let him proceed. The next few shacks were deserted; they were speedily dismantled. The laborers were cautioned to destroy as little as possible. They carefully pulled nails and stacked the lumber neatly, to be removed by the owner. Northward they marched, removing one shanty after another, with or without the help of the proprietor. By a little after noon, the deed was done.

When the army reached Dennis Kearney's shack, they found him busily removing his wares and his platform. When they offered to help, Kearney stepped back in a grand manner and exclaimed, "Let the Romans do it!" Then he gave orders to the park laborers in an imperious manner as to how best to do the job.

Molly Greenlock was beside herself. She danced around in the sand and swore by all the seals on the rocks that when she got her hands on Pixley, she would give him what Paddy gave the drum. But in the end she stood peacefully and watched her castle go the way of Babylon, Carthage, and Troy. That day and the next the road was filled with wagons and carts hauling away the last vestige of Mooneysville by the Sea.

Pixley had won, but Mooneysville had a last hurrah. The following day, close to the Cliff, on a neat mound of earth with a peanut-shell-covered cross at the head, a small sign proclaimed, "Here lies Frank M. Pixley. Keep his grave green." In the center of the grave was a big bottle of whiskey and some glasses. A small sign invited one and all to "help yourself." One of the more gullible in the crowd of bystanders hastened forward to quaff his share. He disappeared into a deep hole that had been cleverly concealed with brush and sand by some diabolical ex-resident of Mooneysville. The crowd roared.

"God help the poor," said Ex-Mayor Con Mooney. A fitting epitaph for Mooneysville, U.S.A.

Stylish equipages on a Sunday outing in the Gay Nineties.

A New Regime

When the new park commissioners met on May 12, 1886, none of their predecessors were present. A letter from Frank Pixley was read, in which he expressed his regrets at being absent, explaining that business in Alaska prevented his attendance. Pixley also noted that there was a deficit of about $800 in the Park Fund.

He wrote that the sum of $49,500 remaining from the Sharon Bequest was on deposit at the Bank of California. With the reading of the will of the late Sen. William Sharon of Nevada, it was found that he had left $50,000 for the beautification of Golden Gate Park. The money was to be spent at the discretion of his executors, in consultation with the park commissioners. The executors' names were Fred W. Sharon, son of William Sharon, and the senator's son-in-law, Francis G. Newlands. Pixley noted that the money was to be used for the construction of a gateway at Stanyan Street, under the direction of the architect John Gash.

Pixley also noted that $10,000 was due to be paid to his friend, W. B. Bradbury, who had built the waterworks and was agitating for his fee. Pixley did not explain how the new commissioners were to pay a $10,000 debt in light of the Park Fund deficit. He earnestly assured the new board that he would be happy to meet with them and give them the benefit of his experience as a park commissioner. His offer was not accepted.

The new board was organized, and Maj. Richard P. Hammond was elected president for a one-year term. The board resolved to hold meetings at least once a month, which would be open to the public. Since they wanted to know as much as possible about their duties, the commissioners requested that William Hammond Hall, the designer of the park and then-state engineer, make a report on the condition of the park. He was also encouraged to make recommendations concerning its future development.

On May 29, 1886, the board met again and passed resolutions stating that the superintendent was accountable for the conduct and efficiency of all employees. They directed the superintendent to give them the names of all personnel who should be discharged. They also stated that all applications and recommendations for positions must be presented to the clerk of the board at the Park Lodge, where the commissioners pledged to keep regular office hours. Commissioner William H. Dimond objected to the firing of any veterans of the nation's wars, but he was overruled by his colleagues, who maintained that incompetent men should be discharged, regardless of their status or political affiliation.

An extensive exodus of men from the park payroll began. The date of Superintendent John J. McEwen's resignation is not recorded and, although numerous mentions are made of "the superintendent," it is not clear whether the references were to McEwen or Hall. It was apparent, however, that Hall's presence was being felt.

The park labor force had grown in number. Besides the superintendent, it included the head gardener, James Taylor, who had been hired in 1883. F. Vincent was in charge of the Conservatory, and Patrick Quigley was foreman of the roads. Patrick Owens had been the nurseryman since the park's beginning. J. L. Howell was the night guard. In addition, the park employed thirty-four laborers. The police force consisted of two men: Officers S. M. Thomson and J. W. Beckwith. Occasionally, the city police force would furnish one or two extra men for weekend duty. Eleven mules and four horses, a few wagons, and three water carts serviced the park.

Engineer Hall suggested that the Sharon Bequest, originally intended for use in building a mammoth Stanyan Street gate, be used instead to provide a playground for children, similar to the ones in Central Park in New York and Lincoln Park in Chicago. After much discussion and consultation with the Sharon trustees, this suggestion was accepted.

Hall also pointed out the need for underpasses at various points to separate pedestrian traffic from equestrian traffic and to separate north–south nonpark traffic from the actual park traffic. Several tunnels under various park roads are presently used for pedestrian traffic, but no grade separations have been made on the Main Drive or South Drive to accommodate the traffic from the Richmond and Sunset districts. The need for such separations was acute in the 1880s, and in the 1980s the need is ever more acute.

Hall mentioned that the park roads were worn out. They had been sprinkled and rolled daily to keep the dust down, but no new rock had been added to the clay base since 1876. They were worn down to their foundations. Much money would be needed to repair this neglect.

Under Hall's early management, all roads, paths, walks, and water lines had been carefully laid out on the park map so that repairs could be made and recorded easily. But in Hall's ten-year absence, water lines for irrigation were laid without any records. Thus, when a line broke, no one knew how or where to turn off the water. This condition still prevails in the park today.

The *San Francisco Evening Bulletin* reported that the new Park Board had requested the previous board to determine the validity of Bradbury's claim. Pixley declined to participate stating that he would serve only if *one* of the previous board members were on the committee and if the present board appointed three other disinterested members. He stated that the two previous members, Rosenfeld and Goodall, would outvote him in the matter. Captain Goodall responded that Hall McAllister, Irving M. Scott, and W. R. Eckart had examined the waterworks and pronounced them "poorly constructed." All three, according to Goodall, were prominent, qualified men, and he did not feel the bill should be paid until the terms of the contract were fulfilled. Rosenfeld replied similarly, and the matter rested for a time.

After Bradbury sealed all the leaks in the reservoir and installed meters according to original plans, his bill was ordered paid, with the exception of $2,000. That amount was withheld until other work was done to the satisfaction of the board.

To the casual observer, the park looked in good condition. Viewed as a group, the trees that had been planted between 1871 and 1876 under Hall's direction appeared healthy and thriving. In reality, the forced neglect of the plantations due to lack of funds was readily apparent. The young trees were merely stems, with foliage at the top and none of the spreading limbs necessary for a beautiful tree. Trees are initially planted close together for mutual protection. As they grow, they are gradually thinned so they can expand horizontally as well as vertically. Since no tree thinning had been done since 1876, Hall recognized that something had to be done at once if the trees were to be saved. A $5,000 appropriation was secured from the Board of Supervisors for this purpose. Hall went to work as soon as the money was available.

The press, ignorant of the nature of growing trees,

took up the cry, "Woodman, spare that tree." They bemoaned the fact that although much money had been spent to create a forest in the park, the park workers were destroying "perfectly good trees" for firewood. Although wood was being burned in the steam plant that pumped water for the park, the trees were actually being cut to allow the remaining ones to grow properly.

Protests poured into the commission office about the destruction of the trees. The public, as usual, believed everything in the newspapers, and refused to listen to any explanations. In desperation, Hall appealed to Central Park designer Frederick Law Olmsted, who happened to be in the city at the time, to make an examination of the tree plantings and give his opinion.

Olmsted later wrote to the Park Commission as follows:

> In noticing, as you ask me to do, what has been accomplished on your grounds, I am able to compare the site for Golden Gate Park, as I examined it last week, and as I saw it twenty years ago, when the question of its selection was being discussed. And now I say that the result thus far obtained in the legitimate line of park creation . . . is an achievement far exceeding all that I have believed possible.
>
> As to the question — the condition and management of the forest tree growths — I consider that Mr. Hall's views are unquestionably sound and his statements sustaining them appear to be moderately made and accurately correct.

The question was also put to John McLaren, a noted San Mateo County gardener. McLaren had at one time been in charge of the James Lick estate on the Peninsula, as well as the Maglee estate and those of other wealthy families. He, too, confirmed that Hall was taking the proper steps to repair the damage done by years of neglect to the forest plantations. Eventually, the public outcry was stilled.

When the new board came to power in May 1886, the newspapers, which had ignored the park during the Pixley years, began praising accomplishments in the park. On June 19, 1886, the *San Francisco Evening Post* carried over a full page on the park. With this new publicity, the park became immensely popular again. In 1882 a careful survey of visitors on one day showed the following: 118 carriages carrying 788 persons, 1,103 buggies with 2,549 persons, 96 equestrians, and 5,704 pedestrians, for a total of 9,131 persons. By April 1886, with three streetcar lines serving the park, more than 47,000 people visited the park in one day by the streetcars alone. The population of the city was about 250,000 at this time.

The *Evening Post* listed more than 225 different persons or families in the parade of horses and carriages in the June 19 article. Even Frank Pixley and his "turnout" were described, along with the Spreckels, the Crockers, the Sutros, Charles Webb Howard, the Stanfords, and the other famous families of the era. P. H. "White Hat" McCarthy, later mayor of the city, had a fine carriage with four matched horses pulling it. Young Dan McCarthy trailed him with his two Shetland ponies pulling a small cart. Another famous family had a large carriage pulled by six sorrel horses. The harness was of russet leather, trimmed in gold; it alone cost $5,000. The carriage, which was lined with pink silk, had been imported from Paris. The horses were driven by a liveried coachman.

During this period, great pressure was still being applied to park officials to build a speed track within the park for the benefit of those who owned racehorses and wanted to drive them fast. Although racetracks existed in the Richmond District (the Bay District Track) and the Sunset District, these tracks were apparently insufficient. Wealthy people wanted a track in the park where they could display their horses.

The pressure of special-interest groups is always hard to withstand. Such groups are influential, and their individual members are usually contributors to political campaigns. In the end, they usually get their way. The park commissioners, however, maintained that no work should be done until $35,000, the estimated cost of the track, had been fully pledged and the money placed in the bank for use of the Park Commission. The horse owners were also required to furnish two men to maintain the track. These requirements postponed the building of the track for a time.

Hall wanted to keep the Speed Track out of the park at all costs. He suggested using D Street (Fulton Street) from Seventh Avenue to Ocean Beach for the purpose, as it was still ungraded and unused as a public street, or building the track adjacent to the railroad tracks along H Street (Lincoln Way). However, these proposals did not meet with the approval of the horse owners, because they wanted to "see and be seen," and they wanted the track in the park. Hall also proposed that the track might be built between South Drive and H Street, where it would not interfere with other users of the park. This plan, too, was vetoed by the horse owners, and the matter remained unresolved.

Special-interest groups had pushed the idea of a Speed Track since Frank M. Pixley's election to the board. Although he was no longer on the board, he was instrumental in getting Joseph Austin appointed. Since both Austin and Hammond were wealthy and had blooded horses of their own, it was only a matter of time before the movement was revived. This time a determined group of men vowed not to be stopped. It included Charles Webb Howard, Leland Stanford, Charles Crocker, J. M. Donahue, Millen Giffity, A. P. Hotaling, William W. Story, Albert Gallatin, Fred C. Talbot, Adolph Sutro, Adolph B. Spreckels, H. B. Cook, Alvinza Hayward, Fred W. Sharon, James G. Fair, and others. The *Examiner* also joined in the fight, proclaiming that the plan was not objectionable in any way. The paper claimed that the very name "Speed Road" was a misnomer, because public sheds, trotting stands, or public houses in connection with the road were to be absolutely prohibited.

The Sharon Building was currently being built in the children's quarters. To distract attention away from the road, M. J. Kelly, the builder, was charged with using inferior stone. These charges were made by a man who had bid on the building and lost. These same tactics had been used successfully in spring 1876, when charges were brought against Hall to take public attention away from the corruption in the building of City Hall. The public is easily fooled, time and again. The charges against Kelly were not confirmed, and the matter was dropped after about two months.

Most of the cost of the Speed Road was subscribed by this time. Although the Park Commission had insisted that the money be fully subscribed, the horse owners persuaded the commission members that they would quickly furnish the balance, so work was begun. The San Francisco Bridge Company was awarded the contract for the work. The road began just west of Strawberry Hill and ran in a southwesterly direction from Broom Point for a distance of 6,400 feet, finally curving back to meet the Main Drive to Ocean Beach. A total of 120,000 cubic yards of earth had to be moved to construct the road, nearly three times as much as was needed to construct the children's quarters.

Charles Webb Howard thought it was perfectly proper to build the Speed Road in the park. In an interview with an *Examiner* reporter, he stated:

> People who have fine horses will speed them. And it is the part of wisdom to provide a place where this may be done with safety, not alone to the stock and the drivers, but also to spectators and the general public. The drives throughout the park, fine as they are, are not of the character to allow of fast driving. It does not take a horseman to know that to drive fast over those rock-like roadbeds is simply to ruin his horse. . . . The knowledge that we have a drive of this character will attract to our city and vicinity the finest stock in our own or any other state.

His view once again ignored the real purpose of the park, to serve as a recreation area for the ordinary person, the work-weary, the convalescent, the young, the poor, and the elderly. The park was converted into a rich-man's plaything, and if that change interfered with the enjoyment of others, what of it? The *Examiner* praised the road

The second Music Stand, dedicated in 1888.

as "an attractive feature." It was pointed out that Chicago, New York, Boston, and other cities were agitating for just such a road, and San Francisco would be the first. But the Speed Road for Central Park suffered an ignominious defeat in Albany. Not so in San Francisco.

In vain, the *Evening Bulletin* raised its voice in editorial protest:

> The gentlemen who are able to possess fast horses do not stand in need of this refreshment as much as some of their less-favored fellows. Their winters are passed in the sunshine of the South and their summers in villas at Lennox, or cottages by the sea. But to the poor and the children of the poor, the park offers the only glimpse of greensward that greets their eyes from one year's end to the next. It seems a cruelty to destroy these pictures of peace that a wise forethought has prepared for them especially to enable a few opulent citizens to enjoy their chosen pastime. And this is especially true, because the park and its scenery add nothing to the enjoyment of these horsemen, who find in the driving itself its own great reward. Some of these gentlemen have famous picture galleries, and all right-minded persons would sympathize with their horror and distress if some vandal hand should cut out a strip of the border of one of their favorite landscapes. But the living picture is just as truly a work of art as the painted, and the cutting away of this broad stretch of verdure and substituting for it something entirely incongruous with its motive and purpose would be an outrage quite as brutal.

All protests were ignored, however, and work on the road continued.

When it became apparent that the new Music Concourse south of the Main Drive would soon become a reality, the bicycle riders of the city demanded that Conservatory Valley be filled in and made into a parade ground where the bicycle riders could also "see and be seen." The head gardener, James Taylor, estimated that the cost for that work would be at least $2,200. After several months of study and conferences, it was decided that when the old

Music Concourse was abandoned, no driving or riding would be permitted in Conservatory Valley. The valley would be converted into a flower garden. The decision was wise, and it has endured to the present day.

Ordinances allowing bicycle riders the use of all the roads in the park were rescinded in July 1886. The cyclists were then denied the use of roads around the Music Concourse and those leading to the Casino. In the future, riders

North Ridge Road in the 1890s.

on these roads would have to dismount and push their bicycles.

Special bicycle paths had been built for the convenience of the riders, but they insisted on the same courtesies as those extended to riders of horses and carriages — that they be allowed to use any road in the park.

Bicycle riding had reached great heights in the 1880s and 1890s. The bicycle advanced in style until both wheels were of the same size, and both men and women could ride. The early high-wheeled bicycle could be ridden only by a skilled person, and even then, it was dangerous to life and limb. Hitting a rock or a depression on the road often sent the rider over the handlebars into a heap.

The long dresses and skirts of the Victorian age were not well adapted to bicycle riding. Soon "the bloomer girl" came into being — to be written about, sung about, praised or scandalized, depending on the point of view. Women were soon riding bicycles at all hours of the day and evening. Editorials and sermons from the pulpits howled over this practice, but nothing seemed to deter the lover of the wheel.

According to the August 4, 1895, *Examiner*, the first bicycle owner on the Pacific Coast was Col. Ralph de Clairmont, who imported his bicycle from Paris in the spring of 1876. On his first ride to the Cliff House, he caused a stampede of horses, but no one was injured. The following year, G. Loring Cunningham received an English bicycle from Boston, and shortly after, Governor Perkins, R. B. Woodward, and J. B. Golly imported their wheels from Coventry, England. These machines were of the high-wheel variety; Woodward's had a sixty-inch front wheel. One had to get the machine going at a good rate and then climb two steps to the saddle.

Bicycle rental shops opened up for business on Stanyan Street and nearby. As the sport grew in popularity, rich men were heard to grumble that one could not tell a rich man's daughter from a "typewriter," or office girl. In December 1895, the *Examiner* reported that this situation would soon be remedied. Tiffany's of New York had agreed to decorate bicycles to order with gold and silver. Soon people would be able to show they had money to burn by the decorations on their bicycles.

Some of the accessories for bicycles that could be purchased included:

TIFFANY BLUE BOOK — 1897 EDITION

BICYCLES

The latest models of the best manufacture, mounted in sterling silver, with silver bell, cyclometer, lamp, watch holder and watch, and silver-trimmed tool bag.

Men's wheels, complete . . . . 325 upward
Ladies' wheels, complete . . . . 550 upward

OWNER'S WHEELS DECORATED TO ORDER AS DESIRED.

BICYCLE SUNDRIES

Adjustable Watch Holders:
Silver . . . . $ 7.

Bicycle Watches:
Tiffany & Co. open face watches,
reliable timekeepers, in nickel
cases . . . .   9.
In silver cases . . . . 10.

Cycling Recording Books:
Assorted leathers . . . . 2.50 to   5.
With silver mountings . . . . 5.50 to 12.
With gold mountings . . . . 17. to 30.

Flasks:
Cut glass, leather covered,
with silver top and cup . . . . 10. to 24.

Scarf and Stick Pins:
Miniature gold bicycles . . . . 3.25 to 3.75
With diamond in lamp . . . .   6.

Tool Bags:
Made to order in assorted
leathers . . . . 20. to 30.

The following verses from the December 8, 1895, *Examiner* are typical of those written about female bicycle riders during this period:

The Bicycle Girl

The Bicycle Girl, oh, the Bicycle Girl
With a spinnaker skirt and a sleeve like a furl;
Such a freak on the wheel, such a sight on the tire
I am certain I never will love or admire.

Her leggings are brown and her hat is the same,
"I say there, old man, can you tell me the name?"
But this is absurd, for I never will like
A girl who goes whizzing about on a bike.

The Bicycle Girl, oh, the Bicycle Girl,
She wears on her forehead a dream of a curl
And the sound of her bell and the hum of her wheel
Is enough to make any man's cranium reel.

The Bicycle Girl, oh, the Bicycle Girl,
She has lips like a ruby in settings of pearl;
And why did she smile as she lightly spun by?
Does she think I could love her? No, never, not I.

It's foolish, I know, though I never have tried,
Confound it, I really believe I could ride.
For the Bicycle Girl, oh, the Bicycle Girl
She has tangled my heart in her mystical whirl.

Numerous bicycle clubs were formed in the city. Bicycle racing became a popular sport, and a journey to Los Angeles or Reno to participate in competitions was commonplace.

The speed limit for bike riding in the park was ten miles per hour. Nearly all cities passed ordinances regulating bicycle speed and requiring lights at night and horns or bells to be sounded when approaching intersections.

In Oakland, after the passages of such an ordinance, the bicyclists paraded through the streets with huge bells attached to their machines which they sounded, making the city a bedlam. Others carried loud fish horns, making a hideous racket. The *Argonaut* editorialized as follows:

We hope the Chief of Police of Oakland will keep on arresting these Yahoos and put them behind bars. Bicycle riders must be taught that not the entire earth and the fullness thereof are theirs, but that there are a few other people on the planet.

When he returned to the park in 1886 on loan from the state engineer's office in Sacramento, William Hammond Hall was asked to locate and employ a competent superintendent. He found such a man — John McLaren of San Mateo County. McLaren was hired in the spring of 1887 and served as assistant superintendent under Hall until Hall resigned again in 1889. According to Park Commission minutes, McLaren was appointed superintendent of Golden Gate Park on July 29, 1890, and held that position until his death in 1943.

According to the book *Master Hands in the Affairs of the Pacific Coast,* published in 1892 by the Western Historical and Publishing Company of San Francisco, McLaren was born in Scotland in 1846. He was educated in the public schools and apprenticed as a landscape gardener. He practiced his profession on several estates in Scotland, and at one time worked at the Royal Botannical Gardens in Edinburgh. When he came to California in 1872, he went to work in San Mateo County on the Howard family estate, as well as the Lick and Maglee estates. In 1876, McLaren married; later, he had one son, Donald, who followed in his father's footsteps and became a nurseryman. Donald and his father owned and operated a nursery on El Camino Real in San Mateo County.

Depending on your source, John McLaren was considered either a martinet or a benevolent dictator. Politicians hated him because he did not take orders. He gave orders, and they were obeyed. He would fire a man for wearing gloves. And he loved scotch. One old-time *Chronicle* reporter said that John McLaren drank a quart of scotch every day but that he never saw McLaren drunk. Visitors to the Lodge were invited to an inner office for "a wee nip."

Most of his workers admired and even worshipped him. Frank Foehr, who retired as superintendent of parks in 1971, says that McLaren always swore at his men, and that swearing right back at him was the best way to keep their jobs. Foehr worked in the park for forty-seven years.

McLaren's battles with bureaucracy were legion. He fought the San Francisco Municipal Railway to a standstill when it planned a streetcar line through the park. He also fought the chief of the Park Police Station when the chief sought to remove an oak tree that was too close to the buildings. McLaren told him, "I'm a reasonable man. Let's compromise, and you move the station." After the battle, which John McLaren won, a reporter asked him to comment on the fight, and he merely said, "Just a wee misunderstanding."

When the city wanted to extend Sunset Boulevard through the park to connect with Lincoln Park, McLaren slyly offered the land at the intersection of Thirty-Seventh Avenue and Fulton Streets to the Police Department for a Police Academy. The Police Department jumped at the offer, and soon a Police Academy stood in the way of the proposed connection with Lincoln Park. The building still stands, but it is now a senior center.

In 1917, when McLaren reached the mandatory retirement age of seventy, a grateful Board of Supervisors wrote legislation that permitted him to remain superintendent of parks as long as he lived. Since he would thus lose his pension, the board also doubled his salary for life. The gruff little man ruled the park with a strong hand for more than a quarter-century after that.

McLaren received many awards for his work in Golden Gate Park. He became world famous as landscape architect for the 1915 Panama-Pacific International Ex-

position. He grew trees years before that event and stored them in the Presidio until needed. He experimented by planting varieties of bulbs at varying depths in the ground, so that one day flower beds would be of one hue; during the night, his men would remove the older plants, and the beds would seem to blossom with a different color the next day. The world came to know him as a "magician with a magic wand." His legend grew until it was said that he "waved a magic wand and created Golden Gate Park out of a desert." This aspect of the legend was untrue. Four different superintendents had ruled before him; by 1887 when he was hired as assistant to William Hammond Hall, more than 700,000 trees and shrubs already graced Golden Gate Park.

McLaren had also been appointed landscape architect of the earlier 1894 California Midwinter International Exposition held in Golden Gate Park. He resigned just after being appointed, when he learned he would have to take orders from the director general of the fair, M. H. de Young, co-owner of the *San Francisco Chronicle*. McLaren took orders from no one, except perhaps his gracious wife.

The war came to Golden Gate Park in 1941. In 1942 McLaren was desperately ill in the Park Lodge. Because of the war, lights were out all over the city, and the Christmas tree in front of the Lodge was dark. But when McLaren asked if the tree could be lighted again, it was done. A policeman, an air-raid warden, and a gardener stayed on duty to make sure the lights were turned off in case of an alert.

John McLaren passed away in his beloved park on January 12, 1943, and his body lay in state in the rotunda of the City Hall for two days. The funeral procession passed through the park on the way to the cemetery at Colma, and his employees stood at attention with heads bared as it passed.

Just after McLaren had become the fifth park superintendent, at a regular meeting of the Park Commission on May 12, 1887, President Richard P. Hammond reported on the completion of his presidential term. He stated that the last session of the legislature had increased the tax levy for Golden Gate Park from 1½¢ to 3¢ on $100 of valuation. This change would double the park's income, allowing proper development of the park.

The grading for the Children's Playground and the new Music Concourse had been completed, and a new bandstand (of the latest design for projecting sound) had been built. The Sharon Building was under construction, and prospects for the future looked bright. Work on reclamation was proceeding according to plan; numerous walks and drives had been laid out. More than 18,000 trees and 10,000 plants and shrubs had been planted.

The drives and walks for the Music Concourse had not been completed due to lack of funds, and the steps leading up to the bandstand were not finished. It was estimated that the steps would cost over $1,700, so they would have to wait. However, the Market Street Cable Road generously offered to fund an increase in the size of the park band to thirty-five players.

Now that money was available, concrete walks were ordered for the central section and the east wing of the Conservatory. Money was appropriated to purchase seats for the new music grounds in June, and preparations were made for the dedication of the new Music Stand and the Francis Scott Key Monument to be held on July 4, 1888.

Superintendent Lynch of the Powell Street Cable Company asked permission to build a gateway to the park at the Seventh Avenue terminus of his road. The matter was postponed for a time but eventually approved. This building still stands at Seventh Avenue and Fulton Street.

On June 16, 1888, the *San Francisco News Letter* severely criticized the park management. The editor admitted that the Children's Playground would be a good feature and that the new Music Stand and Music Concourse were admirable. But he criticized the general appearance of the park, remarking that the grass was brown and that few flowers bloomed there. The editor further said that neither the management of the Casino, nor its surroundings, had improved. The prices charged there were entirely too high for the average citizen, and the Casino was called a "flash" house. The editor also charged that the park commissioners, "worthy and excellent gentlemen" though they were, usually passed their evenings and weekends with their families and did not know what went on in the park.

Two weeks later, the same editor charged that entirely too many dead bodies had been found in the park. People had died by their own hand — or perhaps they'd been assisted by others. The editor suggested that since the coroner paid an honorarium of ten dollars to anyone finding a dead body in the county limits, perhaps the park was becoming notorious in this respect. More police might be needed in the park at night to discourage this situation.

On July 1, 1888, Engineer Hall presented a report of progress since the spring of 1886. He made many suggestions for improvement, including the construction of archways or tunnels under the drives to separate foot traffic from horses and bicycle traffic. The first one, he said, should be built on the path leading from Seventh Avenue to Conservatory Valley. This one was needed because one cable road now came down Fulton Street nearly to Seventh Avenue, and the new line from Point Lobos Road down Seventh Avenue to Fulton was now completed. He suggested three more: one under the road in front of the Conservatory (Main Drive), and two more beyond that, one leading to what is now Laveaga Dell and the other one to the north, leading to the new Music Stand. The tunnel under the Main Drive was built, but two were postponed, and the one under the North Ridge Road was never built.

July 4, 1888, was the dedication of the new Music Stand (where the tennis courts are today) and the Francis Scott Key Monument. More than ten thousand people arrived in the park for the event. Women wore light dresses and shielded themselves from the sun's rays with gaily colored parasols. Children played on the green slopes, dressed in the bright colors of the national flag. The

Dedication of Francis Scott Key Monument on July 4, 1888.

somber male attire was brightened by the dashing appearance of hundreds of military uniforms. The monument was erected to honor the memory of the author of "The Star Spangled Banner." Its $60,000 cost was donated by James Lick before he died. The sculptor was William W. Story, and the statue was made in Italy. After completion, the monument was loaded on a nine-hundred-ton Italian bark, the *Pietro B*, with Captain Minetti commanding. Since the

small ship was not known for speed, the voyage around Cape Horn took 187 days. The ship arrived at the Howard Street wharf on January 25, 1888.

On the day of the ceremony, the platform was filled with the usual civic dignitaries, the Lick trustees, and the Society of California Pioneers. Mayor Edward B. Pond was applauded as he rose to make the acceptance speech. Then followed a one-hundred-gun salute of the Second Artillery

Regiment, California National Guard, and a one-hundred-voice chorus singing all four stanzas of "The Star Spangled Banner." A congratulatory address was next given by Irving M. Scott, and then ten thousand voices joined the band as everyone sang the anthem. It was a stirring occasion, enjoyed by all.

President Hammond reported that many people had suggested a menagerie or zoo in the park. In September 1888, D. H. McDonald was contracted to erect a fence around a proposed deer park near the Children's Playground. T. Duncan of Duncan's Mills, California, sent a letter offering to donate ten deer for the new park, and the secretary was ordered to send a letter of thanks to the donor. The following month, L. L. Robinson offered to donate some deer, and a letter of thanks was sent to him, asking him to hold the deer until a fence could be built. On November 23, 1888, six deer arrived from Duncan's Mills. Ten had been shipped, but four died during the trip, and one looked as if it would die soon.

More than fifteen hundred quail were estimated to be in the park. "The Hermitkeeper" of the gate at Seventh Avenue was responsible for their feeding. Each morning he would come to the same spot and call them, presumably in their own tongue. They would flock about the old man and scold him and ruffle their feathers until he scattered their breakfast of grain on the ground. A sentinel posted in a nearby tree would sound a warning if a dog approached. Then the quail would disappear in a loud whir of feathers and return only when the old hermit sounded the all clear for them.

The following spring, Charles A. Grow, superintendent of the California Ostrich Farming Company, offered a pair of ostriches to the park. They were accepted and ordered to be placed in Deer Glen.

The *San Francisco Examiner*, rising to the front of the newspaper competition in the city, referred to itself as "The Monarch of the Dailies." Since little had been done

The Golden Stairs, built in the 1870s.

Copyright 1895, by B. W. Kilburn.

The Casino after the second story was added, about 1894.

about the proposed Menagerie in the park, William Randolph Hearst determined to do something. And so was created one of the most unusual jobs ever given to a newspaper reporter. In May 1889, Allan Kelly was summoned to Hearst's office where he was startled by the following question: "Do you think you could get me a California grizzly bear?" Kelly replied, "I think I could get a bear if I tried. Do you want him dead or alive?" The reply: "Alive."

Kelly left immediately for Southern California and went to the Ojai Valley in Ventura County near Santa Paula to catch his bear. He secured the services of a guide and three more men, a pack mule, and suitable horses. For six months the five men camped in the mountains, setting traps or cages built of stout logs, and baiting them with a quarter of a beef. It was a rough life. At one point, climbing the side of a mountain on a narrow trail, they came upon a nest of rattlesnakes. The warnings of the snakes caused the pack mule to lose his balance and roll over and over down the mountain. He was unhurt and came scrambling back to the group, who hurriedly examined the pack to see if their snakebite medicine had been broken. It was not, and they each fortified themselves with some of it, just in case, and went on their way.

Finally one morning, their toils were rewarded. One of the traps held a huge grizzly. They had trapped him, but how would they get him out of the trap? They left him there for two days to calm down. Then they fashioned a noose from a chain and put it through the logs. When the bear stepped into the noose, four men hauled away on it. With one whip of his paw, the bear jerked the chain from the hands of the four men and snarled.

Then they fashioned another noose and dropped it through the top of the cage. When the bear stepped in it, the chain was jerked up to his shoulder, and after several hours of struggle, it was secured to the cage. Then the other front leg was caught and secured. Ropes were then fastened to his hind legs, and at long last the bear was spread-eagled on the ground. His captors offered him a stick, which he grabbed in his jaws. Finally, a rope was passed several times around the stick and his jaws.

The next morning the bear was lashed to a crude sled to be hauled down the mountain. It took four days to reach a road where a wagon could be used. Then a stout cage was made, and the bear was transferred to the cage. The cage was hoisted to the wagon, and the men made their way to Ventura and the railroad. There the bear was placed in a boxcar and shipped to San Francisco.

Jubilantly, Hearst called the park and said, "I have a grizzly bear for your Menagerie." Austin replied, "We don't want him." So Monarch, as the bear was named, was taken to Woodward's Gardens to be placed on display. When the Midwinter Fair came to San Francisco in 1894, Monarch was at last brought to Golden Gate Park and lowered into a huge concrete pit that had been prepared for him.

After the fair, an iron cage was built for Monarch behind what is now the Academy of Sciences. The bars were bent in at the top to keep the bear from climbing out, and Monarch seemed satisfied with the situation until someone donated an Alaskan moose to the park. Monarch immediately developed a fondness for moose meat and tried to climb out of his cage. Attendants armed with iron bars beat him back to the ground, and he was confined to a smaller cage until strong bars could be attached to the top of his cage. Monarch was the center of attention for many years. He is said to be the paternal ancestor to many of the bears now at the zoo. He died in 1911, and a taxidermist was hired to preserve his huge body, which was displayed at the Academy of Sciences for many years.

The Menagerie grew and grew. It included a fifteen-acre Deer Glen. Just west of where McLaren Lodge now stands, a small meadow was enclosed with a tall wire fence, and several peacocks and hens were displayed. This area is still referred to as Peacock Meadow.

Maj. Richard P. Hammond was a fun-loving fellow, even if he was a staid park commissioner. From an itinerate ship's captain, he secured a kangaroo. With the help of a park laborer, he took it to the Deer Glen and released it. What happened next was not in the major's plans. The kangaroo briefly assumed a prayerful attitude, as if giving thanks, and then rose into the air and sailed over the fence, to the astonishment of all. He reached the Main Drive and cleared it with one leap just as a man and his wife went by in a horse and buggy. The *Examiner* reported that the driver immediately handed in his application to the Temperance League. His wife fainted.

In September 1890, the commission ordered the construction of an aviary, the cost not to exceed $600. A house for birds may seem strange today, but in the days following the gold rush, birds were scarce. Nearly every tree on the Peninsula had been cut for firewood when San Francisco was a boom town, composed mostly of tents and makeshift huts. When the trees went, so did the birds, with the exception of sea birds. The new Aviary was built opposite the Conservatory on the south side of the Main Drive, and it was an instant success.

Numerous complaints came to the Lodge about the Casino. Charges of drunkenness, fights, and other disorderly conduct were made. Finally the Daemon brothers were notified that their lease would not be renewed, and plans were made to move the Casino building about one hundred feet south, closer to the Main Drive, and to add a second story. The place was to be made presentable, not only in appearance but also in character. But the bad reputation it had already earned could not be erased, and a year later the Casino was empty, a financial failure. For about a year or so, it was used as a natural history museum. Buffalo and other large animals that died in the park were turned over to a taxidermist, then put on display. Swans, ducks, quail — anything that could be preserved — were added to the collection.

Once more a horsemen's group appeared before the board and generously offered to "donate" the Speed Road to the park. The board did not accept the donation. The road was not yet completed, and the fund for finishing it was $8,000 short, including the cost of fencing and running a waterline for sprinkling the road. The horsemen insisted that they had done enough and that the commissioners should finish paying for their "improvement" of the park. General Dimond appeared to be the backbone of the opposition to the Speed Track, insisting that the horsemen should live up to their word and raise the money for the road that was to be for their exclusive use. Then he resigned suddenly from the board, giving the "press of business" as his reason. About the same time, the board voted to ask Superintendent Foley of the house of corrections to loan fifty prisoners to complete the Speed Road. Labor organizations voiced fierce opposition to this plan and the matter was "laid over."

Rumor soon had it that William W. Stow was to be appointed in General Dimond's place. Hall, who was serving as consultant to the park, warned the board that Stow was not the proper man for the job, and that he could not in good conscience work with such a commissioner. But Stow, who wanted to retire, wished to be known not as a lobbyist, which he had been, but as a friend of the people. Stow was rumored to have promised to obtain more money for the park if he were placed on the board. When Stow was elected to the board in September 1889, Hall quietly withdrew from any further connection with Golden Gate Park. The board wrote him several times, asking his advice on park matters, but the letters were never answered.

May Day at the Children's Playground, about 1915.

The Children's Playground

On Wednesday, March 22, 1978, a group of citizens and civic leaders gathered in the southeast corner of Golden Gate Park to rededicate the Children's Playground. Redesigned and reconstructed, it was vastly different from the early Victorian playground dedicated on December 22, 1888. Instead of separate wooden slides for boys and girls, the new slides, for all children, were made of concrete and were part of the steep embankment at the southern extremity of the playground. Swings were made of metal for durability, in place of the homemade wooden swings of long ago. A high metal circular slide of yesteryear was kept, and the Farmyard, with its barnyard fowl and goats, was reinstalled.

The new playground was renamed "The Mary B. Connolly Children's Playground" in honor of the long-time secretary of the Recreation and Parks Commission. Mary Connolly happily took part in the ceremonies that gave well-deserved honors to a universally loved lady and a respected public servant.

Originally called The Sharon Quarters for Children, the playground embarked on a new chapter in a tradition that has endured in the park for ninety years. Thousands of children have danced around the Maypole, scrambled for Easter eggs hidden in the grasses, ridden the donkeys and elephants, and driven the goat carts of long ago. The merry-go-round has thrilled thousands of youngsters. The Sharon Building holds a place in the memories of many mothers and maids who have spent leisurely hours on the balcony, watching future San Francisco citizens indulge in their youthful fantasies.

A child could be a pony express rider on those slow-moving donkeys, fighting off Indians and climbing mountains and fording unbridged rivers, or a maharaja, swaying on the back of the elephant so generously donated by Commissioner Herbert Fleischhacker in the 1920s. So many of San Francisco's homeless orphans experienced the wonder of free days, when benevolent societies of the city paid for those days at the Children's Playground. On those days the Columbia Park Boy's Club and many other groups furnished music and entertainment for the children of the orphanages.

Following the example set by Central Park in New York and Lincoln Park in Chicago, the first park engineer and superintendent, William Hammond Hall, had planned for the Children's Playground to be at Haight and Stanyan streets. But in 1884, in defiance of State Law and Order Number 800, the Park and Ocean Railroad built a huge wooden depot inside the park at that spot and rendered the area unsafe for the use intended.

Many suggestions are always made about how to spend another man's money, and this occasion proved no exception. When the bequest of Sen. William P. Sharon had first been made public, Park Commission president

Frank M. Pixley had wanted to build a huge German-type beer garden and dance hall. Others felt that a glass-enclosed music pavilion would be preferable. Still others wanted a lake to be built; their opponents asked if the Pacific Ocean wasn't enough water to look at. The executors leaned toward a great marble gate at Stanyan Street. After more than two years of controversy, in which the *San Francisco Bulletin* took an active part, the building of the great gate was determined to be the best use for the money. Architect John Gash, who had rebuilt the Conservatory in 1884 after the disastrous fire, was selected to draw up the plans. They were not modest. The words *Golden Gate Park* were to be cut into a huge marble gate — along with the words Sharon — 1885.

The public outcry was immediate and vociferous. The *Bulletin* said one did not need to be told that one was entering Golden Gate Park. Others argued that the gate was merely a fancy gravestone, designed to make Senator Sharon immortal. The controversy raged, but the plans were pushed ahead. Trenches were dug for the foundation, and soon a boxcar load of marble arrived on the grounds. The marble came from the Inyo Quarry in the Sierras, and it was rumored that people close to the situation had a monetary interest in this quarry.

Then came the bombshell. When Governor Stoneman did not reappoint the park commissioners in the spring of 1886, the three new commissioners he appointed were all approved by William Hammond Hall. The governor further decreed that Hall should act as consulting engineer for the new commission. Since Hall was already on the state payroll as state engineer, this appointment would relieve the commission of the need for hiring an engineer.

Hall immediately discouraged the idea of the marble gate. After several meetings with the executors of the Sharon Estate, he succeeded in persuading them that a children's quarters would be more benevolent use of the bequest. The new commissioners were easily convinced of the merits of this proposal.

But with their approval came the problem of where to place the children's quarters. This problem coexisted with the question of what to do about the crowded conditions on the Music Concourse in the west end of Conservatory Valley. Across the Main Drive from Conservatory Valley was a high hill that in the early days reached all the way into the Panhandle. Some of the hill had been removed to create the Main Lawn Valley, but much of it remained. Farther south of the hill, where the Children's Playground is presently located, was a huge freshwater lake. It was decided that this spot offered the most secluded location for the new playground. So the hill was moved laboriously by horse-drawn scraper, and the lake was filled in.

Contrary to common practice by city officials of the day, Hall utilized the Sharon Bequest to prepare both a secluded spot for children and the level ground for the much-needed new Music Concourse. Hall's style was always to make one dollar do the work of two if he could manage to do so.

The removal of the old commission also signaled the end for Park Architect John Gash. The new commissioners called for designs for the Sharon Building, and the plans of architects Percy and Hamilton were selected. In April 1887, bids were called for the construction of the Sharon Building. On May 21, 1887, the bids from four contractors were opened and read. Donald McKay's bid for $19,945 was rejected as not properly filled out. The bid of Gray and Stover for $39,250, accompanied by specimen of stone from Niles Quarry, was read and received. M. Hefferman's bid was not considered because it was not received with a check. The bid of M. J. Kelly for $35,777, accompanied by specimen of stone from Niles Quarry, was read and received, and all bids were taken under consideration. On May 28, 1887, the contract was awarded to M. J. Kelly, subject to approval of the quality of the stone by the architects.

John McLaren, who was hired in May as Hall's assistant, was given his first assignment: to plant trees and

Alvord Lake and bridge from Stanyan Street built in 1889.

shrubs on the site of the new playground. His title was acting superintendent.

The street railroads of the city contributed $4,000 toward the improvement of the children's quarters. This money was spent to build a tunnel under the roadway near Stanyan Street to protect children going to and from the playground. This old bridge under Kezar Drive was the first concrete-reinforced arched bridge built in the United States. During the Park Centennial in 1970, the American Society of Civil Engineers placed a plaque on it.

New problems arose. The architects reported in October 1887 that progress was slow on the Sharon Building and that the time allotted for the contract would expire long before the building was completed. At the November meeting of the Board of Park Commissioners, Kelly was "called upon the carpet" and ordered to hire more stonemasons and speed up the work. Kelly pleaded for more time, explaining that Leland Stanford was building Stanford University and had hired all available stonemasons. In addition, Stanford, who was part-owner of the Central Pacific Railroad, had preempted all the flatcars to haul stone to the university grounds. So Kelly could not secure cars to haul stone, even if he were able to find additional stonemasons. The park commissioners had no choice but to allow additional time for construction. Unanimously, they granted Kelly a ninety-day extension.

Then Hefferman, one of the contractors who had bid unsuccessfully on the building, came forward with the

Tent-covered merry-go-round, about 1889.

George M. Murphy, printer of the park music program, made an offer of $1,000 per annum for the privilege of operating the Children's Playground and the Sharon Building when completed. His bid was accepted in October 1888, with a lease of three years.

The original outfitting of the Sharon Building consisted of refreshment booths, a merry-go-round, six bicycles, six tricycles, six baby carriages, two donkeys, and three croquet sets. The original merry-go-round was covered by a tent, and half the horses were equipped with sidesaddles for proper young ladies. All the other equipment was to be kept in the lower rooms of the building, to be loaned to young patrons of the playground.

At long last, on December 22, 1888, the day of dedication arrived. At 12:30 P.M., President Richard P. Hammond of the Park Commission and his wife escorted Mrs. Francis G. Newlands to the balcony of the Sharon Building, accompanied by her brother, Hall McAllister, Jr. Major Hammond waxed lyrical about the climate of San Francisco, comparing it to the cold, icy parks of the East. He extolled the virtues of Senator William Sharon until the guests began to wonder if he were speaking of the same Senator Sharon they had known. The senator had been well known in the West for his alleged treatment of Sarah Althea Hill, whom he had maintained in a secret suite of the Palace Hotel. She later claimed to be his wife, and that he had reneged on his promises to her. The airing of those charges in court was billed as "The Trial of the Century." By the time the major was finished, little was left for Mayor Pond to say other than to accept the gift on behalf of the city.

The Second Regiment Artillery Band, California National Guard, then played selections. Other men spoke until the children wandered off to explore their new playground. Finally the band played "Dreams of Childhood," and the ceremony was concluded.

The new playhouse was a dream world in itself. It had

serious charge that Kelly was using inferior stone — not at all like the stone Hefferman had agreed to use. The contractor was accompanied by two lawyers. In view of the charges, a meeting was set for January 5, 1888, to review the matter. When the matter came up, Hefferman testified that Kelly was using rock, not from the Niles Quarry but from a San Jose quarry. He further testified that there was no shortage of stonemasons; rather, Kelly would not pay proper wages — and this was the only reason for the lack of skilled artisans.

Many witnesses testified concerning the quality of the stone and concurred that it was good. William T. Johnston, superintendent of construction on the building, testified that he was satisfied with the quality of the stone. It was then revealed that Hefferman was disgruntled because Kelly had not purchased the rock from the Niles Quarry, which Hefferman owned. The charged were dropped.

water fountains, ice cream fountains, soda places, dairy rooms, storerooms for playthings, stables in the cellar for goats, and every possible convenience. Broad lawns for lawn tennis and football surrounded the building. Swings, a merry-go-round, and scores of other devices had been installed for the amusement of little ones.

Col. J. Mervyn Donahue, a local steel manufacturer, donated three thousand bottles of Napa soda water. Davis, the Palace Hotel's manager, donated a gift for the girls; Davis sent up three thousand boxes of candy. And Major Hammond donated three thousand tin horns for the boys. The sounds of the three thousand tin horns annoyed folks all afternoon. And the tooting continued on the streetcars when the afternoon was over. Hundreds of protests were made to the streetcar companies about all the noise.

The following day, Vice President Crocker of the Market Street Railroad was just as disgruntled as his customers: "That was a mean, dirty trick for Dick Hammond to pull on us," he fumed. "If I had known he was going to do that, I would never have given him the money for his tunnel. I did not think he would do that. He never would have done it if Merv Donahue had not put him up to it. Merv Donahue is against us for some reason. You know, he is suspected of greasing our rails over in Oakland at the time the Golden Gate Special came through for the first time." On that occasion, as the assembled dignitaries had waited at the depot to greet the train, the engineer had brought the train up with a flourish. Much to his chagrin, the train had refused to stop on command and had glided on the greased rails for nearly two blocks beyond the depot before it finally came to a halt.

At the March 1889 meeting of the Park Commission, George M. Murphy of the Children's Playground reported that his business was a financial success. Not only had he met all his expenses but he had shown a profit, to be placed in the Park Fund, in the amount of $406.

Genial President Hammond immediately proposed to arrange a grand May Day program for the children at a cost of about $500, which would be taken out of the park's share of the profits. His program was ambitious. The day was to be exclusively for children, and all public-school children under twelve were invited to attend with their teachers. The program was already in preparation: the entrance of the May Queen and her maids of honor; the crowning of the queen; the spring chorus of public-school children; the Maypole dance; foot racing; and baseball and other amusements for the children. Prizes were to be distributed, and the band would be in attendance. Teachers of the respective schools were each requested to designate one girl under twelve to act as a maid of honor. From this group, the May Queen would be selected by lot. Four boys' baseball clubs would participate. Major Hammond's enthusiasm went on and on.

"I move," said General Dimond, "that $500 be appropriated and that the chairman be authorized to go ahead."

"And it is so ordered," continued the major.

A tradition was thus started in 1889 that was to continue for decades. For nineteen years, from 1911 to 1930, Mayor "Sunny Jim" Rolph never once failed to be on hand for the crowning of the May Queen. After placing the crown on her head, "Sunny Jim" would kneel humbly at the feet of the new queen and gallantly kiss her hand. The first May Queen was eleven-year-old Maud Cornish, who lived with her parents at 2242 Howard Street. She attended the Valencia Grammar School.

An *Examiner* reporter described the park on the first May Day celebration as a giant goat ranch, because at least ten thousand "kids" filled the park. As early as 9:00 A.M., the rush began, and every streetcar headed for the park was overflowing. The grassy slopes near the children's quarters were transformed into a mosaic of brightly colored outfits. The leader waved his baton, and the band began to play. But the wind wafted the music over into the Haight Street area, and only those near the band could hear.

The crush at the merry-go-round became so great that Officer Thomson and six assistants had to fight their way in to rescue some youngsters who could not breathe. Finally the merry-go-round stopped, and the music was turned off to avoid further threat of injury.

At 1:00 P.M., the giant crowd was transformed into one vast picnic party. Hampers, baskets, and boxes of every description were opened, and soon happy children with jam-smeared faces and hands full of goodies could be seen everywhere. Mothers fed their own children and then invited tiny strangers to share in the lunch. No finer sight was seen all day than this exhibition of true California hospitality.

Some boys secured a long rope and engaged in a noisy tug-of-war. When a friendly policeman tried to quiet them, they wound him up in their rope and dragged him all over the lawn amid shrieks of laughter from the older folks.

After the crowning of the May Queen, the Maypole dances were completed, and then came the games: tricycle races, sack races, and three-legged races, with prizes for each winner.

The *Evening Bulletin* estimated the crowd of children to be in excess of fifteen thousand. Whatever the number, all agreed that it had been the grandest day for children in the history of the city.

By November 1889, enough profits had accumulated so that it was decided to hold a free day for children on November 19, to celebrate Thanksgiving. By this time the goats numbered fifteen, and six stubborn donkeys were on the scene to entertain the swarm of youngsters. The crowd for this event was estimated between five and eight thousand persons, and they seemed to be everywhere at once. Again the band played, and a great time was had until closing time at 4:00 P.M.

As the news of the Children's Playground spread, the popularity of the place grew. Children swarmed to the Sharon House and playground from all over the Bay Area. On Sundays, people rode the ferries to "The City," hired a rig, and went to Golden Gate Park for a picnic. They visited the new Menagerie, which consisted of deer and elk, as well as Peacock Meadow. They also visited the Buffalo Paddock, near what is now Laveaga Dell. Three buffalo grazed there, two bulls and a cow, the survivors of six buffalo purchased in Utah. The bulls were named Ben Harrison and Bill Bunker, the latter after the crusty editor of the *Bulletin*. The cow was named Sarah Bernhardt, although the bellow of this new Sarah was hardly a compliment to the famous actress.

In October 1891, the commissioners decided to "spruce up the place." The Park Commission purchased the merry-go-round from its original owner, W. S. Tyler. Then they made other improvements: purchase of merry-go-round, $2,500; permanent roof for merry-go-round, $2,500; new walks and paths, $1,400; skating and bicycle rink, $1,000; new benches, $400; new swings, $200; spring boards (teeter-totters), $50; Maypoles, $50; rustic house, $300; donkeys, goat carts, and related equipment, $600; purchase of tables, furniture, and kitchen equipment from the present owners, $1,600. The total was $10,600.

The commission also decided to take over management of the playground. George M. Murphy, the former lessee, was hired as superintendent, and his wife was hired as ticket taker. They lived in the attic of the Sharon Building.

It was the opinion of William Hammond Hall that concessions should not be allowed in the park. He felt that the granting of concessions led to political favoritism, and the concessions led to corruption. Neither favoritism nor corruption, in his opinion, had any place in a public park. All operations in the park should be managed and operated by the commissioners, who were responsible to the governor and ultimately to the electorate. As long as Hall had any influence in the park, these principles were strictly followed. Later they were not.

Two little urchins walked into the refreshment hall one day. Both looked bright and healthy, and both had plenty of ventilation in their pants at the knees.

"Say, how much is ice cream?" asked one in an eager tone. "Fifteen cents," replied Superintendent Murphy. "We ain't got but ten cents," sadly retorted the capitalist of the two. "Well, it's pretty near the Fourth of July," said the genial superintendent. "I guess we can let you have a dish of ice cream for ten cents." So he told the waitress to bring a dish of ice cream. She brought a dish with one spoon, but there were no complaints. One boy eagerly ate two spoonfuls of the delicacy and handed the spoon to his companion for his share. Thus they alternated until the feast was gone. The superintendent had watched the scene with interest, and when the dish was empty, he ordered the waitress to bring another dish for the boys with two spoons.

"But we ain't got no more ten cents!" the boy told the waitress. "Oh! Well, that's all right. Mr. Murphy is giving you another dish," replied the girl. The second dish disappeared even faster than the first. Then they glanced around furtively as though they had done something wrong and shot out of the building like a flash.

The superintendent was known to do this sort of thing often. Sometimes he gave a hapless youngster a free ride on the merry-go-round. At other times he offered a free donkey ride or a goat-cart ride to a wistful-looking boy or girl who evidently did not have the price of a ticket. Murphy was always on the lookout for the unfortunates under his charge. In spite of his largess, the playground always showed a profit at the end of the year. Even with low prices for rides, food, and soft drinks, the Children's Playground began piling up profits. So the benevolent commissioners cut prices in half. Beginning in 1892, tickets were to be two for 5¢, and these ducats were good on the rides, for soft drinks, popcorn, and all other items at the refreshment stand.

Then the commissioners embarked on a money-making scheme. They minted their own money, using a new metal called aluminum. These tokens were somewhat smaller than a half-dollar. On the one side were the words "Children's Playground, Golden Gate Park, San Francisco, Cal." and "Good for one ride." On the reverse side was a picture of the Sharon Building, the merry-go-round, benches, trees, some goat carts, and a wagon drawn by donkeys. These coins were sold, two for 5¢, and about forty thousand were minted in three different issues. Then the price of aluminum increased, and people soon learned that they could buy these tokens, two for 5¢, and sell them for 7½¢. Within a few months the supply of coins dwindled to about five hundred. The commissioners withdrew them from circulation and returned to paper tickets, which still sold two for 5¢ for a long time.

Today this practice has been discontinued. The present price of tickets is a quarter. The donkeys and goats have long since disappeared, and the refreshment stand is operated on a concession basis.

The playground grew popular beyond belief. It was so crowded at times with happy children that one began to wonder where they all were coming from. One reason for the popularity of the place was the museum. Contrary to popular belief, the M. H. de Young Memorial Museum was not the first one in Golden Gate Park. The Sharon Building was the first, followed by the old Casino, west of the Conservatory.

Some now-long-forgotten benefactor loaned many cases of stuffed winged creatures to the park. A large room on the grounds of the Sharon Building had housed the goats for the playing field; when the goats were removed to a larger stable, the room was converted to a museum. Most of the cases remained unpacked for lack of room, but there were numerous exhibits to educate and amuse.

A red-shafted woodpecker, wings spread and head twisted inquisitively to one side, welcomed visitors. Clinging to a branch was a jet black cockatoo, and nearby were red, white, and green birds of the same species. Officer McManus of the park force found a titmouse nest one day. Three tiny birds, abandoned by their parents and left to die were still in the nest. The nest and the birds were

Children's Playground, about 1890.

taken to F. Gruber, the park taxidermist, who preserved them just as the titmouse parents had left them. They too were put on display.

The museum also held a ten-foot-long scarf made from the tail feathers of red-shafted woodpeckers. Since each bird has only two feathers, an estimated twenty thousand birds had been slaughtered to make this curiosity.

The north wall displayed numerous cuckoos from all parts of the globe. There were hummingbirds of every color of the rainbow, including the giant hummingbird of the Andes; birds of paradise; flamingoes; penguins; and

even an auk. A monkey fondled a two-headed calf, and a boa constrictor, wrapped around a four-eyed pig, held the children's attention. On one branch, a parrot conversed earnestly with a one-eyed owl. Foxes and wildcats that had been killed in the park and mounted by the industrious Gruber were in another section.

A miniature museum had also been arranged. The scenes included two rabbits playing cards; a huge rat, arm in arm with a duck; and a sick rabbit being ministered to by a wise-looking cat with an odd pair of glasses perched on its nose. Dozens of other scenes amused and delighted the

Children's Playground, about 1894.

children. Collections of butterflies of every description were found on the west wall. One dark room held many boxes of specimens that could not be displayed due to the lack of room.

This long-forgotten museum was a tremendously popular place and a source of wonder for nearly a decade. When the Casino, west of the Conservatory, was abandoned, it was turned into a larger museum, where deceased buffalo, elk, and moose could also be displayed.

December 26, 1895, saw the first free Christmas party at the Sharon Quarters. The children came by the thousands. In consideration for the donkeys and the goats, the superintendent ordered that only two hundred tickets could be distributed each half hour. This plan helped maintain a semblance of order. The merry-go-round, built to haul two hundred, carried at least a thousand children each trip. Five children to each mount was the order of the day, and the overburdened machine creaked and groaned at each revolution. At 3:30 P.M. the wheels of the merry-go-round crushed through the track and stopped, not to turn again until repaired.

While the band played on the balcony and the don-

Children's Playground, about 1894.

keys added their chorus, the children lined up to be seated in the lunchroom. All children were given glasses of milk and all the tongue, ham, or corned-beef sandwiches they could eat. As they filed out, each child was given cookies, an apple, and a bag of popcorn. According to the *Examiner*, 100 cans of milk were used, 750 loaves of bread, and 1,750 pounds of popcorn.

Out on the recreation grounds, many games of baseball and football were going on simultaneously. When the exhausted park workers, police, and volunteers finally finished work that day, they estimated that fifteen thousand children had been made happy. This celebration began a tradition of Christmas parties in the park that was to last for decades.

Then came a change in policy. The Children's Playground was leased to George M. Murphy, previously the superintendent, for $1,000 per annum. The number of free days was noticeably fewer, and the popularity of the place declined. In March 1898, the lease was extended for three more years at the same annual rental.

In March 1901, it was decided that the Children's Playground would not be leased and that the park commissioners would operate it. A Mrs. Hickok was appointed superintendent, and her son was made her assistant. A month later, the *Examiner* reported that the playground had returned $1,400 to the commission, with about $600 of that amount deducted for expenses.

Just a year later, Mayor Eugene Schmitz appeared at a meeting of the commission and charged that the commission was more than $10,000 in debt since it had taken over and operated the playground. Commissioner McDonald hotly denied the charge. He reported that when the commission took over management, the playground was in a deplorable state. He said that Murphy had done no maintenance, and the entire place had had to be repainted and all equipment repaired or replaced. He stated that the commission had spent $10,000 to $12,000 just to get the playground in operating condition.

Nearly every week a different kindergarten school in the city was given a free day at the playground. Letters from grateful school officials poured into the Park Lodge in praise of the new liberal policy of returning to the children all the profits taken in at the Children's Playground. In June 1902, more than three hundred orphans from the Maria Kip Orphanage, Pacific Hebrew Orphanage, and the Infant's Shelter were given the freedom of the playground, including rides, luncheon, pink popcorn, ice cream, and goodies. A band of fourteen pieces, composed of boys from the Pacific Hebrew Orphanage, furnished the musical entertainment.

In March 1903, Mayor Schmitz charged that Superintendent Hickok had hired a United States Army band to entertain at the Children's Playground, thus denying union men the job. After a fierce argument on the board, her job was declared vacant. The secretary of the commission, Herbert L. Schmitz, brother of the mayor, was appointed superintendent of the playground. Just a month later, the mayor's brother was appointed to the Public Works Commission, leaving vacant the offices of superintendent of the playground and secretary of the commission. President of the Commission Adolph B. Spreckels was authorized to hire whomever he pleased to manage the playground, and a Mrs. Millmore was selected. She had not been in the position long enough to train the Maypole dancers properly. In spite of their imperfection, the May Day celebration was held on schedule, and it was a success.

In May 1905, profits from the playground amounted to $1,085 over and above the May Day celebration and the free days for orphans.

The 1906 earthquake and fire closed the playground for six weeks, and repairs to the badly damaged Sharon Building took even longer.

Boating on Stow Lake in the late 1890s.

The Stow Years

William Hammond Hall's refusal in 1889 to work with the newly appointed commissioner, William W. Stow, and Hall's withdrawal from further work in the park, is certainly understandable. Stow had been head of the lobby for the Big Four railroad kings. In 1876, he and Frank McCoppin had engineered the reduction in the tax rate from 3¢ to 1½¢ per $100 for the park, thus bringing all work to a standstill. When the railroad wanted legislation to favor them, Stow was working behind the scenes to see that it was passed.

Later, as board president, Stow complained that the park had been allotted only $180,000 for the coming year and that it would be difficult to maintain the park on that amount. No one dared remind him that he, through Frank McCoppin, had been responsible for crippling the park for many years by this appropriation of 1½¢ on $100 of taxable property, and that now they had 6¢ per $100 for the same purpose. Stow said the park should be supported liberally from the public treasury and should not have to depend on charity. Now that he had retired from the employment of the railroads, he no longer cared how much tax his former employers had to pay to the city.

In December 1889, a severe storm lashed the area, washing out walks and drives in every portion of the park. The Panhandle became a quagmire, and the nearly completed Speed Road was severely damaged. Since the Speed Road had not yet been accepted by the Park Commission, the damage to it would have to be repaired by the horse-men. These heavy rains and severe storms of 1889–90 caused widespread unemployment in California. The situation was especially bad in San Francisco. Archbishop Patrick William Riordan took the lead in raising money to provide relief, and through donations more than $30,000 was raised to hire the needy. In the spring of 1890, more than a thousand men were hired to improve Golden Gate Park.

The South Drive to Ocean Beach was completed during this period. At one time, more than nine hundred men were at work on South Drive with shovels and wheelbarrows, and eight teams were engaged in hauling rock for the roadbed. The men were paid at the rate of $1 a day. The street railroads furnished free transportation for the men going to and from work, and many organizations cooperated in furnishing free lunches.

In April most of the workers were laid off when the Union Pacific Railroad advertised for two thousand men to work on their road in Nevada and Utah. Six hundred and fifty shovels and four hundred and fifty wheelbarrows were then auctioned off by the Relief Committee.

In January 1890, a financial report was published by the Park Commission which showed park income for the six-month period July 1, 1889, to December 31, 1889, as $60,000. This revenue was nearly twice as much as the park had previously received in a two-year period. Expenditures were listed as follows: waterworks and drainage, $3,632.77; roads and walks, $12,738,87; tree planting and reclamation, $11,240.27; maintaining Conservatory, $3,830.74; nursery, $4,070.50; policing, $3,893.78; and structures, $4,892.39.

Twenty thousand trees and shrubs had been planted within that period. The old Bandstand and the Conservatory had been painted. The report also stated that the Music Concourse would be extended. The commission also felt that by building fences on the beach, the sand could be collected behind the fences and a highway could be built. Although the idea was wonderful, they seemed unaware that William Hammond Hall had outlined this precise procedure twenty years earlier.

The steamship *Alameda,* on a voyage from Australia, brought back a pair of black swans, which in August 1891 were placed in Alvord Lake. Then the steamer *Farrallone* arrived from the Bering Sea with a pair of seals. The sealing schooner *Mattie B. Dyer* also brought a pair of seals that were presented to the park by Ross and Hewlett. A detachment of park laborers and park police were sent with a team and wagon to bring the seals to the park. At the Panhandle the procession was met by Superintendent McLaren; Commissioner Hammond; Captain Sam Thomson, chief of park police; and Hamilton H. Dobbin, captain of the night watch.

The seals were placed in Elk Glen (now Laveaga Dell), where they could disport themselves in Elk Glen Lake. The next morning at dawn, the bull elk came down the pathway, leading his herd for their morning drink. The herd found one of the seals lying in the pathway, sound asleep. The bull elk approached cautiously and was sniffing this strange creature when the seal awoke and let out a tremendous roar. The elk fled to the shelter of the trees.

The llama who lived in the Elk Glen also received the fright of his life. In the past, he had dominated even the elk, but after his encounter with the seal, he remained in the brush for days. The seal merely shook himself and rolled down the bank into the water. The only creatures in Elk Glen that would approach the seals were the Brandt geese, which were familiar with seals from their homeland. The seals were to remain in Elk Glen Lake until the new lake at Strawberry Hill could be finished.

Sea captains tried to outdo each other in bringing exotic birds and other animals, trees, shrubs, and seeds to the park. Donated birds were sent from all parts of the globe. Although hundreds of quail of the eastern and mountain variety had once inhabited this area, native birds had not yet returned to live in the park.

In October 1891, the commissioners advertised for bids on a new and larger aviary. The new birdhouse was to be over three hundred feet long, with an eleven-foot walkway. The western side and the roof would be covered with glass to protect the more delicate species. The bid for construction was awarded to T. M. McLachlin for the amount of $6,249. The new Aviary, completed in spring 1892, remained in Golden Gate Park until the completion of Fleischhacker Zoo in the 1930s. The old Aviary was then moved to the Children's Playground, where it contained mostly pheasants.

The *Chronicle* of March 18, 1892, listed the birds in the new building. They included sparrows, linnets, robins, bluejays, parrots, magpies, bullfinches, meadowlarks, canaries, pheasants, nightingales, and cockatoos. Six cardinals were imported from New York.

In November 1891, one destitute but enterprising San Francisco citizen decided that, although he could not afford a turkey dinner, perhaps he could arrange for some quail for his family. Armed with a slingshot, he went to Golden Gate Park one morning and hid in the bushes near the spot where the quail were known to get their morning meal. Officer McManus of the park police, who was overseeing the feeding operation, noticed that the birds were unusually restive that day. Then he noticed little puffs of dust rising in their midst. Since there was no breeze, he soon deduced the cause of the restiveness. Making a flanking movement, he spied the sportsman and surprised him by notifying him that he was under arrest. The man was booked at the city prison for violating a park ordinance. The following day he was assessed a ten-dollar fine, which turned out to be more expensive than a turkey dinner.

Before he left the park in 1881, Superintendent William Bond Prichard had drawn up plans for a reservoir to be built on the east side of Strawberry Hill. At that time, because of the financially crippling legislation engineered by McCoppin and Stow, the lake was not built. In the 1890s, with Stow on the commission and with four times as much revenue, the reservoir lake was built. To add to the irony of the situation, the lake was named Stow Lake.

The bids for this lake were opened at a regular meeting of the Park Commission on July 28, 1891, and the bid was given to Charles Warren, whose price was 8½¢ per cubic yard of cut.

The walk-through at the Aviary, built in 1892, extended over the tops of trees.

Patronage of the park was so great and traffic was so heavy that it was decided to build a steel suspension bridge from Chicken Point to the new Music Concourse. When completed, pedestrians would be able to go from Conservatory Valley, under the Main Drive via the tunnel, to the Music Concourse and the Children's Playground over the near bridge. John A. Rebling Sons Company was awarded the contract to build the bridge, with a bid of $10,435.

When the steel suspension bridge had been built across the drive at Chicken Point, it was painted in two shades of green. The artist, reportedly trying to capture the shadings of nature, then checkered the structure with decorative squares of carmine and added red stripes here and there. All the bolts in the bridge were painted chrome yellow, and in the center of the span was a round red-and-green plate with the words, "Park Commissioners W. W. Stow, Joseph Austin and R. P. Hammond." The letters were also chrome yellow. William Hammond Hall must have had apoplexy.

The bridge opened for pedestrian travel on February 28, 1892. It became a favorite spot from which to view the expensive horses and carriages that the well-to-do displayed at every opportunity in the park.

In April 1892, Superintendent McLaren's wages were increased from $250 to $300 per month. In addition, he was given a three-months' leave of absence to visit parks in the East and in Europe. All expenses were to be paid, except for the time he spent visiting his family in Scotland. He soon wrote back from Central Park that refreshments for children in Central Park were 50 to 100 percent higher than in San Francisco's Golden Gate Park Children's Playground.

In May the board was reorganized with Stow as president and Hammond and Austin as members. The new president announced that another Casino had been built

Rustic iron bridge, across Middle Drive to the Music Concourse, was built in the 1890s.

near Ocean Beach at the turn of the road and that a wire aviary had also been built there to hold gold, silver, and copper pheasants.

The *Chronicle* reported that an incoming steamer had a new elk aboard to be placed in the park. The biggest news of the year, however, was the report that Sarah Bernhardt, the mother buffalo in the park, had given birth to a buffalo calf. The park workers had planned to name this new arrival "Buffalo Bill." But when the baby turned out to be a female, they decided, and after much discussion, on the name Ruth. The fence around the buffalo paddock was lined with people trying to get a glimpse of Ruth. Sarah, however, was very protective of her offspring, and kept her mostly in the bushes. Ben Harrison and Bill Bunker, the

two male buffalo, walked about the paddock looking innocent and disinterested in the entire proceedings.

Thomas U. Sweeney, one of the wealthy landowners in the sand district, offered to build a stone observatory at the summit of Strawberry Hill, provided that he could place his name on the building. Permission was granted, completely reversing former park policy that the park was to be rustic in nature and that all forms of personal advertisement and self-aggrandizement were to be prohibited.

The old practice of naming features of the park with natural names, such as Deer Glen, the Dairy, and the Promenade, was discarded. Henceforth features were to be named after those who had a hand in them, such as Stow Lake, Huntington Falls, and Sweeney Observatory. Stow was a politician par excellence, and he knew how to get money out of anyone. Most of the lakes and buildings in the park were named after park commissioners or politicians, though few people today are even aware of who these people were.

The following year, when a second story was added to the observatory, Hall commented privately that it was a disgrace to the park. In 1906, when the earthquake reduced the structure to rubble, Hall told his friends, "Apparently, a Higher Power has taken matters into His own hands."

Despite the fact that W. B. Bradbury's controversial waterworks were less than ten years old, they were generally conceded to be next to useless. The Union Iron Works in Cow Hollow was given a contract to build a new waterworks for $16,000. In addition to this cost, the commissioners agreed to have park laborers furnish the founda-

Elk in the Deer Glen, about 1895.

"Ben Harrison" and "Sarah Bernhardt" in the buffalo paddock, about 1905.

tion, a building to cover the pumping machinery, and the chimney for the steam engine.

With the abundance of water soon to be available from Stow Lake, Stow dreamed up the idea of a massive waterfall and set about to find the means to build it. He invited Collis P. Huntington, who had employed him for years, to go for a ride in the park. He showed Huntington the new lake and remarked that a waterfall would be most appreciated by the people of the city, if only the park could somehow find the means to pay for it.

Stow Lake, the Sweeney Observatory, and Huntington Falls under construction, about 1895.

A few days later, Stow received the following note in the mail:

San Francisco, California
April 20, 1892

Friend Stow:

I have often thought of the pleasant ride we had in the park a day or two ago, and somehow I imagine you showed the beauties to me not alone because you wanted me to see and enjoy them, but because you trusted to their silent influence to convince me that I ought to give something toward the cascade you seem to have set your heart upon having.

I have concluded that this is just one of those cases where the money would be well bestowed and as well appreciated; for your beautiful park is a breathing place for the working people and their little ones, and they always prize and are better by the boon of pure air and country scenes. So, as you told me that it would cost $25,000, I will arrange to have that sum paid to you as the work progresses and the money is needed.

Sincerely yours,
C. P. Huntington

Sweeney Observatory, built in 1891.

With the waterfall assured, plans were immediately made to extend the lake all the way around the base of Strawberry Hill and to construct bridges on the north and south sides of the lake to provide access to Sweeney Observatory at the summit.

By early 1893 the lake around Strawberry Hill was completed, and the construction of Huntington Falls was well underway. Twenty thousand trout were introduced into the new lake by the Fish Commission. At the end of the Mechanics' Institute Fair all of the salmon and trout on display at that fair were also placed in the lake, though the success of this experiment is not recorded.

The park continued to be enormously popular. Money was adequate, thanks to Stow's political influence in the state legislature. People from all around the Bay Area made Sunday outings by ferryboat and then by rented horse and buggy or streetcar from the Ferry Building to the park. Stanford University students often rode the train to San Francisco to spend a weekend exploring the beauties of Golden Gate Park.

Soldiers from the Presidio and sailors from the Goat Island Naval Training Station were always in evidence, usually with proud young ladies. Sutro Heights and Ocean Beach were frequented heavily in the mornings, but when the afternoon breeze came up, people hurried eastward to the more sheltered valleys of the park.

In the afternoons, the harried park policemen had their hands full. Often three or four rowdies on bicycles would ride abreast on the park drives, preventing horses from passing. The shouting match that followed often ended with cursing, fights, and a night in jail. Young men with horse and carriage delighted in driving rapidly through mud holes and splashing muddy water on duded-up men and their ladies. When caught at their prank they would apologize profusely; the police could do little to stop it.

Sutro Heights, which overlooks the Golden Gate, the Pacific Ocean, and points north and south, has never been considered part of Golden Gate Park. But in the 1880s, the trip to the park was incomplete without a visit to Sutro Heights. The hill was originally known as Chamber's Potato Patch because all 160 acres of it had been homesteaded by a man named Chambers in the 1840s. He raised the best potatoes ever to hit the markets around the Plaza. But to get those potatoes to the market was something of a struggle. They had to be lashed in bags to a packsaddle astride a mule and carried over the dreary sand wastes of Central Avenue, where a semblance of a road led to the city. Since Chambers could not match the price of the farmers in the Mission District, he gave up his claim and moved to Oregon.

In 1854 C. C. Butler, a man of wealth, arrived in San Francisco from New York. While exploring the land around the city one day, he happened on the potato patch, which he called Strawberry Hill — not knowing about the one in the park. Butler decided that this land would some-day be to San Francisco what Coney Island was to New York City, and he determined to buy it. An agent was sent to Oregon to locate Chambers. Although Butler never disclosed the exact price, he did admit that it cost more to find Chambers than it did to buy the homestead.

Next, Butler built a road to his property in order that people might see it. To secure permission to build his toll road, Butler contacted his state senator, Christopher Buckley — a move that was his undoing. Senator Buckley did not ordinarily do favors unless he derived some benefit from them — in this case a one-third interest in the road and the property. Ultimately the charter was secured, and Butler built a fine road. At the same time, he built the first Cliff House. Even before the road was finished, people drove out to the Cliff House to be greeted by the genial host, J. G. Foster, whose presence became a San Francisco tradition.

All went well for a time, as the tolls were paying off the investment rapidly. But then William Hammond Hall built a road to the beach through the park that could be traversed free of charge. Thus, Butler's next problem was how to get rid of the worthless charter to the road. Since he had a financial stake in it, Senator Buckley managed to sell the toll road charter back to an impoverished San Francisco in 1877 for the princely sum of $25,000.

Possibly to pay William Hammond Hall and the park commissioners back for ruining Butler's ambitions, the toll road was then placed under the jurisdiction of the Park Commission. Maintenance of the road would henceforth come out of Park Improvement and Maintenance Funds. The park commissioners spent money on the road only under threat of violence from nearby residents. The problem remained a source of trouble until the city finally took over the Point Lobos Road.

Then along came a man named Merchant. He had lived on the White Cliffs of Dover and had long dreamed of a home in America where he could look over the waters. He wanted to buy some land from Butler and Chambers so that he could build a $50,000 mansion. Butler and Chambers hastily sold Merchant land for his mansion, but to their chagrin, Merchant built only a little cottage. Every time Butler saw that cottage, he wanted to throw it over the cliff.

Bowed but unbeaten, Butler then proposed that Senator Buckley build a mansion on the bluff to enhance the value of their jointly owned land. The senator consented, and the contract was let. Then came the announcement that the vessel *Commanche* would be launched in Cow Hollow. The senator went to the launching. When one of the ship's hawsers caught Senator Buckley's leg as the *Commanche* slid down the ways, his leg was broken, and an infection set in from which he never recovered. The mansion was never built.

About this time a wealthy man named Samuel Tetlow, who had made a fortune in real estate, was looking for a new home in San Francisco. He spied Merchant's little cottage, and he bought the cottage and all the land around it. He enlarged the house and entertained one and all. An invitation from Samuel Tetlow was eagerly sought by society people, and his home became a meeting place for anyone of social stature. But then came a season of trouble. Tetlow's favorite daughter died in the house, and he no longer loved his home by the sea. He offered it to Adolph Sutro, the laboring man who had built the famous Sutro Tunnel in the silver lode on the eastern slope of the High Sierra. The price was not revealed.

So it was that Chambers' Potato Patch, Butler's Strawberry Hill, Merchant's mansion, and Tetlow's eagle's nest became Sutro Heights. In its heyday, Sutro Heights boasted a huge conservatory of flowers; a maze of green hedges, such as were popular on large estates in the 1880s and 1890s; a huge bathhouse and swimming pool; many amusements from the Midwinter Fair; statuary, trees, flowers, and paths for strolling. Sutro kept the grounds always open free-of-charge to the public, but a charge was

Cliff House and Sutro Heights, about 1905.

made for swimming and the amusements. Pictures of the past glory of Sutro Heights can still be seen at the Cliff House.

The Heights were subsequently bought by the city for a park, but it was never maintained in the same splendor as when the Sutros owned it. The statuary deteriorated, and the entire place returned to weeds and brush. In the 1970s, the Heights were turned over to the Golden Gate National Recreation Area along with Ocean Beach. It is now patrolled by state rangers on horseback.

In June 1893, the board met to discuss a proposal that portions of the Columbian Exposition in Chicago be moved to San Francisco and that a fair be held in Golden Gate Park. The area east of Stow Lake was to be utilized for the purpose — but not over sixty acres. No part of Stow Lake or Strawberry Hill was to be closed to the general public.

The Southern Pacific Railroad Company was granted permission to build a railroad in the park, commencing at Tenth Avenue and Lincoln Way and extending to the fairgrounds, for the purpose of moving exhibits by rail into the park. No passengers were to be hauled on this line. The Ferries & Cliff House Railroad was granted the privilege of building a railroad in the park from Ninth Avenue and Fulton Street to the fairgrounds for the same purpose. They, too, were forbidden to haul passengers in competition with the streetcars. The Southern Pacific Railroad Company built the railroad as agreed, but it does not appear that the Ferries & Cliff House Railroad was ever extended to the fairgrounds.

At a regular meeting of the commission in September 1893, it was decided not to lease the Casino again. It had not been a financial success, although food was sold at high rates. For example, milk, which sold for 5¢ a glass at the Children's Playground, sold for 15¢ a glass at the Casino.

In October 1893, Commissioner Stow was authorized to contract for the building of a boathouse at Stow Lake. No mention was made of asking for bids. Stow appears to have been the dominating influence on the board, as Pixley had been previously.

A number of people appeared to ask that a gate be opened into the park at Tenth Avenue and Fulton Street. It was agreed that as soon as Tenth Avenue was graded and paved, the commissioners would open such a gate, provided the residents of the area furnished $2,500 to pay for the work. During this same period, the commissioners granted George B. Childs of Philadelphia the right to erect a shaft commemorative of the religious ceremonies that took place on the shores of Drake's Bay in 1579.

Work on the South Drive was progressing well in 1893, thanks to the funds donated to employ the needy. It was proposed to extend South Drive directly to Ocean Beach from near Forty-third Avenue, where South Drive turns northward to connect with the Main Drive. The extension was called the Citizen's Road, and men were put to

The first boat house on Stow Lake in the late 1890s.

work on it. It was to be sixty feet wide, with a stone bridge to elevate the railroad tracks from the road. The donated funds were also apparently being used to complete the Speed Road for the exclusive use of the owners of fast horses.

On January 13, 1894, the Salvation Army donated lunches to the men who were striving so hard to feed and clothe their families by working in the park. The grammar schools of the city also helped furnish lunches for the workers. Transportation of the lunches was furnished by the *Examiner.*

On March 25, 1894, the *Examiner* announced that Governor H. H. Markham had not reappointed Richard P. Hammond to the Park Commission but had appointed Irving M. Scott to take his place. The governor reappointed Joseph Austin and William W. Stow. No reason for this change was given in the newspaper or in the minutes.

Later, in May, a special meeting was held at which the superintendent was ordered to purchase a vehicle "suitable for the uses of the Park Commission and such visitors from abroad as may be their guests." Money appropriated for park purposes was clearly being spent for the gratification of the park commissioners rather than for the improvement of the park. Stow was accustomed to riding in style, and not at his own expense.

M. H. de Young addressed a letter to the board tendering several Midwinter Fair Buildings to the city. The secretary was directed to inform de Young that only the Fine Arts Building would be accepted and that the executive committee of the exposition would have to remove all other buildings and restore the site as agreed.

The *Chronicle* noted on a day when rain had cancelled the band concert that the Music Concourse had been filled to capacity anyway. The reporter remarked that it was hard to tell whether people came to hear the music or

Huntington Falls and the stone bridge, about 1897.

to view and criticize the dress and deportment of other people. When the viewers grew tired of looking, they took the places of those who had been on view, while the strollers filled the empty seats in the concourse.

On April 9, 1894, thirty thousand people visited the park in addition to those at the exposition. That day Huntington Falls was put into operation. It was described as being a fall of 125 feet, the water varying from 3 to 12 feet in width. First the water rolled lazily down a fall of 6 feet; then it ran down a picturesque cascade for 150 feet and under a rustic bridge to the main fall — a drop of 25 feet, 12 feet in width. Artificial rocks formed the sides of the falls, and the hillside was ornamented with deciduous shade trees, including elm, maple, beech, linden, and birch. Under these trees, more than ten thousand ferns had been planted, mostly natives.

In 1894, the indignation of the horse owners against bicycle riders reached huge proportions. The horsemen complained that the bicycles were hogging the road, as well as the pedestrian paths. On the other hand, bicycle clubs accused the Park Commission of discrimination against them. They maintained that they had the same right to the road as any other vehicle. They wanted the free use of every road in the park, including the Main Drive, the Music Concourse, and the road around Stow Lake. They felt they had as much right to enjoy Huntington Falls as anyone else, and they were determined to secure that right.

Park commissioners are often sensitive to pressure. In an effort to maintain their commissions, they foolishly try to please everybody, to the detriment of the park. If one keeps in mind the ultimate purpose of a park — to relieve the pressures of urban life — then it is impossible to please everyone without forfeiting the overall restfulness of the park. Just as we do not allow business to intrude on a residential community, or bars to be built too close to a church or school, we should not allow boisterous conduct, profane language, or fast movement within a park, where we go to avoid these things.

The commission ultimately gave in to the bicycle riders and permitted them to use all drives in the park except Stow Lake Drive and the Speed Road. In addition, they were prohibited from using the carriage concourse at the Music Stand on days when the band was performing.

As if to prove the folly of trying to please everyone, a serious accident happened between a bicycle and a horse and buggy just after the new ordinance was passed. John Lyons, who lived on 13th Street, was driving a livery rig back to town one day. At the west end of Conservatory Valley, he collided with a bicycle mounted by H. J. Vollmer, who was riding in the opposite direction. Vollmer was cut about the head, and the horse ran away, upsetting the buggy and throwing Lyons to the ground. Lyons was not hurt badly, but the horse dragged the upset buggy all the way to Peacock Meadow before he was lassoed by Officer Harper. The horseman claimed that the cyclist deliberately ran into him, and the cyclist claimed that the horseman tried to run him down.

In fall 1894, Commissioner Stow stated that since Golden Gate Park had no shade trees, he wanted to remedy that situation. He intended to introduce groves of oak trees all over the park. As a start, he planned to have a grove of full-grown oak trees planted on the site of the exposition. Actually, many shade trees grew in the park, in particular the native Monterey cypress. But Stow may have felt that only maples, oaks, and elms qualified as true shade trees.

Men were sent to the W. H. Howard estate in San Mateo County to box large oak trees and hoist them onto wagons for the two-day ride to Golden Gate Park. The cost to the city was not revealed, but today only a remnant of the planting stands between the Japanese Tea Garden and Stow Lake Drive. The trees furnish people very little shade because that area is seldom seen by visitors. This planting is another case of politicians making decisions that might better be made by those who have worked in parks all their professional lives.

The fence that had surrounded the Midwinter Fair was still intact, and the fair officials were charging people a quarter to watch the buildings being torn down. Since the fence cut off South Drive in two places, McLaren ordered his men to take it down and open the drive to the public. After they had opened up a hole large enough to drive a four-horse team through, they proceeded to the west and repeated their act of defiance, aimed at M. H. de Young, to the fence there. Within an hour, more than twenty-five hundred people had flocked into the exposition grounds without paying a quarter.

The *Examiner* reported on December 31, 1894, that Fritz Scheel, leader of the Vienna Prater Band, had been hired to direct the Golden Gate Park Band. Henceforth A. Spadina — the former leader of the Park Band — would lead the band only on Wednesday and Saturday afternoons, and Scheel would officiate on Sundays. Although Scheel had been in America for two years, during the Columbian Exposition and the Midwinter Fair, he only knew two words of English — "the same." And, according to an *Examiner* reporter, although he had spent considerable time in Germany, he could say only "Gesundheit." But he was given permission to fire any inefficient musicians, and he was authorized to buy new uniforms and to make the band "as fine a military band as exists in the country." The *Examiner* article went on to say that the bandstand would be closed for two weeks and that then Professor Scheel would give a series of entertainments "new to the country" — the classical ballet with grand orchestra. This ballet was not to be a mere exhibition of the "sacred leg of a woman," but "a serious pantomime." Thanks to Stow, big things were truly in store.

On January 1, 1895, the *Examiner* reported that Stow had been ordered to support the candidacy of M. H. de Young for the senate. Although Stow had never liked de Young and made no secret of his dislike, he had no choice. According to the *Examiner*, he could either obey his "boss," Collis P. Huntington, or become a has-been like many another before him. But on February 11, 1895, Stow suddenly passed away in his office in the Crocker Building.

In his column, "Arthur McEwen's Letters," on February 16, 1895, Arthur McEwen gave an uncomplimentary review of the life of Stow, though he did say that Stow was "a lawyer of acknowledged capacity." He also called Stow "the executive arm, politically speaking, of the Southern Pacific." McEwen termed this "foul employment," and he seemed to feel that the job was a waste of talent that might have been put to better use.

Rustic bridge on Stow Lake, about 1896.

Grand Concourse of 1894 California Midwinter International Exposition.

Midwinter Fair

Have you lately been over to Golden Gate Park
Where there's something to please from daylight
  to dark?
But the thing that most pleases just now I declare
Is the site of the wonderful Midwinter Fair.

Where late was a wilderness lonely and drear
A vision of palaces now doth appear
With spires and with towers resplendent and rare
Adorning the site of the Midwinter Fair.

They are coming from Germany, Holland and Spain
From Austria, France and the Lombardy Plain
With laces and velvets and fabrics of hair
The ladies to please at the Midwinter Fair.

Like a white robed beneficent angel it comes
With Labor and Wages to thousands of homes
And the Spectres of Poverty, Want and Despair
Are slain by the Sword of the Midwinter Fair.

This song had seven more verses extolling the wonders and pleasures of the California Midwinter International Exposition, or the Midwinter Fair. Many people called it "the greatest undertaking west of the Mississippi since the transcontinental railroad." Detractors called it "the Midwinter Fake."

In May 1893, the Columbian Exposition of Chicago had been running for two years and was due to close soon. M. H. de Young was one of the California directors of that exposition in Chicago, and he conceived the idea of moving many of the exhibits to San Francisco. His reasons were sound. The nation was suffering from a severe business panic. Many banks had failed in San Francisco, and unemployment was widespread. De Young had observed the effect of the Columbian Exposition on the business climate of Chicago. What it had done for Chicago, it could do as well for San Francisco. He broached the subject to some other prominent Californians who were present at Chicago, and most of them agreed with his idea. But some expressed doubt that they could raise the necessary money. Telegrams were sent to Governor H. H. Markham of California and Mayor L. R. Ellert of San Francisco, asking them to call meetings of the Chamber of Commerce, the Board of Trade, the Merchants Exchange, and other groups to gather opinions on the idea.

It was apparent from the outset that public funds would not be available: no federal, state, or city money could be had. No world's fair had yet been built without public money, but the fair boosters felt the lack of it was not reason enough to give up. M. H. de Young wired from Chicago that he would pledge $5,000 to start the fund. Then he called a meeting of Californians in Chicago, and those gentlemen pledged $41,500. When this news reached San Francisco, it was decided to go ahead with the plans.

A committee of more than one hundred was appointed to canvas the city for money. Businessmen were asked to give all they could. Workers were each urged to donate one day's pay. All social groups and secret societies were urged to donate. The plan was successful. The total amount raised from the public was $344,319.59 (including $2.74 from the newsboys of the city) — enough to build the necessary buildings for the display of merchandise.

Interest in the great exposition was contagious. Although de Young had planned for a local fair, a variety of cities and counties demanded a part, and the fair was expanded to include the entire state. Every county in California had a display, and nearly every state in the Union was represented, as well as thirty-seven foreign nations.

When an area comprising sixty acres just east of Strawberry Hill was selected for the site, opposition arose to this destruction of the park. Determination to have a world's fair overruled all opinions to the contrary. After all, it was argued, didn't Chicago hold the Columbian

Grading the site for the Midwinter Fair in August, 1894.

Groundbreaking ceremony for 1894 Midwinter Fair on August 24, 1893.

Exposition in Jackson Park? The space demanded for buildings grew until nearly two hundred acres were used in Golden Gate Park. The site extended from the Main Drive all the way to H Street, or Lincoln Way. South Drive was utilized as the midway, or fun zone.

Ground-breaking ceremonies were held on the site on August 24, 1893. The parade was the largest yet held on the Pacific Coast. Businesses in the city closed, homes and businesses were decorated with flags and bunting, and all the ships anchored in the harbor were decorated for the occasion.

In addition to the usual military units and bands in the parade, the red-shirted Garibaldi Guard, the Swiss Company of Alpine Sharpshooters, the Lucca Cavaliers, the Royal Carvisieri, the French Zouaves, the Lafayette Guard, and the Guard De Jaurez marched in their picturesque uniforms. At the rear of the parade was a huge detachment of the unemployed, some of whom had already been engaged to work on the project.

When the parade reached Concert Valley, more than sixty thousand people had assembled to take part in the ceremony. Bands played, and cannon boomed their salutes. After the numerous speeches, de Young stepped down from the platform and, with a silver shovel, turned the first earth for the undertaking. At that moment, all the bands played "America," and a long line of teams and scrapers and men armed with shovels came around the brow of the hill.

Work began at once. Water and sewer lines were laid, and the sewer line was connected to the city sewer on Fulton Street. Roads were built, but because of the heavy loads, the soft red rock in the park could not be used. The road around the Main Concourse was paved with rock from the quarry at Telegraph Hill. The area was fenced with a high board fence, and two entrance gates with turnstiles were installed — one near the Main Drive and the other near Tenth Avenue and Lincoln Way.

The engineer of the fair was M. M. O'Shaughnessy, who was the city engineer for thirty-five years and served also as the engineer of San Francisco's Hetch-Hetchy Water System. Specifications for the five main buildings were drawn up, and competitions were held for the best design. The largest building was the Manufacturers and Liberal Arts Building, designed by A. Page Brown at a cost of $100,000. The Administration Building, also designed by Brown, cost $25,000. Edward R. Swain was the designer of the Mechanical Arts Building, which cost $65,000. The Fine Arts Building, the only permanent structure of the exposition, was designed by C. C. McDougall at a cost estimated at $45,000. Samuel Newsome designed the Agricultural and Horticultural Building, which cost $70,000.

The exposition guard was under the direction of Col. W. R. Shafter, First Infantry, United States Army, on loan from the Presidio. At no time did he have more than ninety men in his command. The uniforms were copied from the household guard of the king of Italy. Although each guard was armed with a short, straight sword and a revolver, no incident of any culprit being run through with a sword was recorded. Most arrests were for simple drunkenness and rowdiness. The unfortunates were usually escorted to the gate and ejected. Only 109 arrests were made for serious offenses — a remarkable number, considering that an estimated two and a half million people visited the grounds.

The Fire Department consisted of twenty-five men detailed from the city Fire Department, with J. J. Conlon as acting chief. Their equipment included one Hayes truck, one chemical engine, and two hose carts. The twenty-five fire-alarm boxes scattered about the fairgrounds were seldom used. Other than some grass huts burning, the most serious blaze was a fire in the Vienna Prater Building that totaled $100 damage.

An emergency hospital building was erected in the shape of a Roman cross. Dr. Martin Regensberger, formerly the president of Poly Clinic Hospital of San Francisco, served as its director. All the staff doctors and surgeons were also from Poly Clinic. Other city hospitals alternated in furnishing nurses for the emergency service. A total of 1,935 persons were treated during the fair, and of these, only two died — an Eskimo baby, who died of hereditary syphilis, and a South Sea Islander, who died of pneumonia. Four bone dislocations, sixteen fractures, two concussions, thirty-eight burns, and fifty-three sprains were treated. The staff also saw boils, diarrhea, felons, hysteria, indigestion, malaria, neuralgia, skin diseases, syncope, rheumatism, and other ailments. The major disaster of the exposition was the overturning of the stagecoach at the Forty-Niner Camp; a dozen people were injured in the incident.

The exposition was to run from January 1 to July 4, 1894. The object was to hold the fair in the middle of winter to demonstrate to the world that such an exhibit

Midwinter Fair Police on steps of the Administration Building.

Midwinter Fair Police on steps of the Administration Building.

Midwinter Fair Fire Department with the chief and his driver at right.

Midwinter Fair Emergency Hospital.

could be held in midwinter in California, while the East was suffering from cold and snow: hence, the name Midwinter Fair. But nature took a hand in the plans. That winter the worst snowstorm in recorded history occurred in the High Sierra. Trains were stalled for days in the mountains and had to be dug out by hand. Many of the cars carrying exhibits from Chicago had to be taken back and rerouted through the Tehachapi Pass in southern California. As a result of the storm, the grand opening had to be postponed until January 27, 1894. But the fair opened unofficially on January 1, and people were admitted at a reduced rate.

The *Examiner* reported on January 2, 1894, that people seemed to have lost interest in the park. No crowds were to be found at the Conservatory or the Aviary, and the Children's Playground had very few patrons because of the Midwinter Fair. Even "Beertown," that notorious conglomeration of business establishments on D Street (now Fulton Street), in the vicinity of Seventh Avenue, complained of lack of patronage. Beertown had sprung up during one of San Francisco's periodic "cleanup campaigns." These politically inspired moves seldom eliminate crime, but they do tend to disperse it — in this instance to the Richmond District.

When the official opening day finally came, more than ten thousand people marched in the parade. The mayor of San Francisco ordered all municipal offices closed and asked all banks and businesses to close as well. Four regiments of the California National Guard entered, along with the First Infantry Regiment, United States Army. All of the independent military companies of San Francisco and Oakland participated, as well as civic and fraternal organizations.

The ceremony took place at the grandstand that had been erected on Big Rec. President of the day was James D. Phelan, who gave the opening address. He was followed by M. H. de Young and other dignitaries. Then Mrs. M. H. de Young pressed a button that started the big engines. Wheels began to hum all over the exposition. The united bands played the national anthem, and the crowd joined in the singing. Whistles shrieked, steam sirens wailed, bells clanged, the artillery guns thundered a salute, and the fair was open.

It had taken five years to build the Columbian Exposition in Chicago. San Francisco had built its exposition in less than five months from the breaking of ground.

One of the notable things about the exposition was that all the electricity used was generated on the grounds. Until then, Golden Gate Park had had no electricity. Huge engines turned dynamos, and both direct and alternating current was used at the exposition. To save wire, time, and money, many of the lights in the buildings and on outdoor displays were wired in series of five. When one light burned out, five lights were darkened; but this system created little problem. Most of the moveable displays did not have individual electric motors but derived their power from huge line shafts that ran overhead. Flat belts were everywhere. The power for these line shafts came from large engines furnished as exhibits by private companies at no cost to the exposition.

The most popular concession was the Japanese Tea Garden. It was built by a local merchant, George Turner Marsh, who was building a Japanese estate in Mill Valley at the time. Marsh had been born in a suburb of Melbourne, Australia, called Richmond. He had spent several years in Japan as a young man and had learned the language and studied Japanese history and culture. When he came to San Francisco, he built a home in the sand dunes on the southeast corner of Twelfth Avenue and Clement Street. His new home reminded him so much of his birthplace that he named it Richmond. As the area grew around him, it became known as the Richmond District.

Marsh had four Japanese families living on the Marsh estate in Mill Valley, who were building a Japanese garden there. They had just completed a huge gate for the estate when he was awarded the concession for the Japanese Tea Garden at the fair. Marsh had the gate brought by ferry to the park and reassembled as an entrance to the Tea Garden, where it stands today. The smaller gate to the south came from the Panama-Pacific Exposition of 1915.

Bonsai trees, shrubs, vines, and flowers were imported from Japan to make the concession authentic. Japanese carp were imported, as well as roosters with tail feathers sixteen feet long. The site of the garden was selected because of the fir trees that grew there. Fir trees grew in Japan as well, but in Japan their needles were less profuse and not so close together. The Japanese workers perched for days on ladders, thinning out the fir needles to make the scene accurately Japanese. Such architecture had never been seen in San Francisco. This kind of painstaking labor, so lovingly performed, was unknown. Attention to detail was not thought of in the hurly-burly get-it-done climate of early California.

Kimono-clad ladies and young girls served tea and cookies to a fascinated public for 10¢. As part of the concession, Marsh also had the privilege of "transportation" at the exposition. So he imported seventy-five jinrikishas. This gesture nearly provoked an international incident. The Japanese community immediately formed the Anti-Jinrikisha Society. They maintained that a man might pull people around in Japan, but in America horses were available for such tasks. They felt the concession would be an insult to their emperor, and they served notice that any Japanese who hired out to Marsh for that purpose would be killed. Not wanting to lose his investment, Marsh hired a group of German men, darkened their faces, and dressed them like Orientals to pull the jinrikishas. He observed that the arrangement was better anyway, because the Germans could also speak English and were better equipped to describe the wonders of the exposition to the customers.

The Japanese community was not appeased. They noted that the Japanese flag flew on either side of the Main

The Japanese Tea Garden, about 1904.

Gate — also an insult to their emperor. One of the flags was taken down and replaced with an American flag.

The trouble was not over. A three-story building was put up in the Tea Garden for a Japanese theater, and Marsh imported a troupe of Japanese jugglers and acrobatic dancers. Word got out, and the Anti-Jinrikisha Society went down to the harbor to meet the boat bringing the troupe to San Francisco from Japan. They informed the performers that if they went to work for "that bad man Marsh," they would be killed. This time, Marsh did not concede defeat. He appealed to the police chief, and the entertainers were taken under guard to the Japanese Tea Garden, where they performed until the end of the exposition.

When the exposition was over, Marsh sold his concession to the park commissioners. The commission then hired Makota Hagiwara, who was born in Japan on August 14, 1854, to maintain and operate the Japanese Tea Garden.

In 1900, when the city charter was changed, the Hagiwaras were forced out of the park. Because of the anti-Asian sentiment that prevailed in California until after World War II, Caucasians were hired. After the Hagiwaras left, the board received the following letter from Makota Hagiwara:

January 10, 1900

Messrs. A. B. Spreckels, F. W. Zeile, R. H. Lloyd, Wm.
Thomas and Jaspar McDonald, Park
Commissioners, City

Dear Sirs:

For nearly five years, I have had charge of the Japanese Tea Garden at Golden Gate Park. I have endeavored to perform my work to the satisfaction of all. As to my competency, I have merely to say that I have had thirty-five years experience in gardening — ten years in America and twenty-five years in Japan.

Last year I laid out the Japanese tea house and garden for the Charles F. Crocker estate at Mateo Robles, San Mateo County, and I have received a letter from the executors commending my work.

I have performed similar work for M. H. Huff of San Leandro and received an equally commendatory letter.

I have also laid out a garden for G. T. Marsh at his place in San Francisco and subsequently at his place in Mill Valley.

I challenge any Japanese or White Man to compete with me in my work. All my earnings at the park have been invested in beautifying and improving the Tea Garden.

I have, at my own expense, imported from Japan many rare trees and plants. I extended the Tea Garden more than one half of its original size. I spent a great deal of money in the work.

I have drawn plans for the future improvement of the garden and want to be given a chance to carry this out.

I appeal to you to permit me to retain my position.

Very respectfully,

M. Hagiwara

No record suggests that any response was made to Hagiwara's appeal.

The Hagiwaras went just outside the park and leased the entire block on Lincoln Way between Eighth and Ninth avenues. There they built their own tea garden — and a wonderful, mysterious place it was. Little boys used to peer through knotholes in the high board fence and speculate on the happenings within. The Hagiwaras sold tea and cookies just as they had in the park. George Hagiwara, the grandson of Makota Hagiwara, was born there in 1904.

By 1907 the Japanese Tea Garden in the park was in such a deplorable state that McLaren asked Makota Hagiwara to come back and manage the Tea Garden again. Once more, the Tea Garden bloomed and was for years again a favorite spot for San Franciscans.

In 1909 Makota Hagiwara introduced a "fortune cookie" to his clientele. It was an instant success. Apparently Hagiwara was not familiar with copyright laws and did not bother to copyright his invention. Enterprising Chinese merchants copied the fortune cookie, and it became world famous as San Francisco's Chinese fortune cookie. It is exported even to China.

Makota Hagiwara passed away on September 12, 1925, in San Francisco. His son-in-law, Goro Hagiwara, then managed the Tea Garden until his own death on March 31, 1937. Then Makota's grandson George managed the garden until early in 1942. At that time all persons of Japanese ancestry were removed from the Pacific Coast by presidential order and interned for the "duration." Even the name of the garden was changed to the Oriental Tea Garden, but loyal friends of the Hagiwaras mounted a campaign to restore it to the Japanese Tea Garden. When the war was over, old animosities remained, and the Hagiwaras were not permitted to return to their beloved garden. The maintenance was turned over to park gardeners.

In 1971 George Hagiwara offered over seven hundred

Interior of Japanese Tea Garden in 1894.

The four main exhibition buildings of the 1894 California Midwinter International Exposition.

teapots as a donation to the John McLaren Society to raise money for a plaque honoring Makota Hagiwara. With the help of local newspaper columnists and antique stores in San Francisco and Oakland, the pots were sold, and a fund was established. Ruth Asawa of the San Francisco Art Commission designed the plaque. A suitable rock upon which to mount it was located in Marin County, and on March 26, 1974, a fitting dedication ceremony was held under the Japanese cherry blossoms in the Tea Garden. The plaque stands just to the left of the Main Gate as you enter:

To Honor
Makota Hagiwara
and His Family
Who Nurtured and Shared
This Garden from
1894 to 1942

A frog and some lizards adorn the plaque, with the above words in both Japanese and English. After three generations of service, the Hagiwara family was at last recognized for bringing beauty and joy to the millions of people who visit the Japanese Tea Garden.

Many other exhibits at the Midwinter Fair were beyond description. California was prominently represented with gold and silver ores, coal, and other minerals; farm and orchard produce; the wine industry; and the manufacturing industry. One of the rules of the fair was that all products furnished or purchased had to come from the state to help relieve unemployment. Even the Ferris wheel in Chicago was duplicated and built in California, where it was called the Firth Wheel, after its builder.

The state of Nevada constructed its own building, and the products of that state were much in evidence. The foreign exhibits of glassware, ivory, and other manufactured goods were widely admired.

The Electric Tower, brilliantly lighted at night, had a restaurant on the first landing, with three landings above that for observation. At the top was a revolving light, with which it was claimed you could read a newspaper at a distance of eight miles. It was billed as "the Most Powerful Searchlight in the World."

On a little hill in what is now the Arboretum stood Heidelberg Castle. That little hill is still known as Heidelberg Hill.

One of the concessions was Colonel Boone's Wild Animal Arena. This show consisted of trained pigs who did all sorts of tricks. Trained birds would walk over and pick up the American flag when the national anthem was played. A bird would wave the flag to the cheers of all. Of the bears and all sorts of lions and tigers, the most famous was Parnell, billed as a "man-eating lion" who had already killed two men. One day at feeding time, Parnell leaped on one of the trainers without warning. Other lions joined him, and before they could be beaten back, the poor man was dead.

Since the trainer was a "foreigner," with no known relatives, it was decided to make the most of this tragedy. It was announced that the funeral for the lion tamer would be held in the arena. It turned out to be the most unusual funeral ever held in San Francisco. The coffin rested on two of the pedestals on which the animals did their tricks. Every seat in the vast arena was taken, and hundreds more tried to get in. To the back of the seats stood Indians in war paint, miners from the Forty-Niner Camp, hula girls in native dress from the Sandwich Islands, native dancers from Cairo Street, Eskimos from the Far North, swarthy Mexicans, and a big Cossack with his shaggy hat protruding high above the entire crowd.

Outside, at a distance, a band could be heard playing somber tunes while the minister read the funeral service. When the service was nearly over, and it was time for the afternoon performance, the lions and tigers added their voices to the din. Strong men shuddered and women had to be helped from the arena as the roars reminded them of the reason the services were being held.

Then came the funeral procession. Exposition guards in full dress headed the column. Then came the band, playing a funeral dirge. Keeping step to the rhythm were the Indians, the Turks, the South Sea Islanders, and all the representatives of the different concessions who had turned out to honor the memory of the dead lion tamer. The horsedrawn hearse was covered with floral offerings. Hundreds of people connected with the exposition walked in the long line that reached from one end of the Grand Concourse to the other. They carried the lion tamer's body to Lone Mountain Cemetery, his final resting place. Then they all returned to the exposition, and the show went on.

"Little Egypt" first danced in San Francisco at this fair. As she went through her contortions in front of the leering male population of the city, scandalized women and little boys stood outside and whispered about "those goings on." At a variety of exhibits and restaurants, "decent women" could partake of the exotic food.

One could ride a smelly camel in Cairo Street — with the necessary cash. This feature was the cause of another amusing, but painful, accident. One day, two of the concession employees decided to explore Golden Gate Park on their camels when business was slow. Everyone knows that the horses ridden by the mounted police in the park are the best-trained horses in the world. You can ask any mounted policeman in the park, and he will confirm this.

Santa Ana, the horse assigned to Officer T. H. Kennedy, was no exception to the rule. He never shied at steam whistles, and he hardly noticed bicycles. He even looked kindly at cable cars and electric cars. But camels? Santa Ana had never seen a camel, much less smelled one. When he saw two ungainly creatures coming at him with white-robed apparitions astride, he must have wracked his brain. They were not described in the police manual. Santa Ana snorted, then wheeled in abject terror, forgetting all he had been taught. He crashed blindly into a fence, and in the confusion Officer Kennedy was thrown to the ground with two broken legs. Several weeks went by before Santa Ana and Officer Kennedy were reunited.

In the nineteenth century, considerable differences divided the Republican and Democratic parties. Civil War animosities were still fresh, and they were kept alive by many editors and writers. One of these writers, Arthur McEwen was read as avidly as some columnists are today. McEwen was at the opposite end of the political spectrum from M. H. de Young, and he was not bashful about expressing his opposition.

In his letter of March 24, 1894, McEwen, in one of his milder charges, accused Director General de Young of mismanagement. He charged that the exposition was failing because too many free passes had been issued. To support this accusation, he said that reporters had been stationed at the turnstiles to count the admissions. Of 6,910 people passing through the gates, only 1,952 were paid admissions. He stated that it was incredible that such

a number of passes could have been issued legitimately. He called on Mayor Ellert to dismiss the director and to extend the duration of the exposition because "it would take a good deal more than the three months of April, May and June to rid the exposition of the odor of the de Young management."

In fairness to de Young, the free passes may have been issued to bolster attendance at the exposition. Sometimes what is lost at the admission gate is more than compensated for in sales within the grounds. And it is simple, indeed, to stand outside and criticize. Perhaps the truth lies somewhere between. Certainly, the director general had spent more of his own time and money on the project than had his critic. But it is also true that de Young, as co-owner of the *Chronicle*, stood to gain far more financially in advertising and so on, than McEwen.

The exposition did not lack for music. In addition to the official exposition band, under the direction of Charles H. Cassasa, the Iowa State Band played for opening-day ceremonies. At the end of six weeks, the John Phillip Sousa Band was engaged to play for six weeks. The Mexican Eighth Army Band came for the last six weeks and played for the closing-day ceremonies. Many other bands were there, including the Vienna Prater Band under the direction of Fritz Scheel.

Nearly every day some group, county, state, or nation was honored. An Afro-American Day was held in June. Polish, German, Italian, Chinese, Japanese, and numerous other days were celebrated. The *Examiner* and the *Chronicle* both held special days for children. There seemed no end to the imagination displayed in bringing money into the city. On Sacramento Day, special excursion rates were given on the railroad. In fact the Southern Pacific Company advertised excursion rates from everywhere, provided the eastern roads would cooperate — and they did. Even the exhibitors from Chicago were given special rates to move their exhibits to California.

To list all the features, amusements, and concessions

Camels for hire in Cairo Street.

Children's parade on Chinese Day.

The Mexican 8th Army Band at the Fair.

"Esquimaux" Village and dog team.

The Electric Tower at night in 1894.

of the exposition would be impossible. Many old houses in the city still contain mementos and souvenirs from those exciting days. The San Francisco History Room of the San Francisco Library has a case of souvenir coins, glassware, ivory, pewter, and paper goods on display, dating from the California Midwinter International Exposition.

The financial picture was not bad either. Total receipts were $1,260,112.19. Total disbursements were $1,193,260.70, leaving a profit of $66,851.49. The park received the Fine Arts Building for use as a museum. The fair officials also purchased the Royal Bavarian Pavilion and donated it for use as an annex to the museum. Bronzes, statues, and other objects were purchased for display. The Grand Court, which contained a lot of unwanted pavement, was "donated" to the park. And eleven hundred benches from the fair, which had cost $6 each when new, were donated to the park. According to the balance sheet prepared by exposition officials, the total value of donations to the park was $194,051.49.

It had been agreed at the start that the grounds used for the fair would be returned to the park in as nearly natural a condition as possible. This did not happen. Many concessionaires simply left town, so it was up to the Park Commission to restore the site to something resembling a park once again. The large buildings were torn down and the lumber sold, but since the concrete foundations were not salvageable, they were left for McLaren and his laborers to dig up and haul away.

The Electric Tower with its Belle Vista Cafe on the first landing was left standing. Repeated requests from the Park Commission brought no response from its owners, so one day McLaren and his men placed dynamite charges on two of the legs of the tower. At an appropriate moment, the dynamite was discharged, cutting off two of the legs. The old tower shuddered briefly and then fell with a crash. It was sold for junk, and the money was placed in the Park Improvement Fund.

The Firth Wheel, the Mirror Maze, Dante's Inferno, and many other amusements were bought by Adolph Sutro and moved to Sutro Heights for the amusement of his patrons. The Mirror Maze was later sold to Playland at the Beach, where it remained until the 1960s. The carved oak interior of Heidelberg Castle was sold to Roberts at the Beach, where it lined the boardroom for many years. It was last seen at a flea market in Benicia a few years ago. The dealer who had it for sale did not even know that it came originally from the Heidelberg Castle at the Midwinter Fair.

For a time, people remembered the damage done to Golden Gate Park. Efforts were made to hold the Panama-Pacific Exposition in the western end of the park. But the opposition was too strong, and that exposition was held elsewhere.

In 1978 attempts were also made to hold a state fair in the park in connection with the King Tut Exhibit that would be held at the M. H. de Young Memorial Museum in 1979. Opposition again appeared.

The park still holds a few reminders of the exposition, chief of which is the Japanese Tea Garden. The sunken area in the Music Concourse was graded and shaped as the Grand Concourse of the Midwinter Fair. Beside the drive between the Music Concourse and the de Young Museum is a statue of a nude man holding aloft a sword. The plaque identifies it as commemorating the ground breaking for the exposition. Further north, along the same drive, is one of the fountains from the fair, *The Wine Press*. Little else remains, except the M. H. de Young Memorial Museum. The original museum buildings were torn down in the 1920s. Their replacement is still growing, taking up more parkland with every addition.

Looking south from Arizona Garden, about 1907.

Business as Usual

On March 1, 1895, a former park commissioner, John Rosenfeld, was appointed to the Park Commission to take the place of the recently deceased William W. Stow. Joseph Austin became chairman. Once again a person who wielded great political influence had passed from the Park Commission.

The secretary was ordered to write to Colonel A. Andrews of the Midwinter Fair Committee and order him to remove the Electric Tower from the park. Its demise was described in the previous chapter. The chairman and Superintendent McLaren were authorized to prepare plans and obtain estimates for a new Park Lodge. Edward R. Swain, the architect, was to receive 5 percent of the construction costs as his fee. The original Park Lodge was about twenty years old. Although it had been kept painted and in good repair, it was not considered fine enough to suit prevailing conditions. Park buildings seemed to be taking preference over actual parkland development.

Where the original Aviary had stood, across the Main Drive from the Conservatory, the commissioners ordered a circular enclosure with round pickets, arranged so that the front wheel of a bicycle could be inserted between two pickets. Many of the city's old-timers remember the structure, which was known as Cycler's Rest.

On Sunday afternoons, after the band concert, the cyclists took over the carriage concourse and amused the crowd by performing tricks on their bicycles. One young man would get his machine going at a good rate and then spring upright on the saddle with his arms folded and ride round and round. When he tired of this, he would make his bike spring upright on the rear wheel and then ride around the concourse to the cheers of the watchers. But with their newly won freedom the cyclists became uncontrollable, and a new ordinance was passed in August 1895. Bicycle speed was limited to ten miles per hour, a lamp or lantern was required between sunset and sunrise, and bicycles could not be ridden more than two abreast. Coasting was prohibited at all times.

A concession was granted to S. W. Forman to rent boats on Stow Lake. Forman was immediately to give the Park Commission a bill of sale for the boats. Boat rentals were subject to approval of the board, and Forman was to pay the board rent of $100 per month for one year from May 1895 to May 1896. A year later, the Park Commission canceled the lease, and park employees operated the boat rentals.

Over and over again granting concessions proved to be far more trouble than it was worth. Concessions tended to be given to the friends of park commissioners, with the result that they were poorly supervised. Prices would go up and service would deteriorate until public indignation mounted to the point where the leases had to be canceled. With no one to take over the operation, the Park Commission would operate the facility "in the interim." Because someone on the commission or in some other branch of government wanted the concession given as political favor, the facility was again leased out as a concession, and so the process was repeated. (In my opinion, policies today remain much the same.)

A history of the park would not be complete without a description of the Casino Canal, the popular feature that once circled the hill just west of the Conservatory. The *San Francisco Chronicle* ran a feature story April 8, 1895, entitled "Perils of the Deep."

> The ridiculously cheap passenger rate, which does not include berth and meals, places this delightful, health-giving trip within the reach of all. Six minutes of unspeakable delight reward those hardy souls who dare brave the perils of the vasty deep. The half-mile trip is invariably made with absolute safety to the voyager. About the only danger attending navigation on this pea-green stream is that careless passengers are liable to acquire slivers in their elbows from the wooden banks of the canal. Soundings taken at high tide show but four inches of water in the deepest place. . . . Little children make the passage alone without parents or guardians and with no provisions other than a bag of popcorn and a consuming thirst.
>
> On leaving the dock, the passenger encounters a tumbling maelstrom of foam-created breakers kicked up by the paddle wheel, which creates the propelling current. A boat's length farther on and the danger is left behind. The deathgrips on the gunwales of the boat relax, the heart settles back into its accustomed place and the voyager begins to drink in the scenery.

Today nothing is left of these simple pleasures. Stow Lake, with its rowboats, brought about the end of the Casino Canal. No one can be found who remembers braving "the perils of the vasty deep" around Casino Hill.

In spite of the fact that street sweepings were being hauled to the park, the park still found it necessary to purchase loam. Since all of the nearby hills had been denuded of loam, it became necessary to go farther afield. During the exposition, when the Southern Pacific spur track was in the park, hundreds of carloads of loam were hauled up from San Mateo County. After the spur track was removed, the loam was dumped from the cars along Lincoln Way and hauled by team and wagon to wherever it was needed.

The grounds of the exposition could not be restored immediately, because some of the buildings and all of the foundations still remained. The museum that had been "donated" to the city proved to be an expensive gift. Within a year, the commission was forced to spend $12,000 for an annex because the building was too small.

Ignoring the fact that the site of the exposition had already been designated by William Hammond Hall as Concert Valley, Commissioners Austin, Scott, and Rosenfeld decided to use that area as a new Music Concourse when funds became available.

Granting bicycles the freedom of the park also proved expensive. The commissioners had to make a path beside the Speed Road where bicycles could be propelled without restriction of speed. They also had to build a bicycle path from the eastern end of the Speed Road to the Conservatory to keep the cyclists out of the way of the horses, which also had the freedom of the park. The pedestrian — the true park user — was shortchanged in the process. The poor people who truly needed a park and who could afford neither horse nor bicycle were the least organized group of citizens. Since they lacked political clout, they were usually the last to be considered.

Finally, with mounting protest about horses and bicycles taking over the park, the commissioners laid plans to remove pedestrian traffic from the roads. Three new tunnels were planned in the Music Concourse: one in the southeast corner was to lead to the Children's Playground; one in the northeast corner would lead to the Aviary and Bear Pits; and one at the northwest corner would lead out of the Music Concourse toward the Main Drive. Then the commissioners planned an even longer tunnel, this one under the Main Drive and leading to Ninth Avenue and Fulton Street. These plans, carried out in 1896 and 1897, eliminated the conflict between pedestrians and non-pedestrians. However, the conflict between horsemen and cyclists was not resolved until later, when horses disappeared from the picture.

Many complaints were made about the conditions of the Speed Track. But since the horse owners had never obtained the promised money to complete the track, it had to be funded with park money and funds donated to hire the needy. Commissioner Austin, a horseman himself, wanted to move the old Casino to the west end of the Speed Road and turn it over to the horsemen for a clubhouse. But the other two commissioners overruled him, and the building was sold. The buyer, S. Menzies, who paid $400, moved it out of the park to Twenty-fourth Avenue and Fulton Street, where it remained for years as a roadhouse, catering to horsemen and their ladies. At that time, it was not within walking distance of public transportation.

The *Examiner* reported on February 23, 1896, that many men were being laid off at the park. It appeared that the friends of the late William W. Stow were joining the ranks of the unemployed. The commissioners heatedly denied any connection between the death of Stow and the exodus from the park of many workers. But, as one worried worker explained, Stow was a Republican, and Austin and Rosenfeld were Democrats. Stow had apparently filled the ranks of park laborers with friends, just as Frank Pixley had done ten years earlier.

While Pixley had fired the entire police force in order to give his friends jobs, only one or two men on the present police force seemed slated to go. This exodus had been going on, a few men at a time, for about six months, but on the last day of January 1896, nearly sixty men were let go — far more than usual.

President Joseph Austin professed that he was a friend and admirer of Stow and that politics had nothing to do with layoffs. He said the men had been laid off because the park had no money to pay them. At the same time, however, the commission was spending approximately $40,000 for a new lodge, $7,800 on the Great Highway, $5,000 on a bicycle path, $12,000 to expand the museum, and nearly $40,000 for tunnels under the Main Drive and under the drives surrounding the Music Concourse. Thus, it did not appear to the casual observer that Golden Gate Park was pressed for money. It did look as though politics was still playing a large part in the management of the park.

On March 12, 1896, the *Examiner* reported that Charles Fair had imported the latest thing from Paris — a horseless carriage. It had been spotted on Folsom Boulevard and was described as follows:

> The wheels are similar to those of a bicycle, and the front axle is stationary.
>
> The machinery is controlled by two small levers which extend from a rod projecting through the bottom of the buggy. The levers are handled by the motorman, who sits on a rear seat. The contrivance is very simple. The owner estimates that he can speed along from twelve to fifteen miles an hour.

Fair did not realize at the time that he had just introduced a contraption that was to provide headaches to a long series of park commissioners, city planners, policemen, and pedestrians. Unlike horses, this new-fangled machine did not require hitching racks or watering troughs. It did require acres of parking, as well as superior roadways. Worst of all, it could not be lassoed and stopped by a mounted policeman.

One day McLaren noticed that Gobo, one of the two ostriches residing in Peacock Meadow, seemed to be tired and "off his feed." He had been listless for several days.

McLaren could not figure it out, since he had watched Gobo swallow a tennis ball and several empty tomato cans with no damage. In fact, McLaren had cast a suspicious eye on Gobo when several rails disappeared from the fence surrounding the enclosure. So he ordered Patrolman Dick Lite to keep an eye on the ailing bird. Officer Lite soon found the cause. He spied Gobo in full flight around the meadow, with a group of young, yelling vaqueros, armed with riatas, pursuing him. Officer Lite was able to catch and hold only one of the group. Later in the day Officer Kennedy arrested three more of the culprits. All were released after solemnly promising not to molest Gobo in the future.

A wide variety of soil is found in Golden Gate Park. All the hills around the park have furnished loam to augment the sandy soil of the area. After the Midwinter Fair, more than twenty-five thousand cubic yards of loam were hauled by rail from San Mateo County. A great amount of soil has come from Buena Vista Park. In the early days, after every rain, Buena Vista Park had a habit of sliding down onto Haight Street; the surplus soil was delivered to Golden Gate Park. Clay for Stow Lake and other lakes was hauled from the deposit of clay at Turk and Divisadero streets. Many loads of rock were taken from Alcatraz in the 1870s, to be crushed and utilized for drainage in the park. In the 1890s, thousands of wagonloads of silt were scooped up from the bottom of Mountain Lake near the Presidio to feed the trees. A drought during that period dried up the lake, and, while it was dry, contractors were hired to bring the silt to the park.

On Lexington Day, 1884, the Sequoia Chapter of the Daughters of the American Revolution (D.A.R.) planted a "Liberty Tree" in Conservatory Valley. Soil from the battlefield at Lexington was brought in for the occasion.

On October 19, 1896, the Sequoia Chapter brought thirteen trees to the park, one from each of the original thirteen colonies. Soil from a battlefield of each colony was also brought to be planted with the trees. The trees were planted just east of the entrance drive to Stow Lake from the Main Drive, along a crescent-shaped path. It is not known how many of the original trees are still standing. The day's program opened at 2:30 P.M. with music by the United States First Infantry Band. A small bag of earth from Lafayette's grave was presented by C. S. P. Marais, representing France, and it was planted with a cedar tree from Pennsylvania. A bag of earth from the grave of fourteen-year-old Elizabeth Cook, who rode miles through dangerous countryside to help mold bullets for Revolutionary soldiers, was planted with the charter oak from Connecticut. The program closed with the singing of "America" and a benediction by Rev. George Walk.

An even greater variety of trees was transplanted to Golden Gate Park in 1916, following the Panama-Pacific International Exposition. As a publicity stunt, each time a visiting dignitary came to the city, a troop of cavalry escorted him to the exposition grounds, where a tree was planted in honor of the visitor's city, state, or nation. Since most of these trees were planted in the Presidio, they could not be left there, and they were all taken to Golden Gate Park the following year. The location of these trees cannot be ascertained, but the *Official History of the Panama-Pacific International Exposition* tells that they were, in fact, planted in Golden Gate Park.

When a tree was planted by the guest of honor, he was given a small leather case of jewels from the Tower of Jewels. Gov. Phillips Lee Goldsborough planted a white oak for Maryland on May 19, 1915, and Gov. James F. Sielder planted a cedar tree for New Jersey on May 24. On May 26 Hon. John Purroy Mitchel, mayor of New York, planted an Oriental plane tree, along with soil from Central Park. A tree called a "birch-ash" was planted by Gov. George Washington Clarke of Iowa on June 25, and Gov. Samuel Moffitt Ralston of Indiana planted a maple on June 26.

His Excellency W. L. F. C. Chevalier van Rappard, Envoy Extraordinary and Minister Plenipotentiary from the Netherlands, planted an orange tree in honor of the

McLaren Lodge, built in 1895.

birthday of Her Majesty Queen Wilhelmina on September 1. Soil from Valley Forge was scattered around the roots of the red oak planted on September 4 by Gov. Martin Grove Brumbaugh of Pennsylvania. His Excellency Kai Fu Shah, Envoy Extraordinary and Minister Plenipotentiary from China, planted a pine tree on September 23.

Trees were also planted by Former President Theodore Roosevelt, Former President William Howard Taft, Major General George Washington Goethals, and Secretary of the Treasury William G. McAdoo. Numerous other trees in the park were planted in honor of persons or events, including one to commemorate the centennial of the park, observed in 1970. West of Tenth Avenue, near Fulton Street, is a Memorial Grove of redwood trees to honor the fallen of World War I.

Edward R. Swain, architect for the new Lodge, was ordered to oversee its construction. The carpentry work on the Lodge was awarded to J. F. Logan on a low bid of $11,397. The tile roofing was awarded to Forderer Cornice

The Speed Road as it looked prior to the earthquake, about 1900.

Works on a low bid of $3,820. The contract for the stone work was awarded to J. D. McGilvray, who had furnished the stone for the Sharon Building. The Diebold Safe & Lock Company was awarded the bid to furnish the steel safe for the Lodge.

Plans for the Lodge called for three kinds of heating: steam registers, gas fireplaces, and coal or wood fireplaces. The building was to be lighted with both gas and electricity. The western portion of the building would serve as living quarters for the superintendent, and the eastern portion was to contain offices for the Park Commission, the superintendent, and the Engineering Department. The record does not show when the offices were moved from the Victorian Lodge to the new stone Lodge, but the move was made during 1896.

Commissioner Irving M. Scott reported on plans for producing electricity and lighting the park. He suggested that the light poles be of ornamental design and that all wiring be placed underground. He further suggested that the plant be located near the steam pumping plant and that direct current of the highest quality be utilized. Superintendent McLaren was instructed to prepare specifications for lighting the park and to obtain bids for this work.

In 1897 a Police Station and an emergency Hospital were erected on the site of the old Casino, just west of the Conservatory. The hospital also included stables and a shed to house the horse-drawn ambulance. In May 1897, the Board of Health requested that signs be placed along the Main Drive to designate the location of the Ambulance Station, but the Park Commission refused.

In May 1898, Commissioner Rosenfeld's term expired, and Adolph B. Spreckels was appointed in his place. Spreckels was president of the San Mateo Electric Railway and vice president of the Spreckels Sugar Company. Joseph Austin resigned as president, but not from board membership, and Spreckels was elected president in his place. The following month, Irving M. Scott resigned from the commission. No reason was given, but it was well

known that Scott and Spreckels were not on the best of terms. Gov. James Herbert Budd appointed Frederick W. Zeile to replace Scott on the Park Commission. Zeile was president of the Mercantile Trust Company of San Francisco and a wealthy man.

On November 11, 1898, the first polo match was played at Big Rec in Golden Gate Park. It was a game between the Reds and the Whites, both of which were composed of local horses and riders. The Reds won by a score of 5 to 2.

In January 1899, William H. Metson, an attorney specializing in mining affairs, was appointed park commissioner to replace Joseph Austin. Metson held extensive mining interests in Alaska, Washington, California, and Nevada. He also owned large farms along the Sacramento River, where he raised vegetables and other produce.

In the spring of 1899, Golden Gate Park blossomed with all the known varieties of wildflowers that would thrive in the state. The entire western end of the park had been planted with seeds and bulbs the previous season. Plans were made to continue growing wildflowers for the education and pleasure of those who visited the city's great "fresh air factory."

That same spring, Claus Spreckels, the father of Commissioner Adolph B. Spreckels, offered to donate $60,000 for the erection of a new Music Stand on the site of the Midwinter Fair. A resolution was adopted accepting the gift, and the entire construction was left in the care of Spreckels.

During March of that year, the sailors of the revenue cutter *McCulloch* donated to the park a huge silk flag, eighteen by thirty feet. They had bought the flag in Japan with their own funds and chose to present it to the city where they would be stationed. The flag was accepted by Commissioner Metson, who stated that it would be flown only on special occasions.

En route to the tennis court, about 1915.

A New City Charter

In the fall of 1899, when the city charter was revised, Golden Gate Park came under the direct control of the mayor and Board of Supervisors rather than the state legislature. Commissioners would henceforth be appointed by the mayor of the city, not the governor of the state. The park police were transferred to the jurisdiction of the chief of police of the city. This change put the park firmly within the jurisdiction of the city government.

Instead of three park commissioners, the new charter called for five. On January 1, 1900, the following men organized a new Board of Park Commissioners: Frederick W. Zeile, Adolph B. Spreckels, M. Jasper McDonald, Reuben H. Lloyd, and John A. Stanton. Lloyd, whose real name was Reuben H. Kissane, was a well-known San Francisco attorney. As long as he lived in the city he was known as Reuben H. Lloyd.

Reuben, Henry, and William Kissane were brothers, all apparently born in Ireland. William, the oldest, was allegedly a member of a gang of men who had bought old sailing ships, insured them for the rich cargoes aboard, and then had the ships "disappear" or burn to collect the insurance. Many other crimes were attributed to William Kissane while he was in the eastern United States. He was finally arrested but later escaped. He came to California under the name of Col. W. K. Rodgers and grew wealthy as a farmer in Sonoma County, where he became president of the Board of Supervisors.

Henry Kissane came to San Francisco in the early days and became well known without anyone suspecting that he was the brother of the notorious William Kissane. The mother of the three boys — not wanting to be known as the mother of William Kissane — assumed her maiden name of Lloyd. Reuben, the youngest brother, also assumed his mother's maiden name. Reuben and Henry lived together with their mother at 1010 Folsom Street, San Francisco. Although they professed to be half brothers, they were in fact full brothers.

The story came out during the famous 1880s trial involving Sarah Althea Hill and Senator William Sharon. Sarah Hill was trying to prove she was Senator Sharon's wife, not his ex-mistress. She wanted Reuben Lloyd to testify to her character, but he refused, not wanting to get involved in that budding scandal. In retaliation, Hill revealed that Reuben H. Lloyd was in fact the brother of the infamous William Kissane.

Not a single San Francisco newspaper would print the story, but the *Sacramento Bee* and the *Carson City Morning Appeal* carried huge headlines about it. The *Bee* sold out of papers in San Francisco every day during the exposé. When all the rumors had been investigated, it was learned that Reuben and Henry were quite innocent of any wrongdoing. Reuben continued to go by the name of Reuben H. Lloyd. In 1902 he bought a residential lot at the corner of Fell and Stanyan streets. His was the first of many fine residences on the street bordering the Panhandle.

M. Jaspar McDonald, another new commissioner, had

the distinction of building the first telegraph line connecting San Francisco with Salt Lake City. He amassed a fortune in mining and was prominent in the city, having arrived in 1852. Frederick Zeile studied law but never practiced it. He went into business and was secretary/treasurer of the American Sugar Refinery for four years. Later he managed a thirty-five-hundred-acre farm in the Sacramento Delta. Little is known about John A. Stanton. Philip J. Fay was elected secretary of the new Board of Park Commissioners. Former secretary M. B. Fairman was appointed bookkeeper; her salary was $100 per month. Adolph B. Spreckels was elected president of the new board.

Under the new charter, all the parks and squares of the city now came under the Park Commission. Superintendent McLaren was ordered to fire all the employees of the parks and squares with the exception of the head gardener. Thirty new men were hired to replace those who had lost their jobs. Wages for laborers under the new charter were set at $2 per eight-hour day, which had come into being as the "eight-hour law," along with the new city charter.

The secretary was instructed to contact the chief of police to request that all police officers previously hired by the Park Commission be reassigned to the park.

A new ordinance passed by the board prohibited dogs attached to bicycles from entering the park. All types of automobiles were also denied entrance to the park roads. It was ordered that all people driving automobiles in the park be arrested and their automobiles impounded.

The new commissioners ordered the superintendent, henceforth, to plant trees to obtain a cathedral effect in the park and to report at the next meeting about the kinds of trees needed to obtain this effect. McLaren's remarks about this new method of park management did not grace the minutes. No mention was made of these instructions at the next meeting. Commissioner Reuben Lloyd was reported to be riding around the park, seeking a site where poplar trees might be planted to obtain a cathedral effect. Just why

Lloyd wanted to turn Golden Gate Park into a cathedral was not made clear. But the idea was no more ridiculous than other proposals made over the years by instant experts who had been named to the Park Commission.

At a special meeting of the commission in March 1900, an ordinance was adopted prohibiting all automobiles from using the Great Highway, park roads, or the Avenue in the Panhandle, except automobiles utilizing electric power. Gasoline and steam-powered cars were prohibited, in conformance with a similar ordinance in Central Park, New York. Spreckels stated that he wanted to be on record as opposed to any type of automobile being allowed on park roads.

One day in March 1900, according to the *Examiner*, two young ladies decided to go bicycle riding in the park. Daisy Brown and Helen Davis rode the streetcar to Stanyan Street, where they rented two bicycles. The two cyclists carried with them the proper "bloomer outfits." They pushed their bicycles to the Rustic House behind the Conservatory, where they proceeded to change into the proper attire for bicycle riding. Then they pried loose a board on the Rustic Shelter, hid their street clothing, and went "scorching" off into the western reaches of Golden Gate Park.

Along came Park Policeman G. W. Clarke. His sharp eye spotted the loose board, and he investigated. He found four skirts, some shirtwaists, capes, collars, a waterproof cloak, and a few other items that women forsake when they depart this world. Officer Clarke at once scented a mystery, murder or suicide, and he lost no time. He gathered up the garments and hastened to the police station to give the alarm. A search was launched.

Meanwhile, Daisy and Helen returned and discovered that their clothing was missing. Not wanting to be seen in their bloomers, they hid in the bushes with their bicycles until dusk. Then they fled to the hill south of the park, where they made their way to the home of a friend on

Golden Gate Park at the turn of the century.

Twentieth Street. They did not dare go home in their bloomers, fearing parental wrath. They hid all night at the home of their friend. The following morning they saw pictures of their clothing in the newspaper and read of their awful death in the park. Word was sent to Officer Clarke, who sheepishly returned the clothing, and the girls got properly dressed and returned the bicycles to the cyclery on Stanyan Street.

Golden Gate Park has always seemed to follow Central Park in New York in its policies, so when Central Park placed some of its patrolmen on bicycles, San Francisco

Mounted policeman on Main Drive, about 1905.

attired similarly to the Central Park police. They would wear black sweaters, a short blue coat and knickerbockers trimmed with black braid, black-ribbed hose, and low-cut black shoes laced down to the ingrowing nail. Thus arrayed, the bicycle cop could slip into a flock of scorchers without exciting alarm.

Joseph W. Ahearn and Charles Birdsall apparently fit the bill, so they were chosen. Sergeant Conroy offered to head the squad, provided the chief would give him a three-wheeled bicycle, but he lost out on his bid.

The bicycle cops were not meant to overtake automobiles or runaway horses; they were to control the antics of bicycle riders. The policemen were at a decided disadvantage. They tended to weigh more and were larger than the average bicycle rider, thus presenting more resistance to the wind and slowing their speed. It is not known just how long San Francisco's Finest endured this ultimate affront to their dignity.

Since Gen. Irwin McDowell had served on the Park Commission in the early 1880s, complete cooperation had been clearly established between the officers of the Presidio Reservation and the Park Commission. Most of the trees in the Presidio were raised in the Park Nursery and donated to the military. In return, the military allowed the commissioners to take loam from the Presidio to fertilize the park.

Silt from Mountain Lake was also hauled to Golden Gate Park. But, since the businessman always has an eye open for extra profit, the contractors who hauled the loam tried to obtain a monopoly from their friends in Congress so that they might charge whatever the traffic would bear for loam delivered to the park. This scheme was deplored by the *Chronicle* in an article published on April 8, 1900. The editor pointed out that cooperation between the military and the Park Commission had always worked for the benefit of the general public. He called on San Francisco's congressional delegation to subvert the designs of the greedy contractors. This scheme was another example of

followed suit. The plan was not popular with the mounted police. They pointed out that if they caught a runaway horse and roped it, the bicycle was not heavy enough to stop the horse. They said a policeman would look silly and ineffective on a bicycle.

Police Chief Sullivan held no competition to form his bicycle squad. He simply asked for two patrolmen who were "broken to bicycle clothes." An *Examiner* reporter on March 15, 1900, stated that the bicycle squad would be an attempt to use a public trust to turn a profit for a privileged few.

Prior to the charter change of 1900, the park police were under the control of the Park Commission and subject to park policies and disciplines. But under the revised charter, the police were assigned to the park from various stations, and their attitude toward offenders was entirely different. Prior to the change, those who broke park rules were quietly reprimanded and turned loose. They were seldom arrested, except after repeated offenses. But the city police were not cast from the same mold as the former park police.

On April 15, 1900, Officers Ahearn and Birdsall arrested seven boys for speeding on their bicycles and threw all seven into jail. Much comment was heard on the streetcars about the incident. The *Chronicle* stated that when people took the wrong path or were guilty of the slightest infringement of the rules, they were rudely and loudly reprimanded for the infraction.

Another complaint was that a group of young men gathered near the Music Stand and threw dirt and rocks at people listening to the music. Chief Sullivan was blamed; his system of policing the park was thought to be inadequate. On May 28, 1900, the *Chronicle* reported that the mounted police in the park were so poorly mounted under Mayor Phelan that they could not even catch a runaway team of horses.

Out for a spin on the South Drive, about 1908.

One local resident, George English, reported that he had seen a wildcat dragging a dead peacock into the bushes of the park. English offered to donate his services to shoot the animal. The offer was declined, however, as a citizen with a shotgun in the park might be more of a threat to life and limb than the threat presented by the wildcat.

One of the more important events of the year was the arrival of a baby kangaroo at the Menagerie. The news of its arrival spread quickly, and large crowds gathered to catch a glimpse. Daniel Curran, keeper of the park animals, was proud of his charge and went to great lengths to see that no harm came to the unusual baby. The greatest danger was from stray dogs, he remarked, but he was sure that any dog who ventured near the mother kangaroo would regret the folly.

In June 1899, the park commissioners inaugurated a system of two- and four-horse wagons in the park. The wagons held sixteen passengers and ran from Stanyan Street down the Main Drive to the de Young Museum, to Stow Lake and around it, back to South Drive, over Middle Drive, past the Bear Pits and the Buffalo Paddock to the Children's Playground, and back to Stanyan Street. The fare was ten cents, with all day stopover privileges at any point along the route.

Over the years, many other in-park transport systems have been tried without much success. Parks are primarily for walking, and every time these features are added, they seem to create more problems than they solve.

Mounted Police Capt. Sam Thomson was famous for many years in Golden Gate Park. Besides being a superb horseman, he was a favorite of patrons of the park. No one knows how many lives he saved by catching runaway horses and by rescuing people from the waters at Ocean Beach. He was also noted for his beautiful, silver-mounted Mexican saddle, which was his pride and joy. Captain Thomson had won three $200 prizes in successive horse shows, and he spent the entire amount for his saddle. He attracted so much attention and comment that in July 1899 the commissioners purchased silver-mounted saddles for all the mounted police in the park. These were used for only a few months, because as of January 1, 1900, the city charter was changed. Subsequently the police all came under the control of the chief of police of the city of San Francisco, who couldn't afford to outfit his entire force so richly.

In December 1899, it was decided to move the buffalo to another paddock. Ben Harrison, the patriarch of the herd, did not take kindly to this change of scenery. He broke away but was soon lassoed by Captain Thomson and led back to the others. He made several rushes at the officer and his horse but did no harm. Then, just as he was near the gate, he made another mad rush, and one of his horns caught the horse in the chest. Horse and rider were thrown into the air, and Captain Thomson fell under the horse. The maddened bull again gored the helpless horse, but Captain Thomson managed to extricate himself and escape. Other mounted officers surrounded the captain, while Officers Hammill and Arellanes went after Ben Harrison. After a mile or so of running, Ben was exhausted and went willingly into the paddock with the other buffalo.

Captain Thomson went to his horribly injured horse and, drawing his service revolver, shot it. The captain was taken to his residence on Stanyan Street, and Dr. Shumate was called to attend him. The distinct impression of Ben Harrison's hoof was visible on his uniform. Although he was found to have internal injuries, he was back on his beat in a few weeks.

The last year of the nineteenth century saw the completion of the Chain of Lakes. The North Lake was the first one finished. The year-round pond there was laboriously scooped out with teams and scrapers, and the soil was used to construct a scenic road all around the lake. Six small islands were left in the lake, each connected to the next by a rustic footbridge. Swamp cypress trees from Louisiana were planted on one of the islands, and weeping willow, bamboo, alder, and other trees were planted on others. Ferns, lilies, and iris were also planted on the various islands, so that a different environment was created on each island. A dozen varieties of violets added to the beauty of the scene.

Superintendent McLaren stated:

> When the foliage becomes more abundant and the grass begins to grow, this will be the prettiest section of the park. It has been our object all along to avoid anything which would tend to destroy the illusion of nature. No harsh palms or stiff groupings will be permitted around the lakes, and everything will be done to enhance the natural beauty of the surroundings. On the western slopes we have planted a number of deciduous trees as an experiment. They comprise the eastern sweet gum, maple, ash, tulip and swamp cypress. Under these trees great masses of rhododendrons will be planted.

The Spreckels Music Stand, dedicated on Admission Day, 1900.

The water in the lake requires no feeding, and when the lakes are once completed, they will require no outlay. So far the expense attached to this work is in the neighborhood of $20,000.

When all this work was done, McLaren turned his attention south of the Main Drive, and Middle Lake was completed. After that came South Lake, and the western end of Golden Gate Park began to get attention from the public.

Today Chain of Lakes is radically changed. All the footbridges are gone. The islands are indistinguishable from one another, and the lakes are full of trash, brush, tules, and weeds. The Chain of Lakes today is a scene of desolation and neglect — the product of uncaring commissioners and a penny-wise–pound-foolish city administration.

On Admission Day in 1900, about one hundred thousand people gathered in Concert Valley to witness the dedication of the third Music Stand in Golden Gate Park. The Music Stand was designed by Reid Brothers, Architects, with relief figures over the main archway by sculptor Robert I. Aitken. The total cost was between $60,000 and $70,000. A classic style was used, and it was one of the most imposing music stands in the Western

Sheep grazing in Speedway Meadows, about 1900.

Hemisphere. The height of the highest point was 80 feet, with a 240-foot frontage.

Prof. A. Spadina led the eighty-piece Park Band. For the occasion, Spadina had written an overture entitled "Immortality," dedicated to Claus Spreckels.

In his presentation speech, Claus Spreckels said, in part, "Loving California as I do, and being grateful for the many benefits that have accrued to me during the earnest and active life I have lived here, I have desired to manifest these feelings in some monumental structure which would stand as a memorial of my citizenship among you."

Gen. W. H. L. Barnes, a former park commissioner, accepted the gift on behalf of the city and the Park Com-

mission. Following the oratory, the band gave a concert that was a treat.

Ignoring the fact that the original Casino in the park had been a dismal failure twenty years earlier, the current Park Commission proposed the building of a new Casino in Concert Valley. Plans were drawn up by the architectural firm of Tharp and Holmes, and a picture of the proposed Casino appeared in the *Chronicle* on November 3, 1900. It was an enormous structure, seating 250 patrons inside and at least 1,000 patrons in the courtyard. It was to be situated on the eastern side of Concert Valley, approximately where the present Academy of Sciences stands, and it was to extend from one of the pedestrian tunnels to the other.

On November 2, 1900, the *Examiner* printed a poem written by Wallace Irwin about the proposal. The poem was prefaced with the following headline: "Shall the Park Casino be given over to wine and beer or tea and lemonade?"

When Mr. Zeile's dream comes true
   About the Park Casino
Then will we have a meal that is
   Indeed a peacherino.
We'll revel in the canvasback
   And oysters painted blue
Washed down with wine that sparkles when
   That dream comes true.

There I will take my Mary Ann
   To view the joyous scene
And, midst the spell of music rare,
   I'll feed her like a queen.
Much will we scorn the common herd
   And all the things they do
And shun the beastly "cattle" when
   That dream comes true.

So let me eat my two-bit meal
   And save my humble pence
'Till Zeile's marble palace looms
   A vision of expense.
And, if I save ten cents a day
   I kind of think, don't you?
I'll have a lot to spend before
   That dream comes true.

"Now shall Golden Gate Park have a Casino? And if it has a Casino, shall it be a place where the bubbles break upon the lips of wine glasses; where the bottles are very cold and the birds very hot; where the gourmet may tickle his palate with sauces and gravies and relishes: Or shall it be a Casino where the beer shall foam over stein and beaker; where the pretzel shall tangle the teeth with thirst; where the meftwurst, the sauerkraut and the sausage lay claim to all the gustatory delights? Or shall it be a Casino given over to the lemonade, the ginger pop, the milk shake and the sandwich?"

Prominent ladies of the city joined the controversy. Mrs. W. R. Eckart, president of the Sorosis Club, said, "I am thoroughly opposed to the building of any resort in the park where spirituous liquors of any kind can be sold." Mrs. Lovell White, president of the California Club, added, "I think it would be injudicious to take money from our city treasury for the purpose of erecting a pavilion of the kind Mr. Zeile suggests." Mrs. F. S. Vaslit, of the Women's Christian Temperance Union, stated, "As it is, drinks can be obtained entirely too easily in San Francisco, and such a resort in the park, which would have the approval of the 'bon ton' of our city, would do great harm."

The Casino was never built, but seventy-nine years later the Park Commission is still attempting to open a restaurant and a saloon in the Beach Chalet.

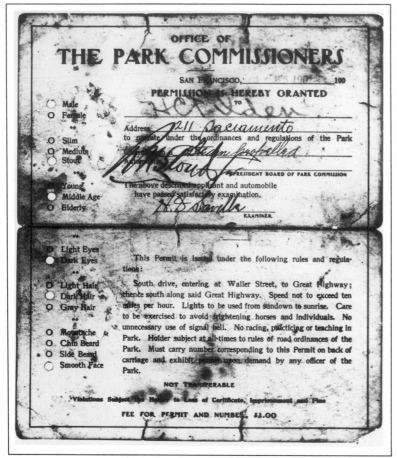

A driver's license, issued in 1901, was required in the park even before a state license.

On April 5, 1901, twenty-five automobiles assembled at Golden Gate and Van Ness avenues so that their drivers could be tested by Engineer Saville of the park concerning their competency in operating their machines. Each driver was put through the paces to show that he could back up, go forward, or swerve to the side to avoid imaginary runaway horses. Fifteen persons, including a number of women, passed the test, but P. Duchin, the sixteenth applicant, failed. When asked to back up, he crossed the sidewalk and crashed into the fence. He was told to become more proficient for the next test.

On June 30, 1901, the *San Francisco Sunday Call* reported on the effect of driving on the modern woman.

> She has arrived — the chauffeuse. She is destined to be one of the "its" of the twentieth century. She is independent with the independence of the times; she is vigorous with the vigor of it; she is ambitious, clear headed and cool, with presence of mind. And what makes her dear to the popular fancy, to the artist and the jingler of fashionable verse, is, above all, her smartness.
>
> For the woman who runs her own automobile is always, if you will notice, crisp and snappy in manner and in dress. This has to come with the use of the machine. It is all in the same spirit.
>
> San Francisco is in line with the rest of the world now. We have our own chauffeuses, and they are growing in numbers. . . . Two of them, Mrs. Moore and Mrs. Baird, have been through the Park's examination. Moreover, they have passed it. Wait until you have seen a Park Examination and you will be more respectful.

When Engineer Saville conducted tests in Golden Gate Park, he had one of his men hide in the bushes. As an applicant's car came along, he was to throw a dummy out in the road. Running over the dummy was cause for denial of a license.

The license cost $2 and was good for three months, subject to renewal at the discretion of the Park Commission. Violations of any park ordinance governing the oper-

A new ordinance governing the use of automobiles was passed in October 1900, allowing all types of automobiles on the South Drive, beginning at Waller Street and ending at the Great Highway. Automobiles were also allowed on the Great Highway south of the park but prohibited on that part between the South Drive and the Cliff House. Speed was restricted to ten miles per hour.

ation of motor vehicles was cause for revocation of the license. When the license was revoked, the culprit had to go before the Park Commission to plead for a reissuance. The *San Francisco Chronicle* reported on November 20, 1901:

> As a result of trying to pass the examination for a permit to use the South Drive of Golden Gate Park, William F. Bowers of the Bowers Rubber Company now possesses a very badly wrecked automobile. This unlucky chauffeur, who had just bought a new auto at a cost of $1,000, took his machine out in the park last Saturday to go through the stunts that the engineer in charge of this detail requires of the applicants for permits. On a wet road Bowers came along with his auto at a speed of twenty miles an hour and tried to turn and clear a ball, representing a baby, thrown in front of the vehicle by the engineer.
>
> It was an impossible feat, and the heavy rig, after running on two wheels for a moment, turned turtle, throwing out the owner and making a complete wreck of the carriage. Luckily Bowers escaped with a few bruises, but not so with his auto, the wheels of which lay on opposite sides of the road, and the vehicle being generally damaged to the extent of $400. Previous to the accident, local automobilists had been complaining of the severity of the park examination.

The *California Horseman*, published in October 1902, had this to say about the automobile:

> Much to the surprise of all patrons of the turf, the automobilists (notwithstanding the number of horses they

A baseball crowd at the stadium in 1901.

scare with their machines) are to petition the Board of Park Commissioners for permission to run their automobiles on the main drives in Golden Gate Park. These beautiful driveways are patronized by women and children who drive their gentle horses to the beach and along the boulevards, but, no matter how gentle these horses may be, the sight of an automobile almost drives them frantic. With fiendish delight the chauffeurs of these ugly, vile-smelling and death-dealing machines wheel around the curves and startle the horses and the occupants of the vehicles. The class of people who manage these monsters never enjoyed riding behind a good horse or took their friends for a drive. They found that in handling a machine they can spread consternation among all they meet. They know the only other pleasure they derive in handling one is to go as fast as the machine will carry them. If the law compelled them to restrict the speed of their machines to a limit of ten miles an hour, all interest in automobiling would vanish.

Park Commissioner M. Jaspar McDonald suggested placing a roof over the lake in the old quarry opposite the Conservatory, known both as Hobo Lake and as Quarry Lake. He further proposed placing every native fish of California in the lake for the education of the public. He did not explain how he hoped to mix river fish with lake fish or warm-water fish with cold-water fish. Apparently it was Commissioner McDonald who needed educating. He also proposed to cover the roof and sides of the proposed aquarium with shrubs and creeping vines so that it would not intrude on the landscape. Nothing further was heard of this proposal, although there were several other propositions to try to raise money for an aquarium.

In March 1901, it was decided to build as many tennis courts on the site of the old music stand as possible. The superintendent was ordered to purchase nets, backstops, and other necessary equipment. The tennis courts became immensely popular from the very first day, and the area devoted to tennis has been expanded many times. Immediately, handball enthusiasts, golfers, and lovers of other sports demanded equal space in the park. Such requests have been a source of much trouble to park commissioners all over the country. In November 1901, four handball courts were opened in Golden Gate Park. Then the park could boast of five baseball diamonds, eight tennis courts, and four handball courts to swell the growing ranks of famous athletes in San Francisco.

In December 1901, the commission donated one of the bull elk in the park to the Elk's Lodge. The animal was shot and turned over to a taxidermist for preparation as a permanent display. Fish and Game Commission representative Vogelsang confiscated the remains, on the grounds that it was illegal to shoot an elk in the state of California. Police Judge Cabaniss found the Lodge and its secretary, Herman Kahn, guilty of having a dead elk in their possession. Kahn appealed the decision, but on May 6, 1902 he withdrew the appeal and paid a fine of $25.

With the election of Eugene Schmitz as mayor of the city, more changes came to the park. Herbert L. Schmitz, brother of the mayor, was appointed secretary to the commission, to succeed Philip J. Fay who had been the secretary. M. B. Fairman was reappointed accountant for the commission. Superintendent McLaren was ordered to look into the matter of a golf course in the park and report back to the commission.

In February 1902, band concerts in the park were discontinued due to the failure of the Market Street Railway to pay their share of the cost, as they had agreed. Commissioner Spreckels was authorized to purchase a shotgun to kill predatory animals in the park. And two rustic shelters were ordered built for the use of pedestrians and bicyclists. In April 1902, President Spreckels announced that the Market Street Railway had agreed to pay $150 per month for the band, and the concerts were ordered to be resumed.

After a great deal of discussion, a "Dutch Windmill"

was ordered constructed in the west end of the park, the cost not to exceed $14,000. The Fulton Engineering Company was granted the bid for the ironwork for the windmill, at a cost of $3,100. Spars of Oregon pine for the windmill were donated by the Pope and Talbot Lumber Company.

In September 1902, Buffalo Bill Cody and his Wild West Show came to town. They set up shop in the sand dunes near the park. No new blood had been introduced into the buffalo herd at the park for years, so Commissioner Lloyd decided to take charge of the matter. The *San Francisco Call* reported the business dealings of Buffalo Bill and Reuben H. Lloyd as follows:

> When a shrewd and clever lawyer like Reuben H. Lloyd starts to swap buffaloes, even with an old-timer in the business like Colonel William F. Cody, better known as "Buffalo Bill," it is a hard race to pick the winner. These gentlemen did swap buffaloes and with full reports of all damage at hand, it appears that the man of the plains hasn't a bit the best of the man whose only experience with buffaloes has been gained at the paddock in Golden Gate Park. The Lloyd buffalo has proved fully as vicious as the Cody animal.
>
> The park commissioners have had in their possession for several years a big bull buffalo that has caused all kinds of trouble. He had brackets placed around his name when he tossed Captain Thomson of the park mounted police over a fence and gored the officer's horse to death. The buffalo was a nuisance. He would not let the other animals in the paddock eat; he was a constant worry and the park commissioners were anxious to give him away to anyone as a pet.
>
> The proposition to exchange bulls was made to Colonel Cody, the plea being that the future welfare of the herds demanded such an exchange.
>
> Now as a matter of fact, Colonel Cody has been looking for somebody to unload his bull buffalo on. The brute terrorized the whole herd. It would not go in and out of the cars and generally made a nuisance of itself. The deal was made and each party thought that it was handing a gold brick to the other.
>
> Twenty cowboys hauled the Wild West buffalo to Golden Gate Park and, reinforced by the mounted police, were able to take the other one back to the show. As soon as the buffalo from the park was landed in the corral of the Wild West Show, he jumped a fence six feet high and, knocking down two tents, took to the timbers above the Affiliated Colleges.
>
> He was dragged back and Sunday night fifty cowboys, ten Mexicans and twenty soldiers got the animal in the car for Salinas. Last night at Salinas the brute gave a big exhibition when he was released from the car. He killed two horses and made such a run that he terrorized the whole town.
>
> Buffalo Bill's former pet that is now at the park is having a hot time. Yesterday afternoon he alternated his amusements by playing center rush with the wire entrance gate to the paddock and chasing the other buffaloes up the trees. The question is: "Who landed the gold brick? The lawyer or the man that owns the Wild West Shows?"

In January 1903, Superintendent McLaren was ordered to begin construction of a new lake south of D Street and east of the new Buffalo Paddock. A total of $21,000 was set aside for this new lake. It would be used for sailing model yachts, as traffic on Stow Lake had become too heavy to accommodate model yachts any longer. The new lake would also be used for irrigation of the west end of the park. The plans called for a lake nine hundred feet long and four hundred feet wide.

In April 1903, Mayor Eugene Schmitz appointed his brother Herbert to the Board of Public Works, which left the Park Commission without a secretary. At a special meeting called to elect a new secretary, M. B. Fairman and A. R. Thomson were nominated, and James de Succa was suggested by Mayor Schmitz. James de Succa was elected. Later, Mayor Schmitz reappointed his brother as secretary to the Park Commission.

The Murphy Windmill, near South Drive, in 1907.

Noting that Professor Gruber of the museum had invented a moth destroyer that had saved the commission thousands of dollars, the board increased the professor's pay from $75 to $100 per month, effective June 1, 1903.

For quite some time, Monarch, the great grizzly bear from Ventura County, had been showing signs of loneliness. It was feared by many that he might die of a broken heart, so the *Examiner* obligingly purchased a female silver tip grizzly from Idaho. When the female grizzly arrived early in 1903, Monarch immediately showed his interest and arose from his lethargy. The female grizzly was placed in an adjoining cage, and Monarch plowed up the dirt in his cage in a most ferocious manner. After he had dug a trench big enough for two bears his size, without attracting any attention from the female, he proceeded to lie down in the hole and gaze longingly through the bars.

Mrs. Monarch was in no mood for him, and she even vented her displeasure on a photographer who was trying to conduct the interview. The following day, the two bears were put in the same cage. They romped and played together for an hour or more. Then Mrs. Monarch decided that her husband was getting too familiar, so she reared up on her hind legs and boxed his ears very soundly. Monarch walked away and plowed up a few more yards of earth, all the while muttering to himself. Later in the day, harmony was restored in the cage.

When President Theodore Roosevelt had announced his plans for a visit to San Francisco, the superintendent had been instructed to provide fresh flowers for his hotel room each day that he was in the city. On May 13, 1903, President Roosevelt alighted from his carriage and, with a bronze shovel made specially for the occasion, broke ground for the monument of President William McKinley to be located at the Baker Street entrance to the park Panhandle. Among the groups assembled were the Grand Army of the Republic, the Spanish-American War Veterans, and the Society of California Pioneers. Then everyone left to prepare for the evening festivities at the Mechanics' Pavilion.

A design for a Dutch cottage at the new windmill was approved. The caretaker of the windmill, in addition to his regular duties, was ordered to plant a garden to raise vegetables for the animals in the Menagerie. The Dutch Windmill was a huge success. Commissioners Spreckels, Lloyd, and Aaron Altman, who had been appointed by Schmitz in 1902, had taken a lot of ridicule because they had insisted on building the windmill. They had been told that the wind was unreliable and that the wells at the beach would soon run out of water, but neither prediction came true. After all that pumping at the rate of twenty thousand gallons per hour, the water level had not dropped. The power furnished by the wind was more than adequate for another pump to be ordered. The water was pumped through a ten-inch main to the reservoir on Strawberry Hill, and the overflow was directed back to the Model Yacht Lake.

Spring Valley Water Company was charging the city $1,050 per month for enough water to irrigate seventy acres of park. The new mill was pumping enough water to irrigate one hundred acres of land, and the entire cost of the mill was just over $16,000.

Commissioner Altman was authorized to design a clubhouse for the Model Yacht Lake, as well as a convenience station for the use of the members. A letter was received from the Model Yacht Club stating that conditions at the new lake were ideal and asking what the name of the new lake would be. President Spreckels suggested that it be called "Model Yacht Lake." Commissioner Sullivan suggested "Spreckels Lake." When the matter was put to a vote, Spreckels Lake was adopted.

The Speed Track in the park had become an abomination. There was never enough help to patrol it, and the horsemen did little to police themselves. Bicyclists refused to stay off, and pedestrians, at considerable risk, often wandered onto the track. The cooling off sheds were not kept adequately clean because the horsemen expected park employees to clean up after them.

Finally the park commissioners decided to do away with the track and to construct a stadium with a trotting track on the outside, a bicycle cinder path inside the circle, and space for polo and football in the center. Superintendent McLaren estimated that it would cost at least $50,000. He was ordered to build the stadium, but no more than $25,000 of park money could be spent on it. The rest would have to be raised publicly. This plan proved to be merely a dodge to pacify the taxpayer who would later furnish the money.

It was proposed to build a concrete grandstand all the way around the track. Each year, $5,000 was to be spent to build a section of concrete seats. When it occurred to someone that a telescope would be needed to see what was going on at the other end of the stadium, the plan was abandoned. President Spreckels donated $1,000 to start the project, and the unfinished "stadium" still stands, a monument to a new set of Park Commission foibles.

The exact date of the establishment of the Bowling Greens is not known. It is believed that the games, confined to Saturday afternoons, started in the park in 1902. In 1903 the sport increased in popularity and games were held every evening, as well as on weekends.

In January 1904, the commission of M. Jaspar McDonald was not renewed. McDonald had had many disagreements over the way the commission conducted business, particularly the management of the playground and the way the books were maintained for the park. The policy of negotiating contracts with businessmen without competitive bidding had been the cause of many bitter arguments.

The San Francisco Board of Supervisors, who by law were supposed to approve all park contracts, eased out of that responsibility with the time-worn argument that the

Visiting Deer Glen by auto.

Board of Commissioners had "exclusive control and management of the parks." This same argument was made by the Park Board so that their business dealings wouldn't be scrutinized. Time after time, the city attorney affirmed this policy, even though contracts were being granted without a majority vote of the park commissioners. W. J. Dingee was appointed by Mayor Schmitz to replace McDonald.

On January 14, 1904, Spreckels Lake was filled with water for the first time. No official ceremonies were held, but President Spreckels and Superintendent McLaren joined in opening the valve.

In February 1904, new regulations for automobiles were adopted by the commission. All types of pleasure automobiles were allowed on the South Drive from Waller Street to the Great Highway, and on the Great Highway. On the straight stretches of roadway, the speed could not exceed ten miles per hour. On curves, the speed was limited to eight miles per hour. On the Great Highway, speed was limited to six miles per hour. All automobiles were required to have their license numbers displayed on the front and rear of each machine, with numbers not less than five inches in height.

Profane language was prohibited in the park, as well as gambling, loitering, sleeping, camping, and selling. Males over ten years of age were prohibited from using the ladies' rest rooms. Swimming at the beach without bathing suits was also prohibited. Swimming in or polluting park lakes was forbidden. Trapping or killing wildlife was forbidden, as was the building of fires.

All commercial vehicles, horse drawn or motor driven, were denied the use of park roads — including any vehicle carrying dead bodies, as well as any funeral procession. The list of things prohibited in the parks and squares was several pages long. It was evident that conduct in the parks had reached the point that drastic meas-

ures were required. If any horse or team should exhibit any signs of fright due to a motor vehicle, the driver should stop that vehicle and remain stopped until all danger passed. Section Eight read as follows: "Words used in this ordinance in the present tense include the future as well as the present. Words herein used in the masculine gender include the feminine and neuter; and the singular number includes the plural; and the plural the singular." In other words, the ordinance was all-encompassing.

Dog racing was a popular sport at the Ingleside Track (now Urbano Drive) in the Sunset District. One of the fleetest hounds was a dog named Connemara, who was a favorite among the bettors. But Connemara grew tired of racing, and one day at the end of a race he had won, he kept right on running. He fled out the gate and headed toward Sutro Forest. An extensive search was made for him, as he was valued at several thousand dollars, but Connemara was not found.

Soon after his escape, chickens, cats, and even pigs were found slain in the area near Sutro Forest. Then the remains of peacocks were found in the park, and Connemara was discovered to be the leader of a pack of dogs. These wild dogs had decimated the poultry farm owned by the Tivoli Cafe, just west of Sutro Forest. The night watchman there, Herman Swanson, swore that at least forty dogs had joined the pack. He stated that the boldest and the apparent leader of the pack was a huge greyhound; the majority of the pack were mongrel dogs.

The *San Francisco Call* reported that a group of coursing men had organized to capture Connemara because of his great value. The mongrels would be shot. The police were also given orders to shoot any wild dog found in the park.

In September 1904, the *Call* reported a dramatic rescue at Ocean Beach. John Warner of the life-saving crew partook of the cup a little too freely, and his new-found courage prompted him to bet that he could swim out to the

President McKinley and party being escorted through the park in 1901.

schooner *Maggie*, which had gone aground a distance from shore.

Captain George H. Varney of the Life Saving Station had warned him several times to stay ashore, but he plunged into the breakers and was soon beyond the reach of his captain. One huge breaker tossed him head over heels, and he was observed to be swimming with less than his usual vigor.

Captain Varney then rushed to his rescue about the same time that Officer Greggains of the mounted police spotted Warner struggling in the water. The officer spurred his horse to the rescue, swinging his riata over his head all the while. The rope fell over the shoulders of the swimmer. The officer then took a couple of turns around the horn of

his saddle and dragged the nearly exhausted Warner ashore. Captain Varney, who was also getting tired, grabbed the rope and allowed the horse to bring him to safety, as well. Officer Greggains was a Native Son of the Golden West and had grown up on a California stock ranch. He remarked that roping men was not much different from roping cattle.

The superintendent reported that garden hose purchased from the West Coast Rubber Company did not last more than a week and was worthless. The secretary was ordered to notify that company the contract had been canceled, and action would be taken to collect the amount of the bond put up by the company. M. Earl Cummings presented his commission to fill out the unexpired term of Commissioner Altman, who had resigned.

President Spreckels presented the park with a new type of water-sprinkling wagon he had observed and purchased in Vienna, Austria. The tank was made of reinforced steel, and the water was pressured by compressed air so that any amount of water could be sprinkled on the road. The compressed air was furnished by a pump under the wagon operated by a gear attached to the rear wheels. The water could be spread evenly up to a radius of one hundred feet. A test was conducted under the supervision of Park Engineer Irwin, Adolph B. Spreckels, and Superintendent McLaren. All were highly pleased with the new sprinkler and resolved to see if the new machine could be used to spread oil on the roadways to settle the dust.

At the January 1905 meeting, William H. Metson presented his commission, replacing that of Frank J. Sullivan. Mayor Eugene Schmitz called attention to the new appointment, saying that certain commissioners in the past had not worked harmoniously with the others. His reference was to the opposition to the Dutch Windmill. The mayor said, "The two commissioners who planned and carried out this successful enterprise, which has done so much for the Golden Gate Park, were accused at one time of misusing public money."

In May a meeting was held to discuss the misuse of the park by automobiles. Commissioner Lloyd said that since the South Drive was made hideous at night by speeding and reckless driving, auto privileges should be restricted. Mayor Schmitz urged that the automobile drivers be given more privileges. President Spreckels suggested 8:00 P.M. as the closing hour on the Main Drive. Schwerin, president of the Auto Club, suggested 10:00 P.M. Lowe wanted the park open to drivers until midnight. All the good and law-abiding auto drivers wanted to know why they should be punished because rowdies, harlots, and hoodlums rioted at night on the park thoroughfares.

Finally it was decided that McLaren and Schwerin would prepare regulations to present to the board. Commissioner Lloyd would prepare regulations for the board, and some sort of compromise would be reached. The Auto Club also promised to hire policemen to help enforce driving rules. As a result of conferences between Commissioner Lloyd and Schwerin of the Auto Club, a new ordinance was adopted to be tried for sixty days. It would become permanent if the auto drivers performed to the satisfaction of the Park Commission.

The new ordinance permitted automobiles on all the park roadways except in the Panhandle from 6:00 A.M. to 11:00 P.M. They were prohibited on the Great Highway from Fulton Street to the Cliff House between 6:00 A.M. and 6:00 P.M. The Main Drive between the Garfield Monument and Twenty-first Avenue was closed to automobiles on Sundays. The Music Concourse, Strawberry Hill, and the North Ridge Road were also set aside for the exclusive use of horses and carriages. Speed on the Great Highway, Middle Drive, and the Main Drive was limited to eight miles per hour. On the South Drive, the speed limit was set at fifteen miles per hour. Both autos and horses were prohibited on the beach north of the Lurline Baths saltwater pier.

An electric car with solid rubber tires, about 1900.

That portion of the beach was reserved for the exclusive use of pedestrians.

The Park Emergency Hospital reported that one Tessie Leffler, a domestic at 1422 Divisadero Street, who recently arrived from Poland, had blown out a gas light instead of turning off the gas. She awoke in the hospital, sadder, wiser, but not much hurt.

The hospital also reported that Emil Sportono, son of a well-known poultry dealer, had been trying to imitate a telephone lineman and had fallen from the pole and broken his arm. The arm was set at the hospital, and the boy went home with his aspirations somewhat diminished.

T. Kearny of Fresno appeared before the board and complained that it had taken his chauffeur two days to secure a license to drive in the park. He was informed that five thousand people owned cars in California and four hundred thousand did not, and the latter had to be considered first.

The Board of Fire Commissioners appeared and demanded that their autos and fire engines be granted the full and unrestricted use of park drives. They were informed that they could use the park drives only when answering emergency calls.

Commissioner Lloyd announced that a friend of his, Samuel Murphy of the San Francisco Bank, was willing to donate $20,000 to build another windmill for the pumping of water in the park. The offer was accepted, and new wells were drilled in the southwestern corner of the park. Commissioner Dingee donated three hundred barrels of cement for the construction, granite for the door, windowsills, and slate shingles. Pope and Talbot again donated the spars for the new mill, and an engineer named Stutt was hired to draw up the plans.

On September 26, 1905, the *San Francisco Call* reported an "elopement" in the park:

> Despite the fact that they had been carefully reared and watched, four black hen turkeys belonging to Elmer Rooker of 429 Ninth Avenue eloped Saturday afternoon with two peacocks from Golden Gate Park. When they were first missed Rooker refused to believe that they had gone back on their bringing up. He thought they had been forcibly abducted by some hungry person, and he reported the loss to the park police station.
>
> Policeman Pidgeon was detailed to hunt up the missing fowls. He found them in Golden Gate Park in the company of two sporty peacocks, arrayed in their gaudiest apparel. Pidgeon gave chase, but the elopers and their escorts eluded him. When last seen they were headed for Strawberry Hill.

On November 4, 1905, the *San Francisco Call* came out with sensational charges of corruption on the part of Herbert Schmitz, brother of the mayor; Abe Ruef, the power behind the mayor; and the mayor himself. It was alleged that the secretary of the commission, Herbert Schmitz, had passed the word to park employees that if they did not contribute a day or two of pay to the mayor's re-election campaign, they would be dropped from the payroll. The *Call* reported that money was collected from park employees November 2 and 3 — payday having been allegedly moved up in order to collect the money prior to election day. The managers of the opposition party, called "The Fusion Campaign," had reportedly notified the Park Commission of the misdeeds of their secretary.

The Park Commission meetings of November 5 and 24, however, made no mention of the charges. Abe Ruef was later sent to prison. Mayor Schmitz was jailed on charges of corruption later, but he remained the mayor for some time to come.

On a spring day in 1906, the lookout at the Life Saving Station in the park noticed that the Dutch Windmill was running after 5:00 P.M., the usual time for stopping the sails. Captain Varney sent two of his men over to investigate. They found the body of the keeper, John L. Hansen, lying on the platform of the windmill. They removed Hansen to the Life Saving Station, and medical help was summoned. He was pronounced dead shortly afterward. Three of his ribs had been broken, and his skull had been fractured. It appeared that he had climbed the windmill to oil the mechanism and had been struck by one of the sails and knocked to the platform.

Hansen's home was only a few yards from the windmill. His wife was waiting for him to come home from work when the news reached her. No mention of the death was made in the Park Commission minutes.

Superintendent McLaren reported that the new Murphy Windmill was nearing completion and that seven thousand feet of ten-inch pipe would be needed. The sec-

Spinning through the park on South Drive, about 1902.   *Ladies with their rented car and driver on South Drive, about 1903.*

retary was instructed to advertise for bids for the pipe. No bids were received, so President Spreckels was authorized to secure pipe on the open market, even if he had to purchase it in the East.

The superintendent was ordered to detail two men on the South Drive and two men on the Great Highway to get the license number of cars that were speeding and to have the drivers arrested. The commissioners decreed that if the violations did not cease, all privileges for automobiles in the park would be rescinded. But when nature took a hand, automobiles were soon found throughout the park delivering food, water, and medical supplies.

Earthquake-damaged Sharon Children's Building in 1906.

The Great Disaster

Golden Gate Park became a haven for thousands of people following the earthquake and fire of April 18, 1906. To make matters worse, the Emergency Hospital was wrecked by the tremor, and people had to be treated under primitive conditions in a makeshift tent hospital.

A Registration Station was established in the Panhandle near Fell and Baker streets so that people going into the park could let their families know where they were. This Registration Station was operated by the *San Francisco Call* as a public service. The *Call* reported on April 21 that about two hundred thousand people were encamped in Golden Gate Park, most of them without shelter of any kind. Many had left their homes without blankets, and it was cold. The week following the disaster brought a lot of rain to add to the discomfort and the illnesses. General Frederick Funston of the Presidio furnished all the tents that were available in the area. Calls for help went out to Fort Lewis, Washington, for more tents to shelter the homeless.

Immediately after the disaster, food was distributed from one of the tennis courts. The food was donated from other cities all over the country. A large food-distribution center was established near Page and Stanyan streets by the Relief Committee, and soon all had adequate food.

By April 25, the *Call* reported that the number of refugees in the park had dwindled to forty thousand, most of whom were housed in tents. Blankets and bedding had arrived in the city. On April 29, the *Call* reported that Major McIver, commanding the Fifth Military Division, had erected barracks in the park. Six hundred people had been transferred from tents to two-room barrack apartments. Construction was continued until all the refugees in the park were housed in barracks. Two permanent camps were established in the park. One was in Big Rec, and the other was built on the old Speed Road that ran southwesterly from Strawberry Hill to the west end.

Automobile regulations were forgotten. Every available automobile was commandeered by authorities to bring food and other necessities to the needy.

Damage to park buildings was extensive. The Superintendent's Report for April read as follows:

The following report for the month of April is respectfully submitted: The principal matter of importance to report this month is the damage done to the park buildings by the recent earthquake. The Spreckels Temple of Music is much damaged, the heavy stone cornice having been shook off, and in falling entirely destroyed the balustrades along the front, in addition the stonework is badly shaken at the corners. Mr. Reid of Reid Brothers Architects estimates the damage and cost of restoring it at $15,000.

The Sharon Quarters is entirely ruined, the east wing having fallen outward and the roof losing the support of the walls collapsed entirely . . . making a total of $11,000 for repairing the Children's Quarters.

157

The Museum building is also badly wrecked; the north wall of the Midwinter section is down, and the south wall from the door level will have to be rebuilt. To restore this whole structure will cost for brick $4,000, for carpenters $4,000.

The Emergency Hospital building is also badly shaken, many of the stones having been thrown out, and the main entrance archway is badly wrecked. The cost of repairing will cost for stone and brickwork, according to the estimate of Mr. McGilvray, $2,500; for carpenters, etc., $1,500; a total of $4,000.

I asked Mr. Coxhead the architect that planned the granite bridge [Stow Lake] to look into the cost of repairing the broken balustrades and coping including concrete work; he reported the cost at $7,500.

The Curator's Cottage is slightly damaged. . . .[T]he cost of repairing will be about $800.

The Beach Chalet has not suffered much and can be repaired for about $2,000.

The pumping station stood the earthquake very well; none of the walls are cracked and the pumps and pipes remain intact.

The windmill towers both stand well, neither of them have a cracked wall and both stand exactly level. The tower of the old mill seems to have been moved about four inches west as shown by the ten-inch cast-iron pipe being parted to that distance.

The Park Lodge had its chimneys thrown down and some minor cracks in the walls and some plaster is broken in the upper rooms.

The boathouse sustained no injury. The Sweeney Panorama is entirely wrecked; the easterly end is down, and the entire structure is broken and out of plumb.

The pipe system of the park was badly shaken and hundreds of breaks occurred in all of our pipes from twelve-inch mains to the smallest branches. A large force of men was employed day and night repairing the breaks and keeping water in the pipes to supply the thousands of refugees that camped in the different sections of the park. The Spring Valley System being out of order, teams and water wagons were put to work hauling and delivering water to the residents of Richmond and Sunset Districts.

Many of the roadways and walks, especially where built on filled ground, subsided in some places to the extent of a few inches, and in many cases to the depth of a foot or more, necessitating the digging up of the macadam, filling up with sand and replacing the rock and afterwards rolling into condition. A large force of men and teams is engaged in this work and will be for some time to come.

At a special meeting of the commission on May 29, Superintendent McLaren was instructed to proceed with restoration work and to halt any new work in the park. In spite of the damage to the Music Stand, the Golden Gate Park Band was requested to assemble near the Music Stand on the first Sunday in May to give a concert.

A company of soldiers assigned to guard duty in the park was instructed to locate a level spot and pitch their tents. Following instructions to the letter, they located on the bowling greens, and before anyone noticed what was happening, the sergeant had laid out neat rows of tents on what must have been a dream of a soldier's campground. No more level spot could have been found anywhere. Superintendent John McLaren was an avid devotee of lawn bowling. It is just as well that his remarks were not recorded for posterity when he saw his ruined bowling greens. It was estimated that it would take at least a year to restore the lawn to its original condition for bowling.

The Second Regiment, California National Guard, pitched their tents on the tennis courts, but they were soon evicted. The park commissioners decided that since the Big Rec had been taken over for the refugees, they would preserve all other facilities for recreation, due to the large numbers of people living in the park. The children's tennis court had been taken over for a soup kitchen, but when the army unloaded lumber for barracks in the other courts, the lumber was moved almost immediately at the grounds keeper's request.

The Park Commission unanimously passed a resolution thanking Mr. and Mrs. John McLaren for "the magnificent and efficient manner in which assistance was ren-

Refugee tents in Conservatory Valley near the Arizona Garden.

dered by them to the homeless, who had applied at the Park Lodge for food and shelter during the trying days immediately following the great conflagration.''

Superintendent McLaren's report for May 1906 read as follows:

> Ten days ago work was resumed on the grading of the new athletic grounds [Polo Field]. The big fill across the old speedway is well under way and will be finished during the present month. The big hollow at the southwest end is about filled, and in a few days will be ready for the surface soil. The delivery of street sweepings being discontinued; manure will have to be hauled from the stable yard for the fertilizing of the infield and for the enriching of the sand slopes. Fortunately we have a large quantity of fine material on hand that is well suited for this work.

> A large force of men is engaged in repairing the underground water sump at the pumping station. . . .

> The repairing of this sump will take at least three more weeks to finish. After finishing the work I would suggest that the repairing gang be sent to the old windmill and straighten the sump at that point. This reservoir also has been twisted badly and nearly half filled with sand. Considerable of the planking will have to be redriven and braced, and the sand removed by centrifugal pumps.

> A force of ten men are still engaged in repairing broken water pipes in the neighborhood of Strawberry Hill. Another gang of three men are repairing small breaks at the

The ruined eastern end of the Sharon Children's Building, April, 1906.

westerly end, and still another gang is engaged in the same work in the easterly sections.

Six teams are still engaged in the filling up and leveling of roadways that were constructed on filled land.

As most of the city squares are almost entirely covered with tents and shacks for the sheltering of people whose homes were burned, leaving very little grass space to be taken care of, I have notified the Spring Valley Water Company not to turn on the water in the following squares: Union, Washington, Portsmouth, Lafayette, Hamilton, Jefferson, Marshall, Columbia, South Park, Garfield and Bernal, Duboce and Lobos. This will reduce our water bills $900 per month, leaving only Alta Plaza and Alamo Square to be watered at present.

The ground surrounding the children's building is now clear of rubbish, and the fallen stone all safely piled. I

would suggest that the merry-go-round and the goat and donkey track be opened, charging the same rates as heretofore, viz. two rides for five cents.

I would also suggest that the Japanese Village be opened as formerly, and that the village be rented to someone who will pay a fair rent for the privilege of selling tea and Japanese cakes with such restrictions as your Honorable Board may consider just.

I would suggest that bids be called for fuel oil, hay and grain, lime, cement, and other supplies, as the yearly contracts have expired. With the exception of the fuel oil, I would suggest that bids be called for delivery in San Francisco, our teams to do the hauling.

In addition to the above, 5 men were employed in the conservatory, 4 in the museum, 11 in the nursery, 9 at the pumping station and electric light plant, 28 in the city parks and squares, 2 at the city and county hospital grounds, 6 in the maintenance of lavatories, making a total of 314.

The *Call* noted an amusing sidelight to all the destruction. The business community of Cincinnati, Ohio, had hired Oliver E. Conner, Jr., to visit San Francisco to determine the cause of the disaster. After his tour of Golden Gate Park, he went back to his home town with startling news, which was printed in the *Cincinnati Enquirer*. Conner had found the strongest evidence of an extinct volcano under Strawberry Hill, which is in the center of Stow Lake. He had found that a spring which had once existed on the slope of Strawberry Hill had disappeared. Nobody bothered to tell him that Huntington Falls had stopped operating because of broken water mains, and he went back to Ohio convinced that he had found the cause of it all. The *Enquirer* story was reprinted in its entirety in the *San Francisco Call* on Sunday, June 17, 1906.

Damage to school buildings in the city was extensive, and since the school auditoriums had not been certified as safe, graduation ceremonies for the schools were held in the Music Concourse on June 2, 1906. Seventeen hundred children from the public schools received certificates of graduation from Mayor Schmitz, according to the *Call.* The one somber note of the day was the sight of the seven hundred homeless children from the tent schools of the park. They were in sharp contrast to the gaily dressed children who had not lost their homes and their clothing. This sight was overcome, however, by the good music of the band and the enthusiastic community singing of the crowd. Estelle Carpenter stood on a chair to lead the singing of "San Francisco Evermore," with the children and the spectators all singing heartily. Superintendent Roncovieri, the first speaker, referred to the occasion as one of the great events in the history of education.

In July 1906, Superintendent McLaren was ordered not to allow any more camps to be built in the city's parks and squares. The camp barracks on the old Speed Road would house a thousand refugees, and twenty-four hundred apartments were being built on what is now Park Presidio Drive.

A man named Callaghan, the owner of a building at the corner of Market and McAllister streets that had been wrecked, offered to donate all the stone necessary to rebuild the Park Emergency Hospital. His offer was gratefully accepted by the Park Commission.

The Relief Committee of San Francisco recommended spending $100,000 to hire unemployed men in the refugee camps to grade what is now Park Presidio Boulevard for the twenty-four hundred barracks apartments. Commissioner Lloyd proposed that the city and the park furnish

Refugee tents near McLaren Lodge, April, 1906.

jobs for all unemployed men in the camps. He proposed that all men who refused to work be evicted. "They will become so addicted to receiving their subsistence for nothing that they will become confirmed paupers," said Commissioner Lloyd. Former Mayor James D. Phelan, then-chairman of the Relief Committee, agreed with Lloyd. The plan was put into effect at once. All able-bodied men had to accept work or move out of the camps.

Mayor Schmitz immediately disagreed and ordered the chief of police to detail two men to each camp to see that no one was evicted. Commissioner Lloyd and the mayor argued so intensely over the matter that when Lloyd's commission expired, he was replaced on the Park Commission.

The crowd that gathered in Golden Gate Park on July 4, 1906, was reportedly the largest that had ever assembled in the park. In addition to being a national holiday, it was the occasion of the dedication of the new Stadium, or Polo Field, in the park. The parade formed at the Baker Street entrance of the Panhandle, led by Grand Marshal A. M. Wilson and a platoon of mounted police. Then came troops from the Presidio headed by the Third Artillery Band. Following that came the U.S. Navy Band and the cadets from the Naval Training Station at Goat Island. After the military came a civilian band and carriages carrying the mayor and other dignitaries. Carriages, automobiles, and thousands of pedestrians followed the organized groups, all determined to march behind Old Glory all the way to the Stadium.

At the scene of the dedication, two thousand children, seated in a close group, sang the national anthem, waving American flags to the music. After the program, thousands of picnic baskets were opened, and San Francisco enjoyed one giant picnic in the park. The afternoon brought a full program of athletic contests for children, college athletes, and the various athletics clubs of the Bay Area. Military contests and races had been planned for the police and

firemen. Although many punches were thrown in the boxing contests, few landed with any real effect.

The hundreds of children attending the tent schools in Golden Gate Park did not have the essentials taken for granted by the average student. The older boys made makeshift benches to sit on. Few textbooks were available. Classes were usually held on the lawns in various parts of the park. Instead of learning to compute speed in the usual ways, they learned how long it took a snail to go a given distance. They learned how long it took for a bird's egg to hatch and how fast a duck can swim. They learned about all the living creatures that crawl, fly, swim, or walk.

When rain forced them into their tent schools, they used makeshift blackboards. For erasers, they had blocks of wood with scraps of velvet wrapped around them. Students learned the names and habits of all the living things. For the most part, their education did not come from any book but from observing life around them. They fed crumbs to the birds and watched the bees gather nectar from the flowers.

At times, teachers would sugar-coat the history and geography pills by taking classes to the Japanese Tea Garden. Zoology lessons merely involved short walks to the Buffalo Paddock, the Deer Glen, or to watch the kangaroo cover ground with a series of immense bounds. Botany was also easy. A visit to the Conservatory and a talk with a gardener there would fill a child's mind with more lasting knowledge in an hour than he or she could absorb in a week in the ordinary classroom. It was much easier to divide or multiply ducks or rabbits than dull numbers, especially if you had names for each. The park teachers less frequently heard the favorite recitation of the ordinary school:

> Multiplication is my vexation.
> Division is just as bad;
> The rule of three it puzzles me
> And fractions drive me mad!

Ruins of the de Young Museum, April, 1906.

Refugee tents and barracks in "Big Rec," 1906.

The adults found life in the refugee camps a bit wearisome, but the children loved it. Armstrong, the school principal, had the children following him around like the Pied Piper of Hamlin. He rode his horse to school, and throngs of children ran to meet him every morning. "Mr. Armstrong, may I lead your horse?" And then after school, they came tumbling out of the tents to catch him before he rode away. "Please, Mr. Armstrong, may I have a ride?" He would always oblige until the hour was late.

After watching him ride away, the children trooped over to the "farm" near Ninth Avenue and Lincoln Way to tend the vegetable garden plots McLaren had assigned to them. Each child had been allotted a plot ten feet square. Each plot had ten feet each of radishes, beets, lettuce, and turnips. Each little garden was outlined with sticks and string, and the name of the child who tended it was printed on a sign attached to the string. The rest of the plot could be planted to suit the imagination — flowers or vegetables. The whole group had responsibility for an acre of potatoes.

Underprivileged? Not one child would agree.

By January 1907, all the refugees in Golden Gate Park had been transferred to other camps in the city, principally to the huge camp between the park and the Presidio on what is now Park Presidio Boulevard. Men and teams were employed to plow the ground at the campsites and to prepare it for reseeding. Superintendent McLaren made an unsuccessful attempt to collect $175,000 from the Relief Committee for damage done to the parks and squares.

In February 1907, McLaren reported that the work of restoration on the Emergency Hospital and the Sharon Building was nearly completed. Repairs to the Music Stand were also nearing completion. The walls and roofs of the museum were repaired, but the interiors were not yet ready to be opened to the public. In April 1907, the Bowling Green was restored, and play was resumed. Tournaments were not scheduled, however, until the ground became more firm.

On November 10, 1907, the de Young Museum was opened to the public for the first time since the earthquake. With the reopening of the museum, the park had nearly recovered from the disaster. The lone exception was the severely damaged Francis Scott Key Monument, which was not restored until 1909.

In addition to the refugees, the park commissioners had the usual problems. In 1906, Superintendent McLaren was authorized to rent out the Japanese Tea Garden on a concession basis. Not until the following year, was he able to persuade the Hagiwara family to return to the garden and to build their home there. The family lived in the Tea Garden until 1942, when the city bulldozed their home.

In July 1906, the Presbyterian church was denied permission to erect a tent in the park for church services. Through the efforts of Commissioner Lloyd, Frederick A. Robbins, a resident of the city traveling in Japan, donated two large and handsome Japanese stone lanterns to the Japanese Tea Garden. A letter was received from A. W. Torrey, mayor of Eureka, asking for the donation of a pair of elk. The request was granted.

Susanna Brown, a former city resident, had donated $5,000 to the park for the purpose of erecting a gate in memory of her late husband, Richard Brown. Commissioner Lloyd was appointed to accept the gift on behalf of the commission. The design of architects Lansburgh and Joseph was accepted was accepted for the gate, and the memorial was installed at Eighth Avenue and Fulton Street.

Commissioner Cummings proposed that a stone fence be built along the Stanyan Street frontage of the park. He was sure that stone from damaged downtown buildings could be secured free of charge. The suggestion was adopted, and the superintendent was given full power to act in the matter. Today the stone fence runs from Fell along Stanyan to Fulton, then west on Fulton for a few blocks.

In September 1906, the bicyclists demanded that they be given complete freedom of the roads in the park. The following month a new ordinance was prepared that allowed the bicyclists to use the roads, and the bicycle paths were reserved for the exclusive use of the equestrians.

Shreve & Company offered to donate a bronze lion to the park from their burned-out art room. J. D. McGilvray offered to donate a stone base for the lion, and both offerings were accepted. The lion is located on the Museum Drive, just off Kennedy Drive, near the two stone sphinxes that mark the location of the first museum.

Commissioner Metson was appointed to write the Auto Club stating that unless the club would cooperate with the board in enforcing the automobile ordinance, the

Ruins of Sweeney Observatory on Strawberry Hill, 1906.

board would revoke the ordinance and withdraw all driving privileges now enjoyed by club members.

At the November meeting the commission notified the Auto Club that they would meet on November 16 to consider again restricting automobiles to the South Drive and limiting speed to ten miles per hour at all times. At the same meeting, Louis Sloss was thanked for his donation of all the copper needed for the dome of the new Murphy Windmill. In January 1907, Superintendent McLaren was directed to prepare an estimate of the cost of constructing a new reservoir west of Strawberry Hill for the new windmill.

The board reorganized, and John C. Kirkpatrick replaced Reuben H. Lloyd, whose commission had expired. On a motion by Commissioner Dingee, William H. Metson was elected president in place of Adolph B. Spreckels, who did not desire re-election to that position.

The San Francisco Driving Club formally dedicated the horse racing track at the new Stadium on May 12, 1907. Many races were held, and the newspapers noted that great impetus would be given to businessmen supplying hay and grain, as well as to harness makers and wainwrights.

The new Stadium was the scene of another huge celebration on July 4, 1907. Thousands came to the park to hear the speeches of the prominent men of the city and to hear the music of the Golden Gate Park Band directed by Paul Steindorff. Estelle Carpenter again led the children in singing our national anthem. The children waved small American flags in unison as they sang. Carpenter then led the crowd in singing patriotic national songs.

At the July 25 meeting of the commission, the union leaders of the city appeared to request use of the Main Drive for a parade and the Stadium for a labor rally on Labor Day. Permission was granted.

At the suggestion of the *Call,* arrangements were made in August 1907 for an automobile ride in the city for 150 residents of various homes for the aged. Details of the trip were worked out by the ladies' auxiliary of the Auto Club. Shiny new cars were loaned for the occasion by the auto dealers of San Francisco, and the event took place on August 15. Forty new cars were lined up on Van Ness Avenue, and at 11:00 A.M. the ride began. The route taken led out Van Ness and over to the Presidio. Then the tourists went through the Presidio and out to the beach, where a stop was made at the Cliff House. Sandwiches, peanuts,

and candy were distributed and devoured as eagerly as if all were young again. After the pause at the Cliff House, the group reassembled for a spin down the Great Highway and back home through Golden Gate Park.

Many of the elderly had never seen automobiles before and could not fathom these self-propelled vehicles. One eighty-two-year-old woman, who could remember nothing but bicycles refused to go, saying, "The idea of an old lady like me straddling one of those things!" She finally consented to go after being assured that automobiles were perfectly decorous and had comfortable cushions.

Many reports had been made of poor police protection in the park. The secretary was ordered to send a list of all park foremen to the chief of police, with a request that they be made "special" police.

On September 18, 1907, William H. Crocker and A. J. Molera appeared before the commission to request that the Academy of Sciences be allowed to erect a temporary building in the park for the purpose of storing and exhibiting the Academy's library and museum. Permission was granted, with the understanding that plans for the building were to be submitted to Commissioner Cummings and Superintendent McLaren and that it was to be built under their supervision.

Dr. W. Ophuls, president of the Board of Health, called attention to the large number of rats in the park. The superintendent was authorized to spend not more than $1,000 to exterminate the rats. Superintendent McLaren was also authorized to purchase the amount of sheep he deemed necessary to keep the grass cropped in Golden Gate Park.

The Society of Colonial Dames of America, resident in California, presented a sundial to the park in October 1907, in honor of three early navigators of the California coast: Fortuno Jiminez, Juan Rodriguez, and Sir Francis Drake. The sculptor and designer of the beautiful sundial was

Earthquake-damaged Spreckels Music Stand, April, 1906.

Commissioner M. Earl Cummings, who had worked on the marble and bronze piece for two years. Music for the dedication was furnished by the Presidio Military Band.

In 1907, scandals in municipal politics, centering on Abe Reuf and Mayor Eugene Schmitz, finally resulted in a new mayor. The new chief executive, James Taylor, immediately clashed with Park Commissioner William Dingee, a supporter of former Mayor Schmitz. As a result, Dingee resigned, and the new mayor immediately appointed former Park Commissioner Reuben H. Lloyd. Lloyd presented his credentials at the November 27 meeting of the commission.

The board decided that the park had suffered long enough from lack of police protection. Commissioner Lloyd was authorized to interview the chief of police and try to secure more cooperation from that department. It was a dim prospect, because the Park Commission had twice refused to allow the city to construct a criminal courts building in Union Square. However, Lloyd was not merely a good buffalo trader; since he could be persuasive in other fields, great hope was held out for the park.

The final story of the park's early history came with the dedication of the monument to the founder of the Franciscan Missions of California. The *Call* of November 18, 1907, described that event:

> With impressive ceremonies the statue commemorating the deeds of Padre Junipero Serra, founder of the Franciscan Missions of California, was unveiled in Golden Gate Park yesterday afternoon. The actual pulling aside of the canvas cover which had shrouded the monument was done by Tevis Paul Martin, eight-year-old son of T. P. Martin of the Pacific Parlor of the Native Sons of the Golden West. Mayor Taylor accepted the statue for the Commonwealth of San Francisco and a letter from ex-Mayor James D. Phelan, who presented the monument, was read.
>
> It seemed as though all the world had determined to make of the day one to be long remembered by those who attended the services, impressive in their very simplicity. Golden Gate Park, always beautiful, shone resplendent in the glory of a slightly westering sun as speaker followed speaker, extolling the life of the man whose memorial towered above them.
>
> Gathered about the base of the statue when the Reverend Father Philip O'Ryan, representing Archbishop Riordan, opened the services with prayer, were approximately three thousand people of all walks of life, of all nationalities and kindred and tongues. The thirty-foot statue of bronze towered above the crowd of pretty California women whose gay dresses made a flower garden of the place. Behind in the background was the museum, its Egyptian facade in somber contrast with the green of the trees.

Washday in the park after the Great Disaster.

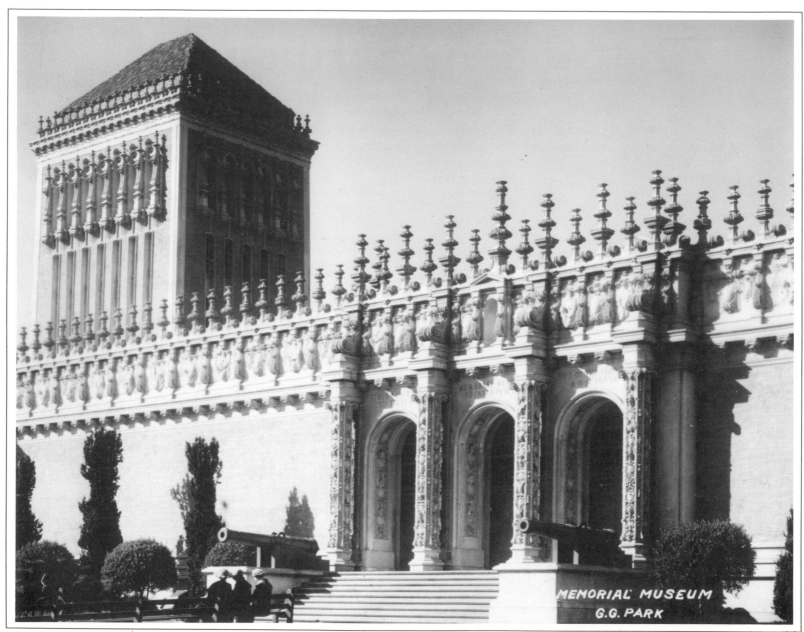

MEMORIAL MUSEUM
G.G. PARK

The new de Young Museum, dedicated in 1921.

Beyond the Earthquake

The years following the Great Disaster of 1906 brought an immense building boom to San Francisco. Everyone was in a hurry to get the city built up again as quickly as possible, and *expediency* was the word of the day. The time was ripe for making improvements. The streets could have been widened, for example, or made to curve *around* the hills instead of going straight *over* them. Civic planning could have been applied to great advantage. But expedience prevailed over logic. Buildings and streets were built helter-skelter. People wanted buildings that were bigger and better than those destroyed by the earthquake and fire — and they wanted them as soon as possible.

At the time of the earthquake, Golden Gate Park had already been so firmly established in accord with William Hammond Hall's original design that all the homeless fire victims could be accommodated. Then, when they left, the parkland was to be returned to its intended use — a place of relaxation amid green spaces rather than site of a refugee camp. The eastern part of the park, closest to the growing city, was developed and cultivated. It held walks, gardens, buildings, ponds and rustic bridges, and areas set aside for specific activities. By 1887 the park held most of the major buildings its designer had intended it to have — a small Victorian Lodge for offices and the superintendent's living quarters, the Conservatory, a small shell-shaped music stand, the Children's Playground building, and the Casino, a one-story restaurant which was subsequently moved from the park. Today, more than twenty-eight acres of parkland are occupied by buildings, exclusive of comfort stations and nursery buildings, and more than 200 acres have been paved over.

The western section of the park, extending toward Ocean Beach and the Pacific, was called a wooded area. Although it was planted and cultivated, it was to remain less developed and less formal — a natural woodland area with walks and drives but no buildings. The entire park was intended to provide the inhabitants of the city with a place to play and refresh themselves. A trip to the park could be very inexpensive, so that poor as well as rich could take their leisure there.

But the expansion fever that took hold in downtown San Francisco, after the earthquake and fire, spilled over into the park in the following years. The 1907 request of William H. Crocker and A. J. Molera for a temporary building to house the library and museum of the Academy of Sciences until the permanent building on Market Street could be repaired had not yet come to fruition because of lack of money.

Then, in 1910, the voters of the city approved a ballot measure that allowed the Academy of Sciences to put up a permanent building in the park. This first building, called the North American Hall, was opened in 1916.

The next building to become part of the park was the

M. H. de Young Memorial Museum. Its modest beginning had been the small, quaint Fine Arts Building of the 1894 California Midwinter International Exposition. This building soon outgrew its walls, and additions were made to it up to the time of the earthquake. The original building was severely damaged in 1906 and did not reopen until 1907. Then a new and larger building was planned to go between the Fine Arts Building and the Japanese Tea Garden. The cornerstone was laid in 1917, and in 1919 the new building was formally presented to the Park Commissioners. The Deed of Trust, dated February 22, 1919, contains the following paragraphs.

By the Grace of God, in the name of humanity and education, this Deed of Trust is made in the Year of our Lord, Nineteen Hundred and Nineteen.

WITNESSETH:

I, M. H. de Young of the City and County of San Francisco, State of California, as a token of my deep love and affection for this city and its people, do hereby give and grant, alien and confirm unto Curtis H. Lindley, John A. McGregor, M. Earl Cummings, Sigmund Greenbaum, and A. B. Spreckels, members of and constituting the Board of Park Commissioners of the City and County of San Francisco, State of California, and to their successors in office forever, all of my right, title, and interest in and to that certain building known as the new Memorial Museum, which I have caused to be erected in Golden Gate Park in said city and county, and to each and every and all of the contents in this and other attached buildings, consisting of various and sundry oil paintings, watercolors, statuary, European and Oriental antiques and handicraft of all kinds, including various ceramics, armors, and textile fabrics, also silver and gold exhibits, precious stones, coins and medals, which I have caused to be placed and installed in said building.

To have and to hold the same in trust, nevertheless for the uses and purposes and with the powers hereinafter mentioned, namely:

First, to keep and insure and maintain the said building and the said contents therein as a museum for the free use, benefit, and enjoyment of the people forever:

Second, if by any chance changes in the laws, the jurisdiction or control of said [park commissioners] or their successors . . ., over said Golden Gate Park shall pass to any other board or body of persons, to execute any instrument or do any act necessary or requisite to transfer said building and said contents therein to said other board or body of persons in trust, for like uses and purposes and with like powers:

Third, the principal condition being that all my gifts are to be for all time maintained in this and connecting buildings in Golden Gate Park. That they are not to be removed or loaned. The building is to be opened every day in the year. *There shall be no charge for admission.* [Emphasis added.]

Any deviation from the conditions of this Deed of Trust shall act as a forfeiture, and all the property so given shall revert to me or my heirs and assigns.

Both the science and art buildings have grown since they were first built, and more buildings have been added to the park. In 1923 the Steinhart Aquarium was built. The Simpson African Hall came next in 1936. In 1952 the Hall of Sciences was built. These buildings completed three sides of a square, and in the 1960s another building, Cowell Hall, was proposed to close the fourth side. Once again, it became necessary to move the Francis Scott Key Monument, which resulted in a ten-year squabble with City Hall to get the monument restored in 1977.

The de Young Museum has mushroomed beyond its original site. The early Fine Arts Building was torn down in 1927, and the location of its original entrance is marked today on Museum Drive by two stone sphinxes. They are copies of the original bronze statues which were probably melted down for their ore. The Brundage wing was added to the de Young building in 1965, to house the art collection of Avery Brundage, a gift to the city of San Francisco.

Steinhart Aquarium, gift of Ignatz Steinhart, about 1925.

The new de Young Museum.

Model yacht club house near Spreckels Lake, about 1940.

It encroached severely on the Japanese Tea Garden. The Park Board may have felt it proper to reduce one Oriental treasure in the park, because the new wing would house other Oriental treasures. Present plans call for another large extension of the complex. That building program will cover the parking lot between the museum and the Main Drive (John F. Kennedy Drive).

One cannot deny the value of these buildings to San Franciscans; no one would want to live in a city without museums. But need they have been placed within a park that was intended as a place of refuge from the city? Instead of a park within a city, the parkland is beginning to look like a city within a park.

One of the biggest building sleights-of-hand ever put over on the people of San Francisco was the construction of Kezar Stadium. In the early 1920s, the son of Mayor "Sunny Jim" Rolph was attending Polytechnic High School, which is located near the park. He wanted a stadium in which to play football. The easiest place to put such a stadium was in Golden Gate Park, and an expert — Henry Beaumont Herts of the firm of Herts and Robertson of New York City — was brought in to justify this incursion. The *Chronicle* of March 18, 1922, reported on his comments: "Golden Gate Park is the only logical place in San Francisco to construct the stadium proposed by the members of your Park Commission. . . . I cannot understand the opposition on the part of certain people of this city against the erection of the stadium in Golden Gate Park."

It is worthwhile to remember that another *expert* from New York City, Frederick Law Olmsted, once said he believed it impossible to grow decent trees in San Francisco.

Perhaps we should learn to beware of park experts from New York City. But Herts also had local support.

The *Golden Gate Pathfinder* of March 19, 1922, quoted Mayor Rolph as saying, "The stadium can be built in Golden Gate Park for $300,000 if this site is purchased. It would cost $1,000,000 to build it elsewhere."

He was speaking of some land adjacent to a corner of the park, owned by the street railways, that had been used as a "roundhouse." The land was no longer needed by the railroad for its steam trains due to electrification of the line, and it was now convenient to sell it back to the taxpayers for $82,000.

In the same article, President William H. Humphrey of the Park Commission was quoted as saying: "The Railroad Commission has valued that site at $82,000 and it has been assessed at $67,000. It provides a natural bowl for a stadium in one of the most sheltered parts of the city, and a stadium could be built there that would be a credit to the city architecturally. *There would be no high and ugly walls surrounding it.*" (Emphasis added.)

What was not brought out was that the nursery and horse barns located in that section of the park would have to be moved into Big Rec, the large public playing field. The users of the park would lose over half of that recreation field as well as the southeast corner of the park. Apparently the city planners did not believe even at that late date that the auto would ever replace the horse, for no provisions were made for parking at Kezar.

As soon as the football field was built in the natural amphitheater that would eliminate the need for walls, "high and ugly walls" were built surrounding it. It quickly became a professional football field rather than a field for high school football. Today, it stands unused as a strangely enduring monument. To tear it down would cost more than it cost to build in the first place. And another chunk of park is permanently lost.

But there have been several victories for the park too. When the Panama Canal was finally completed, a great competition was held between cities to determine who would be granted the privilege of having the Panama-Pacific Exposition. San Francisco won the competition, and the promoters of the exposition naturally wanted to hold it in Golden Gate Park.

Once again experts were brought in to prove that Golden Gate Park was the only logical place for the exposition. After all, it was pointed out, the land west of Strawberry Hill was nothing but a wilderness. And of what earthly good was a wilderness? As no bridges yet spanned the bay, ferry slips were proposed to be built at Ocean Beach so that people could be brought directly to the fair from Alameda and Marin counties. No one explained how a ferryboat could be tied up in the huge breakers that roll in from the Pacific. This problem was evidently thought to be a minor one that could be solved later.

On October 14, 1911, President William Howard Taft broke ground in the Polo Field in Golden Gate Park for the exposition. Some people in the city, however, still remembered the destruction the Midwinter International Exposition of 1894 had brought to the park some twenty years earlier. Strong opposition developed. William Hammond Hall wrote a long piece opposing the site. He pointed out the obvious disadvantages of transportation both by rail and ferry to the park. He also observed that people always want to retain the buildings that are proposed as temporary. Many others joined the fight, and, for once, wiser heads prevailed. The site adopted for the exposition was in Cow Hollow, part of what is now the Marina District of San Francisco. Ferries could come and go there sheltered by the natural bay.

When the 1915 fair was over, the Palace of Fine Arts stood on government land (the Presidio), and the United States Army wanted it moved. They proposed moving it to Golden Gate Park. Again, objections were raised. Through the San Francisco delegation to Congress, the army was persuaded to cede the land to the city so that the building could remain where it had been built and Golden Gate Park could be saved from giving over more land to building sites.

The victory was not total, however. The entrance to the Japanese Garden at the fair was moved to the park, where it constitutes the south gate to the Japanese Tea Garden. The portals of the Siamese Pavilion were also brought to the park and placed in the tea garden. This structure is the only one in the garden that does not represent Japanese architecture.

Water from the park partially supplied the 1915 exposition grounds. Just east of the Beach Chalet, a huge sump was dug. It was fourteen feet wide, thirty feet deep,

The Anglers Lodge and casting pool (in about 1944) was built with WPA funds.

and three hundred feet long. A filtering plant was installed to filter the water, which was them pumped to Mountain Lake on the southern edge of the Presidio near Fifth Avenue. From there it flowed by gravity to the fair site in the Marina. After the fair, the sump was filled and forgotten. In the late 1970s, during the drought, the park turned brown for lack of water because by then most of the park had been hooked up to the Hetch-Hetchy water system, and the underground supply had been forgotten.

Contrary to popular belief, city parks do not usually suffer from a lack of money. In fact, they seem to suffer more when too much money is available. When money is plentiful, politicians look around for ways to spend it — and they seldom spend money on things that cannot be seen and pointed out. For instance, an adequate water system is usually contained in underground pipes. They certainly work well enough and are a great boon to the park, but it is difficult, nonetheless, to point with a gesture of pride to a water spigot as one's contribution to society. Buildings — offices, museums, restaurants, and the like — are big, sturdy obvious things that can be pointed out to voters. Anything new must be strikingly modern. Rustic or old-fashioned bridges and shelters which blend in with the woodland setting are much less obvious, so they are seldom built.

One would think that Golden Gate Park suffered during the Great Depression of the 1930s, when people had no money even to pay their own property taxes. Not so. This period was the greatest in the entire history of the park as far as construction went. Federal and state money, available in abundance, was used to create jobs. To be sure, people did need work, but both the Golden Gate and the Oakland Bay bridges were under construction. So was the San Francisco Airport and Moffett Field to the south. But with additional "free money" available for building, the natural area of the park was sacrificed.

In 1932 the Police Stables were built. In 1933 the first water reclamation plant in the United States was built — to reclaim water from sewage. While reclaimed water is useful in irrigating the park, water could be pumped from underground wells at a more favorable rate per million gallons, and the land used for the reclamation plant could be restored to parkland. During this period also, the huge Richmond sewage treatment plant was also built, with federal money, in the west end of the park — the area that was to remain natural. While the city needed the plant, the park certainly did not. Not only was parkland taken, but large areas of land around the plant became unuseable for park purposes because of the stench that rose from the plant.

It is easy to see how parkland gets taken up for non-park use. Many people think that parkland is wasted space, that it should be sold and put to other more "practical" uses. As a city grows, especially a city with the strong natural boundaries of San Francisco, almost all the available land is bought up and used. The remaining land, if any remains, becomes very valuable. Then hungry eyes focus on the city's parklands — land that is both open and already "owned" in some sense by the city. With some finagling a site can be got — and isn't it a perfect spot for the new You-Name-It? Each year brings something new to the park, taking another bite from the parkland itself. Every day brings one or two proposals to London's Kew Gardens, as well, for something new to be put in the park. The parklike setting has been maintained against such pressure only because "we bloody well keep it that way," to quote one of its caretakers.

In 1936 the Nineteenth Avenue-Park Presidio connection was built through the park. This road effectively cut the park in two. The city had been able to construct a tunnel under Twin Peaks in 1915 and another under the hill on Broadway, but it apparently had no means to build a tunnel under just four blocks of sand to keep the park whole. It would have been, and *still is*, very simple to dig a trench wide enough for a road, build a concrete tunnel, and cover it over with soil, trees, and shrubs. When Park-

Presidio Drive was extended through the Presidio to Golden Gate Bridge, the federal government demanded — and got — a tunnel under the golf course. But the city fathers and the Park Commission were not able to do the same to keep Golden Gate Park in one piece.

In 1937 the Anglers Lodge and casting pools were built as well as a parking lot for the anglers' use. The year 1938 saw a new clubhouse built for the Model Yacht Club at Spreckels Lake. Buildings, not open space, had assumed supremacy in the scheme of things. That supremacy prevails today.

In 1946 a new boathouse was built on Stow Lake. It was not a rustic building, such as the one being replaced. A modern building was chosen, on the theory that times change. But what doesn't change is natural beauty and the need people have for it. The only possible excuse for urban parks is that they allow us to get closer to nature. If we wanted to live continually with modern features, we would not need parks at all.

A major reorganization took place in city government in 1947. At that time, the Playground Commission was housed in a little office above the Civic Auditorium. It had just a little bit of land and few playgrounds under its jurisdiction. But in that year, the Playground Commission succeeded in getting a proposition on the ballot that gave it millions of dollars. The bond issue passed, and the city was presented with an interesting situation. Its Playground Commission had lots of money and no place to spend it. The Park Commission, on the other hand, had a lot of land and no money. No possibility remained for getting another bond issue passed. Only one thing remained to be done, and it was done in 1949, at the next election.

The Playground (or Recreation) Commission was combined with the Park Commission, and since the Playground Commission had the money, the new unit was called the Recreation and Parks Commission. Other cities, making the same move, termed their groups the Park and Recreation Commission, perhaps reflecting an emphasis on parks.

With more money available again, a huge building program was launched. The first thing built with the bond issue money for playgrounds was an office building — the McLaren Lodge Annex. This large, rather drab two-story addition to the old Lodge, complete with full basement, was erected in 1950 and is still not fully used.

Next, four playground buildings were put up at Ocean View, St. Mary's, Potrero Hill, and in the Sunset District. These buildings have never been mentioned in architectural magazines. They have no particular redeeming social importance and are, in fact, nondescript. But they were important to the architect who was chosen to design them. He was paid to design the first building. Then three more *identical* buildings were put up, according to the Engineering Department files, using the same plans. The architect was paid three times more for designing those too.

Money in itself is not the answer to all the problems of urban parks. The proper use of park money could begin a move toward change. Parks tend to suffer more permanent damage when an abundance of money is used indiscriminately. Today emphasis is on CETA money, HUD money, Urban Beautification money, and state bond issue money. The department has more money than it can logically spend, but that money is being spent on features which are often very expensive rather than on maintenance. Mechanical equipment necessary for park upkeep is not maintained, ostensibly for "lack of money." Lawns have not been mowed for as long as three weeks because "there is no money to repair lawnmowers." One can see gardeners mowing huge lawns with small 20-inch mowers. Valuable labor is being wasted that could be spent advantageously in more creative and productive gardening work.

Trees have been neglected to the point that limbs break even when there is no wind. Older buildings have

Golden Gate Park Centennial Parade on October 17, 1970.

Tunnel under Main Drive at 10th Avenue.

been let go. Growing sheds behind the Conservatory are being held up by log chains and steel cables. Yet the Recreation and Parks Commission goes on building new buildings and neglecting the old. The office force in the park appears to be larger than the gardening force. Golden Gate Park has lost thirty-five gardeners and assistant gardeners in 1979, but no reduction in "executive assistants" and "assistant superintendents" is apparent. Some of the assistants even have assistants, but gardeners are as scarce as hen's teeth.

The park has been used in many ways over the years it has been in existence. During World War I, trenches were dug in the park, and men practiced "going over the top." Later, tennis became a widely popular sport. If one could afford a string of polo ponies, one would use the lovely polo field in the park. The 1930s brought the building boom supported by various public works programs and the World War II manpower shortage. The job of being a park gardener was not considered essential to the nation's defense; gardeners were called up along with everyone else, Their call to duty led to the hiring of the first women gardeners in Golden Gate Park, a practice John McLaren did not approve of but could do little about.

Many prominent park commissioners were appointed over the years and their names became widely known — Fleischhacker and Spreckels among them. Women had been active on the Playground Commission when it was combined with the Parks Commission; they began serving on the combined board too. In particular, Mrs. Sigmund Stern, who was a Park Commission member for years, became known for her many contributions.

The 1950s may have been a quiet time for the park as well as the country, but the 1960s certainly weren't. A migration that started with the Bohemian population from North Beach to the Haight-Ashbury District ended with teenaged runaways from all over the country coming to San Francisco. The hippies, or self-styled "flower children," adopted a lawn on a hillside near the Children's Playground. It became known as "Hippie Hill." When to the notion of park administrators, this area became overpopulated, an ingenious park superintendent covered Hippie Hill with fresh manure, ostensibly to fertilize the lawn but actually to rid the hill of its "undesirable" element. The manure was effective, though not very pleasant to the nostrils.

The crime rate in and around the park grew uncontrollable in the late 1960s. A scooter patrol was formed in 1970, the hundredth anniversary of the formation of the first Park Commission. This patrol consisted of twelve men, mounted on Honda motorbikes that ran with almost no noise at all. These policemen could appear on the scene without being heard, and sixty-nine felony arrests were made in the park during the patrol's first month of operation. Word soon got out. Within a few months, criminal arrests were reduced to a trickle and most of the officers were reassigned. Yet another change in park policy had come and gone.

Now, in the early 1980s, with Golden Gate Park's problems still unresolved, the delights of the Japanese Tea Garden may no longer be free to visitors. Alan Cline, an astute observer of park problems and policies, reported in the *San Francisco Examiner* on January 31, 1980, that discussions had begun with regard to "imposing the first fee since Makato Hagiwara [and others] molded the classical garden for the 1894 California Mid-Winter Exposition." Cline notes that the subject is touchy because "the word is out from City Hall to get out and raise revenues . . . or else."

The Great Highway in the 1960s.

Epilogue

The design and layout of Golden Gate Park has been changed many times since its creation to accommodate the differing needs of the people it serves. Some of the changes have been necessary and wise. Most have not. Many have been prompted by a sense, though perhaps misguided, of the public good. Other changes in the park have been the result of self-seeking and personal greed, pure and simple. To hope for an end to decisions made in this way is unrealistic. But it may be possible to develop a sense of public trust rooted in everyone's need for wide open space and an area of greenery in which to relax. To reiterate the words of William Hammond Hall, "Destroy a building and it can be rebuilt in a year; destroy a city woodland park and all the people living at the time will have passed away before its restoration can be effected."

Golden Gate Park is a vast public treasure. It is meant to be used well, cared for, and then passed on to the descendants of its users so that they too will have access to a true park within the city of San Francisco. Only then will the public trust have been carried out with honor.

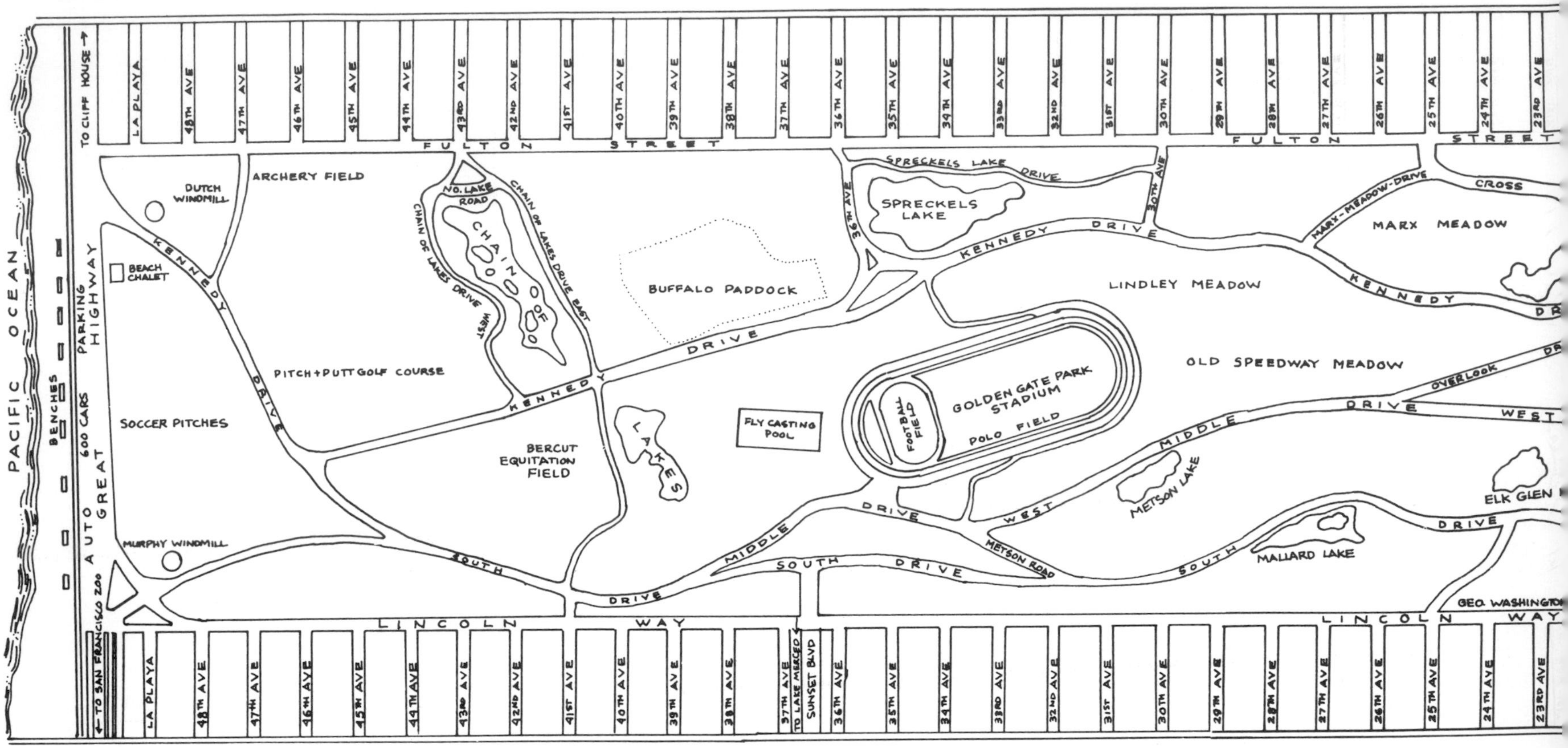

PACIFIC OCEAN

BENCHES

PARKING 600 CARS

AUTO GREAT HIGHWAY

TO CLIFF HOUSE →

TO SAN FRANCISCO ZOO →

LA PLAYA

48TH AVE 47TH AVE 46TH AVE 45TH AVE 44TH AVE 43RD AVE 42ND AVE 41ST AVE 40TH AVE 39TH AVE 38TH AVE 37TH AVE 36TH AVE 35TH AVE 34TH AVE 33RD AVE 32ND AVE 31ST AVE 30TH AVE 29TH AVE 28TH AVE 27TH AVE 26TH AVE 25TH AVE 24TH AVE 23RD AVE

FULTON   STREET   FULTON   STREET

DUTCH WINDMILL

ARCHERY FIELD

BEACH CHALET

KENNEDY DRIVE

NO. LAKE ROAD

CHAIN OF LAKES DRIVE WEST

CHAIN OF LAKES DRIVE EAST

CHAIN OF LAKES

PITCH + PUTT GOLF COURSE

SOCCER PITCHES

MURPHY WINDMILL

BERCUT EQUITATION FIELD

LAKES

KENNEDY DRIVE

BUFFALO PADDOCK

FLY CASTING POOL

SPRECKELS LAKE DRIVE

SPRECKELS LAKE

30TH AVE

36TH AVE

KENNEDY DRIVE

MARX-MEADOW-DRIVE

CROSS

MARX MEADOW

LINDLEY MEADOW

KENNEDY DR

OLD SPEEDWAY MEADOW

OVERLOOK DR

WEST DRIVE

GOLDEN GATE PARK STADIUM

FOOTBALL FIELD

POLO FIELD

MIDDLE DRIVE

WEST DRIVE

METSON ROAD

METSON LAKE

ELK GLEN

MALLARD LAKE

SOUTH DRIVE

GEO. WASHINGTON

SOUTH DRIVE

MIDDLE DRIVE

SOUTH DRIVE

LINCOLN   WAY   LINCOLN   WAY

LA PLAYA

48TH AVE 47TH AVE 46TH AVE 45TH AVE 44TH AVE 43RD AVE 42ND AVE 41ST AVE 40TH AVE 39TH AVE 38TH AVE 37TH AVE TO LAKE MERCED SUNSET BLVD 36TH AVE 35TH AVE 34TH AVE 33RD AVE 32ND AVE 31ST AVE 30TH AVE 29TH AVE 28TH AVE 27TH AVE 26TH AVE 25TH AVE 24TH AVE 23RD AVE

Golden Gate Park today.

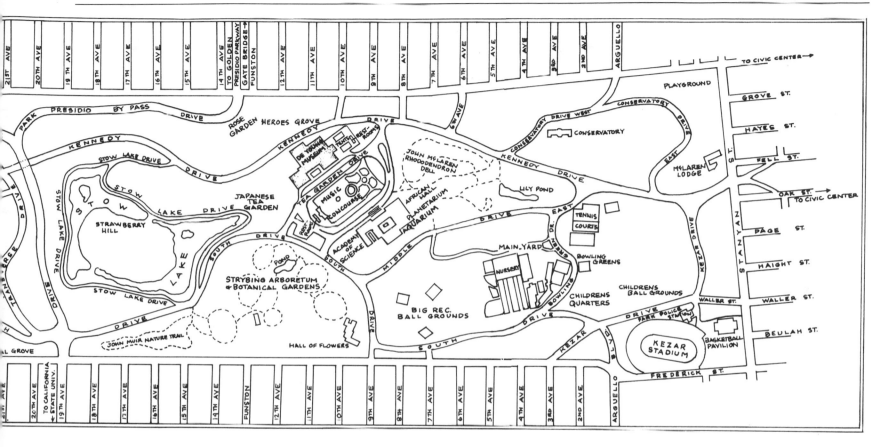

Works Cited

Argonaut, January 19, 1878 ff.

California Architect and Building News, September 1893.

California Historical Society, William Hammond Hall Letterbooks.

California Horseman, October 1902.

California Horticulturist, 1870–1871.

California Senate and Assembly, Report of the Special Committee, 1876.

Carson Daily Appeal, January 23, 1876 ff.

Charles Carter's Real Estate Journal, August 1870 to December 1894.

H. S. Crocker Company, The Official History of the California Midwinter International Exposition, 1894.

Daily Alta California, January 13, 1876 ff.

Dewitt's Guide to San Francisco, 1883.

Dewitt's Guide to San Francisco, 1898.

The Golden Era, "Valuable Services," 1/2/1869; "The Park Swindle," 1/30/1869; "The Outside Land Assessment," 2/20/1869; No Title, 3/6/1869; "The Outside Lands," 3/13/1869.

Golden Gate Park News, July 4, 1888 ff.

William Hammond Hall, "Recollections of Early California Engineering," portions of a speech given to the American Society of Civil Engineers, date unknown.

Hawthorne, November 28, 1893.

Illustrated Pacific States, "Golden Gate Park," March 10, 1888.

Knights Templar Triennial Conclave, Pacific Coast Guide and Program, 1883.

The Land of Sunshine, vol. 9, no. 4, September 1898. "A Transplanted Tea Garden" by Willard M. Wood. Also June 1898 to December 1900.

Marin County Journal, December 16, 1875 ff.

Mechanics' Institute, Twentieth Annual Report, June 10, 1876.

The Mill Valley Independent Journal, May 1, 1908.

News Letter, 1870 ff.

Outside Lands Committee, Report to Board of Supervisors, December 7, 1868.

Out West Magazine, June 1908. "Life in Golden Gate Park" by Gibson Adams.

Overland Monthly, "The Parks of San Francisco" by Charles S. Greene, March 1891. "Golden Gate Park" by Richard Gibson, March 1901.

The Pacific Rural Press, August 6, 1881 ff.

Park Commission Minutes, April 1870 to 1908.

Park Commission Publication, The M. H. de Young Memorial Museum.

Park Commission Reports to the Legislature, 1871 to 1880.

Park Commission Reports to the Supervisors, 1870 to 1908.

San Francisco Chronicle, October 1875 to 1908.

San Francisco City Directory, 1868 to 1908.

San Francisco Daily Morning Call, July 1875 to 1908.

San Francisco Evening Bulletin, July 1868 to 1908.
San Francisco Evening Post, April 1886 ff.
San Francisco Examiner, July 1878 to 1908.
San Francisco Examiner, Press Reference Library, 1912.
San Francisco Municipal Reports, 1865 to 1908.

San Francisco WASP, April 30, 1881 to 1902.
Santa Fe Railroad, Passenger Department, *Santa Fe Route,* 1901.
Weekly Colusa Sun, March 10, 1878.

Index